King of Two Worlds

King of Two Worlds
Philip II of Spain

Edward Grierson

G. P. Putnam's Sons
New York

Library of Congress Catalog Card Number: 74-78401

SBN: 399-11384-3

Created by Walter Parrish International Limited, London, England

Printed in Great Britain

Contents

Preface

On the whole the English-speaking peoples have been extraordinarily good at forgiving their enemies. Bonaparte was a hero to the Whigs during his lifetime, long before he became a cult anywhere. The Eighth Army deeply respected Rommel. Hitler has had his apologists, and even George III is not now the bogeyman he once was in the United States. But one enemy – Philip II of Spain – remains largely unforgiven on both sides of the Atlantic. Perhaps he came too close to defeating the English and pre-empting the vigorous freedom-loving stock that was about to colonize the northern half of the New World. Certainly of all those foreign aggressors since the Norman Conquest who have dreamed of invading the British Isles, he was the only one who took the project seriously and actively set out to achieve it.

Much of this resentment of Philip is unjust, for one of the many paradoxes of his life is the steady support he gave England in his earlier years. In seeking to keep her alliance he married one Queen of England and proposed (if not too pressingly) to another. He protected Elizabeth Tudor in the dangerous times before her accession and continued that protection afterwards in his European diplomacy in the face of constant rebuffs and humiliations. Not till goaded too far by what he regarded as English piracies in the Indies and aid to his rebel subjects in the Netherlands did he finally send out his Armada.

Our hostile response to him is not only unfair, but it deprives us of understanding of one of the most intriguing and enigmatic men who ever sat on a throne: the lover of justice who was implicated in at least two murders; the peace-loving man who spent the last eighteen years of his life in almost continuous aggressive war against his neighbours; the semi-recluse who married four wives; the pious collector of sacred relics who was also the world's first crowned bureaucrat. If he had been simply the bloodthirsty bigot of Protestant tradition he would have been far less interesting. But he was a much subtler and more humane, more sympathetic, person. That he was also capable of what seem to us appalling crimes is part of the fascination of his life and of the society into which he was born. For whatever he was, only sixteenth-century Spain could have fashioned him.

Chapter ·1

Early Years

In the sixteenth century Spain was the most formidable of European powers. Her rise had been rapid. For nearly eight centuries large tracts of her territory had lain under the rule of Moslem conquerors from North Africa. Almost submerged at first under the Islamic tide, her Christian peoples had fought back in the long struggle of the *Reconquista* until in 1492 the last Moorish enclave in Granada had been surrendered to the 'Catholic Kings' Ferdinand and Isabella.

There were several Spains. Isabella's kingdom of Castile, which with Leon covered most of the peninsula (apart from Portugal) as far south as Toledo and the Andalusian plain, was an entity quite distinct from Ferdinand's Aragon along the Mediterranean coast with its capital at Saragossa on the Ebro. There was also the Pyrenean province of Navarre. By the marriage of Ferdinand with Isabella the first great step towards unity had been taken; and by a series of dynastic accidents, some fortunate, some tragic, their elder grandson, Charles, came to inherit not only their Spanish lands and the Aragonese possessions in Italy, but also, through his Austrian Habsburg father, the seventeen provinces of the Netherlands with the Franche Comté (the county of Burgundy). By bribery on a heroic scale he was also elected to the overlordship of Germany as the Holy Roman Emperor Charles V. As if this were not enough for any one human being, a few years before Charles's birth a Genoese seaman named Christopher Columbus had presented himself at Isabella's court and had proposed a fanciful scheme to reach the East Indies and their spice trade through the back door, by sailing westward into the unknown. By this chance Spain had stumbled on an empire in the Americas beyond the wildest hopes of the down-at-heel adventurers, the Conquistadores, who set out from Columbus's Hispaniola in search of El Dorado, the legendary 'gilded man'.

The conquests of Cortes over the Aztecs in Mexico and of the Pizarros and Almagro over the Incas in the Andes of Peru, achieved by a handful of men in armour over armies often out-numbering them by many hundreds to one, remain among the most astonishing events in history. They were triumphs of courage and endurance, aided by luck, brutality and cunning. From nothing, in a matter of a few decades an empire was carved out which stretched from the

The empire was not built without sacrifice; Gonzalo Pizarro aided his brother in the conquest of Peru, only to fall out with his masters, and lose his life at their hands.
Mary Evans Picture Library, London.

Caribbean, through California, Mexico and the Isthmus of Panama to the Atlantic coast of Colombia (the 'Spanish Main') and down the Pacific seaboard of Ecuador and Peru as far south as Chile. In many ways it was to prove an embarrassment – the success of the enterprise attracted not only a horde of Spanish-born scoundrels who needed a deal of curbing by royal viceroys, but also corsairs from less fortunate 'have-not' nations like the French and the English, who were unimpressed by the way the Pope had chosen to divide the New World between Spain and Portugal. Even the wealth that flowed from it was a doubtful blessing which swamped the old economy of Europe under a flood of coin and sent the cost of living spiralling.

However in the short run the wealth from the Indies regenerated Spain. At first it was a mere matter of gold dust washed by slave labour from Caribbean streams and treasure looted from Aztec and Inca kings, but soon very much larger resources came to light: metal from Mexican mines and the huge silver mountain of Potosi in what is now Bolivia.

Before these discoveries were made and the treasure fleets of galleons were organized to bring specie from the Mexican Gulf and the Isthmus to the home ports on the Guadalquivir, Spain had not been abundantly blessed by nature. There was rich soil in the temperate north, in the Valencian coastal strip and in Andalusia, but much of the land was infertile, mountainous and in La Mancha semi-desert. The central plateau was subject to extremes of heat and cold. Its principal product was wool from the flocks that travelled the drove roads criss-crossing the plains.

This austerity of landscape and climate, together with a tradition of militant Christian faith born of the struggle against the Moors, had bred a hard and enduring people. The men who conquered Mexico and Peru and formed the the nucleus of the armies which had taken Granada, and who for a century afterwards were to rule the battlefields of Europe, were either impoverished minor gentry or illiterate adventurers from further down the social scale. The great territorial landlords, whose ambitions had at one time threatened to tear the nation apart, had been tamed and were content to serve the King as his viceroys in Italy and the Indies and in military and diplomatic posts across the world. A favoured few among them served at the heart of affairs on the various Councils which under the crown ruled Spain and her empire, but in the lower echelons the nobility were being gradually elbowed out by the appearance – as in France and England – of a new bureaucracy of 'men of the robe' who fattened on an expanding apparatus of government. From this same class came the army of churchmen in the sees and parishes and various religious orders that proliferated throughout the country, often in bitter rivalry with one another. Supporting the whole edifice was the Dominican stronghold of the Holy Office, the *Suprema*, the Spanish Inquisition, which was concerned with enforcing orthodoxy on every human soul within its reach.

Tightly governed by Church and Crown, the Spanish people still retained some of the appearances of freedom. Castile and Aragon had their own parliaments (Cortes) where representatives met to vote grants (*servicios*) to the King in return for the privilege of airing their grievances. The Cortes in Aragon comprised four orders: municipalities, clergy, gentry and nobility. In Castile there were only delegates from eighteen towns. There were trade guilds, that of the sheep-breeders (the *mesta*) being extremely powerful. As the Indies trade built up, a whole complex of services and courts grew up with it and found their natural centre in the great *entrepôt* of Seville. Landless peasants were moving to the towns, where those who failed to get employment in trade or the armies found outlets for their energies in the ranks of the bravoes roaming the streets. It was – particularly in Andalusia – a boom situation superimposed on an economy and life-style essentially frugal. Apart from a few centres like Granada, Segovia and Toledo (famous for its armour), and the ports where shipbuilding flourished, industries were not highly developed. Around Valencia a rich agriculture had been built up on the backs of Moorish labourers, but elsewhere it was often a matter of scratching a living from thin soil. Many of the old centres of prosperity in the north of the country were in decline, and generally among the ruling classes there was an aversion to work and trade.

It was a country where the free circulation of goods, capital and ideas was everywhere met with barriers. One has only to look at a map to see how nature had cut off Spain from her French neighbour by the Pyrenees and had divided her up internally – by the Sierra Guadarrama and Sierra de Gredos between Old and New Castile, the mountains of Leon in the north-west, the Sierra Morena and Sierra Nevada in the south – into pockets of provincialism between which communication was never easy. The rights and customs (*fueros*) of

Aragon were not those of Castile. A real frontier still ran between them which even royal officials had to recognize and respect. The powers of the Inquisition often conflicted with those of the state, particularly in Aragon which had its own ancient juridical traditions. Basques and Catalans had not even a language in common with each other or with the Castilians of the central plains. The conquered Moors (*Moriscos*) in the mountains south of Granada were nominally 'New' Christians, but in fact as irreconcilably Moslem as their ancestors in the days of the Emirs. There remained the sea, but even there the Mediterranean, though largely ringed to the north by Spanish possessions, was no Spanish lake but increasingly at the mercy of the fleets of the Ottoman Turks and their Barbary Coast pirate allies. Even the nation's triumphant history had contributed to this sense of isolation and self-sufficiency. The victory over Islam had been hers alone; the Indies were her own back yard. The new wealth of the world came from her mines. Even the Spanish Inquisition was a separate establishment, distinct from the Papal body that looked after souls elsewhere.

What image would embody the spirit of this varied people? The teeming city of Seville, with the ships home from the Indies at their berths downstream at Sanlucar? Pilgrims on their way to Santiago de Compostella, the shrine of Spain's patron saint? Bullfights in the squares of dusty provincial towns? The Inquisition at work in the sombre pageant of an *auto-de-fé*? Students at the university of Salamanca? Religious processions? Mule teams on the stony tracks that wound their way up into the sierra through winter snows or the burning August heat? Here was a land of infinite promise and variety, and yet

Spain and Portugal

by some paradox it was growing more and more blinkered and inward-looking. Its king was an Emperor wearing the crown of Charlemagne, yet Charles's internationalism, his foreign birth in Flanders and many absences abroad, occasioned more reproach than praise.

In fact Spain felt in need of very little from outside. Once an oppressed and occupied nation, she had fought her own way to the mastery of a large part of the known world. For nearly half a century nothing she had attempted had failed. Was she not favoured by God and His saints, the agent of the divine will? Perhaps here, in the realms of the spirit, lay the real good and evil genius of the nation. St. Teresa was a young girl in Avila. The founder of the Jesuits, Ignatius de Loyola, was preparing himself for his life work. Tomas de Torquemada, the first Inquisitor General, was not long dead. Into such a country, on 21st May 1527, the future Philip II was born at Valladolid, in the arid lunar landscape of the Castilian plain.

In the life of this most complex being certain contradictions were present from the start.

He was the only son of the Holy Roman Emperor Charles V, who under other crowns was a mere king (Charles I) of Castile, Leon and Aragon. Charles was not the sole ruler of these territories, for still living behind bars in the castle of Tordesillas was his mad mother Joanna (*la Loca*), whom the Castilians had refused to disinherit. The child, Philip, who in the course of a long life was to seem the very incarnation of Spain, was the son of a Flemish-born father and Portuguese mother and had the fair hair and blue eyes of the typical Fleming together with the protruding jaw widely supposed to be a legacy of the Habsburg family but in fact derived from the ducal house of Burgundy, a cadet branch of the kings of France.

His birth had been the signal for an outburst of popular rejoicing. His father had taken him in his arms exclaiming with pious and triumphant joy: 'May our Lord God make you a good Christian. I beg our Lord God to give you His Grace. May it please Him to enlighten you, that you know how to govern the kingdom you shall inherit.' Shortly afterwards the news reached Valladolid that on 6th May the imperialist troops in the service of Charles, 'the Most Catholic King' as his papal title went, had brutally sacked Rome and made the Pope a prisoner. It put a hasty end to the festivities. The child was baptized with solemn splendour in a chapel of San Pablo at Valladolid by the Cardinal Archbishop of Toledo, Primate of Spain, with the herald crying, 'Hear ye! Hear ye! Hear ye! Don Philip Prince of Castile by the Grace of God', and in after-life was to be regarded in Protestant demonology as the arch-papist; and yet for at least the early part of his reign Philip was to be often enough at odds with the Papacy and on one occasion actually at war with it. The richest ruler in Europe, with the gold and silver of the Indies at his disposal, he was to suffer three State bankruptcies.

Such contradictions were part and parcel of the situation into which Philip had been born as heir to so many lands, honours and duties. The Holy Roman Empire whose crown his father wore was a contradiction in itself: a typically misty German hankering after the reality of that world order of the Caesars

The Family of Philip II

```
Ferdinand V  =  Isabella I
of Aragon        of Castile
                     |
Juana  =  Philip I                    Manoel I
(la Loca)                             of Portugal
   |          |- - - - - - - - - - - - - - - -|
Eleanor   Catherine = John III   Charles V = Isabella    Mary    Ferdinand I = Anna
                      of Portugal  Emperor   of Portugal           Emperor      of Bohemia
              |                       |                                         and Hungary
       Maria of Portugal                                        Maximilian II
                                                                   Emperor

Margaret    PHILIP II = 1. Maria of Portugal   Maria = Maximilian II   Juana   Don John
of Parma               2. Mary Tudor             |                             of Austria
(illegit.)             3. Elizabeth of Valois  Anne of Austria                 (illegit.)
                       4. Anne of Austria
```

which the Germanic tribes in the fifth century had played a major part in destroying. Still holy, in the sense that it was Christian, and still an empire, though an elective one, it had never even in its creator Charlemagne's day been Roman, and the Popes usually feared and hated it for its interferences in Italy. Since in its development it no longer amounted to much more than nominal suzerainty over the patchwork of German states, it had little importance in terms of power, but it still had great prestige and there was no lack of candidates for its throne. As time was to show, Charles was never able to pass the imperial succession to his son: it went to his brother and *his* descendants in the Austrian branch of the Habsburgs. But even without the Empire, in all conscience Philip's inheritance at birth was impressive enough, and it was to grow larger. Certain formalities of popular acceptance by the Cortes or parliament of Castile had to be gone through before he could be officially heir to this heartland of Spain; but these had been met before he was a year old. The Aragonese waited rather longer, but their acceptance of a Spanish-born prince who was a great-grandson of their own Ferdinand the Catholic was never in doubt. In Italy Philip was heir to Naples and Sicily and was soon to have Milan. Through his great-grandmother Mary, daughter of Charles the Bold, who had married the future Habsburg emperor Maximilian, came the inheritance to the old fragmented 'middle kingdom' of Burgundy, comprising the Netherlands and the county of Burgundy, the Franche Comté, along with a more shadowy claim to the duchy of Burgundy with its capital of Dijon, which Charles was for years to try vainly to reclaim from France. There was the disputed territory of Navarre on the Pyrenean frontier. There were Spanish islands in the Pacific discovered by Magellan in 1521, to be called the Philippines, and others in the

Caribbean that stemmed from the voyages of Columbus. Six years before the child's birth Hernando Cortes had completed the conquest of Mexico, and during the boy's infancy the Pizarros were adventuring in the high Andes to the still more incredible conquest of the Inca empire in what is now Ecuador and Peru.

The indirect dynastic ties were almost as impressive. The King of England had a Spanish wife, whose daughter, Mary Tudor, had been engaged as a child to Charles and as an ageing spinster was to marry Philip. Portugal was almost inextricably bound to Spain through a network of marriages. Philip's mother, the Empress Isabella, had been a Portuguese princess; his first wife was to be another; and in the end he was to inherit the crown of Portugal. One of his sisters was to marry a Holy Roman Emperor. His aunt married the King of France; he himself was to wed a daughter of France and to try to put the child of that union on the throne in Paris.

Dynasties counted for everything. Almost the whole of Europe apart from the Balkans, where the Ottoman Sultan ruled, was tied in a noose of family entanglements which, before the rise to political power of parliaments and peoples, really settled the destinies of the continent by marriage contracts and the births of eligible brides and bridegrooms who could in effect be auctioned off at the tenderest ages. Much therefore depended on the qualities of a ruler and his family. And deep in Philip's character, the fruit of early training in the duties and qualities demanded of a prince, lay a concern which was to become

The world of Philip's birth: a chart drawn by Girolamo Verrazano on vellum in the early 16th century.
Courtesy the National Maritime Museum, London.

Philip II's mother, Isabella of Portugal, painted by Titian.
Photograph, Giraudon, Paris.

a fanatical dedication to the principles of government. It is a notable coincidence that Niccolo Machiavelli died in the year of Philip's birth. What had been laid down in *Il Principe* ('The Prince') was not published in its author's lifetime and received scant respect for another two centuries, but already the germ of political science was in the air, and there is a world of difference between the casual lessons in statecraft which earlier kings had provided for their successors and the infinite pains which the Emperor Charles took to prepare his son for an inheritance which was also a profession, a burdensome one, of which he himself had begun to weary.

Opposite: Titian's painting of the Emperor Charles V at the height of his power after the Battle of Mühlberg in 1547. Courtesy of the Prado, Madrid.

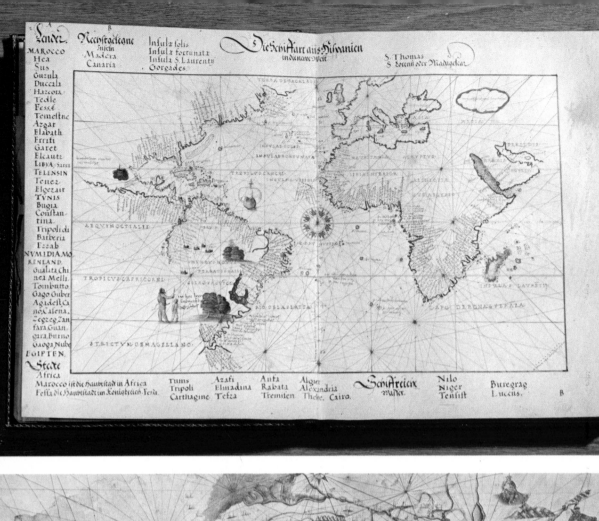

On the surface Philip's early childhood was happy and uneventful. We have charming glimpses of him as a blond cherub being carried in a kind of cart or riding on a donkey through the streets of Spanish towns to the plaudits of loyal and admiring crowds. He was fortunate in parents who loved him and whom he loved in return – the letters and gossip of the times and Philip's own tributes much later are conclusive proof of a relationship of trust and affection rare among the ruling houses of Europe. Of course immense care was taken with his education. At the age of seven he was given a household of his own. A professor from the university of Salamanca, Juan Martinez Siliceo, was put in charge of his studies, and he had the services of a grandee of the old school, Don Juan de Zuniga, Comendador Mayor of Castile, to instruct him in the knightly pursuits of fencing, hunting and jousting. It was an age when physical prowess was expected of rulers – had not his own birth been celebrated by the Emperor by killing a bull with his own hands in the arena? Twice a week they went out hawking or shooting with the long bow, and Zuniga diplomatically reported the prince's skill at these sports and his excellent seat in the saddle, while in the classroom the professor from Salamanca was busily earning himself an archbishop's mitre by praising the scholar's diligence at Latin and Geography.

In reality the boy's responses were curiously uneven. Every lesson his father taught him in statecraft was learnt and was to be applied throughout his life: indeed one could almost have deduced most of the events of the coming reign from the instructions that Philip had received from the Emperor in his teens. The encouragements of other tutors were less regarded. Under the Emperor's eye in Flanders Philip was to appear in the lists at tournaments and break lances with the champions of his time, but it was a sport he found thoroughly uncongenial. He was to retain some interest in shooting, but only of the most sedentary kind. Dancing he enjoyed. He liked painting and sculpture and was to develop into a considerable connoisseur and patron of art. He was interested in history and mathematics, but in spite of his father's constant exhortations to learn foreign languages he never mastered more than Latin and a smattering of French. It was as though subconsciously he was rebelling against Charles's expressed wish: 'I would have you perfect'. Undoubtedly he was a very different man from the convivially minded Emperor. He was not wholly lacking in animal spirits, for whatever the truth of the gossip about his midnight jaunts and womanizing in Brussels, he certainly from the age of eighteen kept a mistress in Spain and by the time of his marriage to Mary Tudor was sufficiently a man of the world to cause his poor wife tortures of jealousy. But there was a lack of robustness about him, perhaps the legacy of an attack of smallpox when he was nine. The strain of mental instability running through the Spanish royal house, which had shown itself as outright madness in Philip's paternal grandmother and great-great-grandmother and was to be echoed in the tragic career of his son Don Carlos, can perhaps be seen in vestigial form in his father's premature senility and retreat to Yuste, and even in his own withdrawal,

Opposite, above: This map showing Europe, Africa, the Atlantic, and North and South America is from a book of twenty-five charts on vellum dated 1554. It was drawn by a Venetian, Johan Baptiste Agnese.

Below: A portolan chart of the Mediterranean and the north-east Atlantic attributed to Angelo Freducci Anconna and dated 1550.
Both courtesy of the National Maritime Museum, London.

forty years later, to the cloistered calm of the Escorial. Long before that moment came, a succession of watchful Venetian ambassadors had commented on his grave, inward-looking nature and his love of solitude. But it would be wrong to see heredity as the root cause here, for a great part of it must have come from the loss of the boy's pious, loving mother when he was only twelve.

The Emperor had been deeply affected by this death. He had lost not only a wife but a political ally and helpmate virtually irreplaceable as Regent of Spain during his absences from the country. The Empress had died at a most inconvenient moment. Her children were still young, and the only other members of Charles's family to whom he might turn were either married to foreign kings or were engaged, like his brother Ferdinand in Vienna and his masterful sister Mary in the Netherlands, in duties from which they could not possibly be spared. No European rulers of the time (with the exception perhaps of the Ottoman Sultans, who customarily slaughtered brothers and half-brothers in making their way to the throne) would have dreamed of looking beyond their families if they could help it when choosing viceroys for really crucial posts. The death of Isabella meant that her son now had an important role to play not only as Regent of Spain, but also as part of the Spanish link with Portugal. This link was now a tradition in both ruling houses, despite the mutual dislike and distrust of the Spanish and Portuguese peoples. Philip had now become a piece of vital importance on the European chessboard: at the age of thirteen he was therefore made Duke of Milan; before he was sixteen he became Regent of Spain and negotiations were afoot for his marriage with the Portuguese Infanta, a girl of much the same age as himself.

In coming to these decisions the Emperor had been guided by pressing dynastic and political needs. Since he was about to leave the peninsula on one of his endless round of visits to central Europe, he had to have someone whom he could trust in Spain, and he had to re-insure himself by a renewal of the Portuguese alliance. But he was not unaware of what he was asking of his son. He remarked sadly that the responsibility of the Regency and marriage must make the boy a man long before his time. 'You are still young', he wrote, 'to bear so great a burden.' To live up to the following advice was one of Philip's most enduring aims:

> Be a friend to justice. Command your servants that they be moved neither by passion nor by prejudice, still less by gifts. . . . In your bearing, be calm and reserved. Say nothing in anger. Be easy of approach and pleasant of manner.

The very accents of Polonius. Touchingly, the Emperor goes on to add that it is impossible to think of everything, since in politics there are more exceptions than rules, but above all his son must always try to pursue 'the straight path', have a good judgment and 'do good works'.

To help guide him in this task a powerful trio of advisers had been assembled in the shape of Spain's most formidable grandee, Don Fernando Alvarez de Toledo, Duke of Alva, Cardinal Tavera, and the Comendador Francisco de los Cobos; but a warning in the Emperor's most solemn manner went with them. Los Cobos liked money too much; Alva was a great soldier, but ambitious and not above trying to trap an unwary prince through the agency of women. Philip must beware of everyone: 'Depend on no one but yourself. Make use of all but rely exclusively on none. In your perplexities trust always in your Maker. Have no care but for Him.' In the years ahead the Emperor was to offer other advice on every topic under the sun, but the key to Philip's developed theory and practice of kingship lies here, in words he took closely to heart. 'Depend on no one . . . Make use of all . . . .' This assumes that the ruler will be of the competence and calibre of Machiavelli's 'Prince'. But suppose he is not?

These instructions, which Philip carried out to the letter, were in fact a recipe for disaster both in the Netherlands and in the planning of the 'Enterprise of England', the great Armada of 1588. However in 1543 all that lay far ahead. It was a time of rejoicing as the young Regent prepared for his marriage to the Infanta Maria of Portugal, who brought with her the enormous dowry of 900,000 crowns: one of the few financial triumphs of the Emperor's reign. Papal dispensations were required, for the bride was doubly related to her bridegroom: her mother was his father's sister, and her father, King John III, was his mother's brother. Even the Pharaohs would have been hard put to it to better such a degree of consanguinity – to be improved on many years later when at his fourth marriage Philip contrived to wed his own niece.

This first bride was a girl five months younger than her husband: no beauty, with high arching eyebrows and a rather weak chin. Certain ill-intentioned persons working against the match had said even unkinder things, making it necessary for the Spanish ambassador in Lisbon (who had arranged it) to issue a series of sharp *démentis* on the subject of the girl's looks. She was 'more stout than slim', it was true, he wrote, but taller than her mother and outshone by none of her ladies at the Palace. Furthermore, her disposition and temper were 'angelic'. She was liberal, gracious and very fond of clothes, liked dancing and was uncommonly healthy.

However, controversy over the personal charms of the Infanta was forgotten in all the splendours of the marriage ceremony. The university city of Salamanca was chosen for the occasion. On 11th November 1543 the bride, swathed in gold and silver with a purple velvet mantle and hat with a plume to it, made her state entrance into the town, riding side-saddle on a richly caparisoned mule and surrounded by a brilliant retinue. According to one story, Philip himself, masked and with his hat pulled down over his eyes, had come out to take a preview of his wife as she rode under the triumphal arches through the torchlit streets; according to another he had followed her in disguise all the way from Badajoz on the Portuguese frontier and watched her ride in from the windows of a house overlooking the route. Next evening the young couple were married by the Cardinal Archbishop of Toledo, and for several days the rather solemn little town gave itself over to a succession of bullfights, tournaments, banquets and balls at which the Regent and the Princess danced elegantly together at the head of a glittering court.

Little more than eighteen months later Maria died in childbirth. She cannot have been wholly without influence on so young a husband. Yet she remains a shadowy figure, remembered only as the mother of Don Carlos who was to pose great problems for Spain. Apparently overcome by this death, the widower,

Philip's first wife, Maria of Portugal: this effigy stands to the right of the altar in the church at the Escorial.
Photograph, MAS, Barcelona.

still only eighteen, went into retreat at the monastery of Abrojo. Less in keeping with the pious and solitary nature usually attributed to Philip, he soon returned from the cloister to the arms of his mistress, Doña Ana de Osorio.

This liaison was common knowledge in Valladolid, and for a while there seems to have been something approaching consternation at Charles's court far off in Germany at rumours that the infatuated heir might even wed his mistress. One of Philip's trio of advisers, the supple and understanding los Cobos, hastened to reassure the Emperor that his behaviour was nothing more than boyishness. Like the early mistresses of Philip's great-grandson, Louis XIV, who shared many of his tastes, Doña Ana was ultimately to be despatched to a convent, but only after ten years of semi-marital bliss, and for the time being at least she was an influence for good in keeping the young widower happy and contented under the burden of care increasingly imposed on him.

For the Regency of Spain was no sinecure. The Emperor loved his son but he wanted work out of him. Deeply involved in the problem of Germany and the divisions the Reformation had caused between its Catholic and Lutheran princes, he was in constant and often desperate search for money. These were the days before the output of the Mexican and Peruvian mines had come to the rescue of the treasury. The Cortes of Castile and Aragon had been squeezed dry already. The Emperor was turning reluctantly to the notion of forced loans, and los Cobos had hit on the splendid plan of selling licences to Spaniards to ride mules, otherwise forbidden in the interests of Spanish horse-breeding. But there was hardly a ducat to spare, and already Philip had resisted his father's cries for cash by reminding him of the 'depths of calamity' to which the people had been brought and the deplorable state of the country. 'The prisons', he wrote, 'are full, and ruin hangs over all.'

Apart from Seville and the ports on the Guadalquivir, the trading centres for the *Carrera de las Indias*, Spain was to remain a poor country throughout Philip's reign. But her poverty suited her. Don Quixote and Sancho Panza do not have two *reales* to rub together, but they adventure more richly in the realms of the spirit and imagination than almost any other characters in fiction. So it was in the actual world. Spain's poverty in no way prevented her from being the most powerful of European nations in the period from her capture of Granada in 1492 to her defeat at Rocroi, a century and a half later, when to the astonishment of contemporaries her hitherto invincible infantry was at last cut down on the battlefield. Her people were tougher and more enduring than other Europeans precisely because of the harshness of their climate and the frugality of their lives. And this went for the *hidalgo*, the country gentleman, the stock from which the Conquistadores had been bred. One remembers again Don Quixote:

> His diet consisted more of beef than of mutton; and with minced meat on most nights, lentils on Fridays, and a pigeon extraordinary on Sundays, he consumed three-quarters of his revenue. The rest was laid out in a plush coat, velvet breeches, with slippers of the same for holidays, and a suit of the very best homespun cloth which he bestowed on himself for working days.

With such men, under the Duke of Alva as commander, the hard-pressed Emperor was in 1547 to win the victory of Mühlberg over his Protestant foes in Germany. It gave him a breathing space which he planned to use by sending for his son to join him in Brussels, bringing as much money with him as he could lay his hands on. To prepare him for the journey and to brief him in Spanish policy, the Emperor sat down in January 1548 to compose the longest and most famous of his letters of instruction.

> The first and most solid foundation of your conduct must be absolute trust in the infinite bounty of the Most High and the submission of your desires and actions to His blessed will . . . thus you will earn His help and aid in the development of all necessary graces in reigning and governing well.

The Emperor goes on to urge his son to look for peace, not war. It makes ironical reading in the light of Charles's own campaigns in Germany, Italy and Africa and the almost constant warfare waged by his son against one adversary after another and sometimes several at once – the Turks, the Barbary pirates, the Papacy, France, England, rebellious subjects in the old Moorish kingdom of Granada and in the Netherlands, this last a war that went on for forty years after Philip's own death. But we can be sure that the instructions were sincerely meant. Charles knew the ruinous cost of war and warned his successor in the strongest terms about it. And it was advice sincerely received. Venetian ambassadors were usually right, and a whole succession of these observant men were

Two high-relief portrait medallions: On the left, Philip's father, the Emperor Charles V, is wearing the Golden Fleece; on the right is Prince Philip, as he then was.
Courtesy the Hispanic Society of America, New York.

to remark that Philip was at heart a peace-loving and defensively-minded soul who would only take to war if driven.

Though only forty-eight, the Emperor, a great valetudinarian and a sufferer from gout, stomach cramps and a dozen other ailments, was already anticipating his own death or at least discussing the possibility with his successor. His letter, which is packed with accurate information and sage advice over the whole political spectrum, is fascinating proof of how even the wisest of men can be confounded by events beyond their control. Philip is told to keep a close eye on French corsairs in the Caribbean. Not a word is said about English privateers, for Hawkins and Drake were names still unknown. The Netherlands-born Emperor praises the 'great affection and fidelity' of the seigniors and lesser nobility who were to lead the fateful rebellion of the provinces against his son. Forty years before the Armada he stresses the importance of keeping on good terms with England.

Yet these were really secondary matters when compared with the need to counter French ambitions in Italy and the Low Countries, and the Turkish threat by land and sea. On these points the Emperor dwelt at great length. If possible, peace should be kept with France, and even the family claim to the Duchy of Burgundy must not be pressed to the point of war, though it should never be abandoned. In central Europe Philip must support his Habsburg uncle and cousins against any further advance of Ottoman power. And as future ruler of Naples, Sicily and Spain, he must *at all costs* support his naval ally Genoa and maintain a strong fleet of galleys to hold the Turks and the Barbary pirates well away from the northern shores of the Mediterranean. If this advice had not been faithfully followed Malta might have fallen to the Turk, the decisive battle of Lepanto might have been lost, and Spain herself might have seen an invasion from North Africa, supported by a rising of the Moorish population of her eastern seaboard, which could have reversed the verdict of the *Reconquista* and given Andalusia back to Islam.

On the whole it was a remarkable *tour d'horizon* by a ruler of worldly experience who was also a devout believer in the supremacy of God's will. The end of the letter reverts to the mood of the beginning:

> I pray that God will protect you and that He will direct all your desires towards the fulfilment of His service, so that having reigned and governed in accordance with His wishes, you will end by attaining to life immortal.

Armed with this advice, and leaving behind him a new Regent of Spain in the person of his Austrian cousin Maximilian,* recently married to his sister the Infanta Maria, Philip tore himself reluctantly from the arms of his mistress and rode across Aragon to Barcelona, paying a brief visit to the Benedictine shrine of Montserrat on the way, and then to Rosas, where in the autumn of 1548 he embarked for Genoa in a fleet of fifty ships commanded by Spain's redoubtable Genoese ally, Prince Andrea Doria. Milan received him warmly as its Duke, and passing over the Alps he was met at Bruchsal on the Rhine by an escort of cavalry. Thus he wound his way northwards to Brussels and reunion with his father.

In an age devoted to ceremony, the state entries of emperors, kings and princes into their territories were obvious set-pieces of propaganda, and this first appearance of Charles's heir in the Netherlands provinces was carefully staged to impress. Philip rode in a cavalcade between the imperial general, the Duke of Savoy, and the Cardinal of Trent, representing the secular and heavenly arms of militant Catholicism. Behind them came the Duke of Alva, the Bishop of Arras (better known to history as Cardinal Granvelle), and the local-born counts of Egmont and Horn.

If the Gods of Olympus in an inspired moment had vied with one another to produce a masterpiece of tragic irony, they could hardly have done better than this. Granville, acting as Philip's most trusted adviser, was to bring the Netherlands nobility (those loyal and faithful seigniors) to a state of revolt. Alva was to bathe those peaceful provinces in blood, and in the course of his governorship to send the Counts of Horn and Egmont to the scaffold in the *Gran' Place* of this same town of Brussels through which they were all riding in such apparent amity.

Perhaps the writing was already on the wall and had been there ever since the marriage of Charles's Spanish mother and Burgundian father had led (after a death in the male line of Castile/Aragon) to the union of Spain and the Netherlands provinces in the person of Charles himself. This unexpected and unnatural connexion was to prove fateful for everyone. Ways of life were entirely different. The seventeen provinces of the Netherlands were the remains of that Middle Kingdom between France and the states of Germany that had arisen when Charlemagne's empire had been divided among his sons. In the fifteenth century under the dukes of Burgundy it had almost become a viable kingdom. Now it was fragmented again, but still independent of its powerful neighbours

* Maximilian was the son of the Emperor's younger brother Ferdinand, King of the Romans, head of the Austrian branch of the Habsburgs. Both Ferdinand and Maximilian were to become Holy Roman Emperor in turn.

This bronze medal, executed by Leone Leoni, was issued at the time of Philip's journey through northern Italy in 1548. The reverse is shown. Hercules is encouraged by Virtus to scale a rocky height while Voluptas tries to detain him with pleasures of idleness.
Courtesy the Metropolitan Museum of Art, New York.

on either side, as indeed in the shape of the Benelux countries it remains to this day. In the northern provinces, in the sixteenth century, the culture was Germanic: in the southern or Walloon provinces it was French. The only tie with Spain was the ruler they had come to share. There were windmills in plenty on the plains of Holland and Brabant, but not even the craziest knight in these fat pastures would have dreamed of tilting against them. Great guzzlers and drinkers, given to worldly pleasures and display, the first bourgeoisie in the bud, the inhabitants of the Low Countries had nothing in common with the sober, reserved and pious man who by a freak of fate was soon to be called to rule over them.

In some ways Philip was to be much more successful than his father. He ruled Spain better and was more loved and respected there. It was he and not Charles who turned back the tide of Turkish advance in the Mediterranean. But where the Netherlands were concerned he lacked the instinctive understanding of the people which came of his father's Flemish birth. For all his Burgundian look, he remained Spanish to the core. Nor did he have that *bonhomie* and warmth of personality which made the Emperor, even in defeat,

Opposite: Prince Philip painted by Titian in 1551. Not appreciating Titian's almost impressionistic technique, Philip is said to have thought the portrait looked hastily painted. Courtesy of the Prado, Madrid.

Overleaf: This altarpiece, La Gloria, *was commissioned by Charles V in 1551 and delivered in 1554. It shows the Spanish royal family (Charles, his wife and son) in the top right-hand corner supplicating the Trinity. Old Testament figures including Noah and the Ark, and Moses and the Tables of Law, can be seen in the left foreground.* Courtesy of the Prado, Madrid.

a sympathetic and popular figure. Charles's gluttony was famous throughout Europe: it earned him nothing but approval, where Philip's austerity was derided outside Spain. Though he was to have three more wives than his father and at least as many mistresses, he never produced two such splendid bastards as Margaret of Parma and Don John of Austria, grand chips off the old imperial block who were to be standing credits to the Emperor's memory long after he was dead.

This lack of the common touch and even of ordinary human failings was to cost Philip dear. The mature man was to become a far more benign, ubane figure than his first appearance on the European stage suggested, but for many of his subjects this was the image they remembered – a stiff, proud, sullen, arrogant prince, sadly lacking in the vitality which had made popular rulers, indeed national totems, of such monsters as Francis I and Henry VIII. Even his two widowed aunts, Mary, Regent of the Netherlands, and Eleanor, Queen Dowager of France, who were with the imperial court in Brussels and might have been expected to enthuse over him, found him disappointingly 'small of body compared with the Germans' and by inference only half a man.

All these judgments were unfair. At his father's wish, Philip had not failed to take part in tournaments and masques, to show himself to the people of the Netherlands provinces, and to swear in the most solemn manner to respect their bewildering number of traditional customs and privileges. The whole exercise had been mounted with the utmost pomp and ceremony, Philip being accompanied on his tour of provincial capitals by the Regent and her court, their every move recorded for posterity in a book entitled *El Felicessima Viaje del Principe Don Felipe* by a member of Charles's secretariat. In his classic biography W. H. Prescott describes the triumphal arches and the inscriptions that lined the route and found their way into 'The Most Fortunate Journey' as proofs of the love and devotion of the Netherlanders for their future ruler:

> They were both in Latin and in the language of the country, and they augured the happy days in store for the nation when, under the benignant sceptre of Philip, it should enjoy the sweets of tranquility and freedom. Happy auguries! which showed that the prophet was not gifted with the spirit of prophesy.

Yet for Philip all these earnest attempts to please and conciliate were in vain. 'Not very agreeable to the Italians, not very acceptable to the Flemings, odious to the Germans,' noted the Venetian ambassador sourly of this extended good-will tour. The young man had even tried to ingratiate himself with the northerners by swigging beer, a drink he detested. It made no difference. He could not help looking both arrogant and ill at ease: a deficiency in style which disturbed the Emperor, uneasily aware that all this propaganda had somehow failed of its full effect. The Netherlands roundabout however had been only one facet of the plan. Behind the visit to some of his patrimonial provinces by the heir apparent to Spain, the Indies, half of Italy, the Franche Comté and the Nether-

Overleaf: A suit of armour made for Philip II in Augsburg, Germany, in 1552.
Courtesy of the Armeria Real, Madrid. Photograph MAS, Barcelona.

Opposite: The original portrait by Titian, painted in 1553, hangs in the Prado; this copy is in the Palazzo Barberini in Rome.
Courtesy of the Galleria Nazionale, Palazzo Barberini, Rome. Photograph Scala, Florence.

lands, had lain something deeper: a project for winning for Philip the reversion to the Holy Roman Empire itself.

That Empire was still in theory elective. The shadowy successor of the real empire of Charlemagne, it still amounted – or *had* amounted before the advent of Martin Luther – to the spiritual leadership of Germany. By bribery of the Electors on a massive scale Charles had prevailed a quarter of a century earlier over the claims of the Kings of France and England, to win the accolade for himself. The spread of Protestantism in northern and central Germany had gravely compromised the standing of a Catholic emperor, as had the advance of Ottoman Turkish power into the heart of Europe, but the imperial crown was still the most glittering of prizes and it had long been Charles's wish to secure it for his son.

Unfortunately, his brother Ferdinand had been busily establishing a rival claim. Of the two brothers Charles was the more Germanic, having been born in Flanders, whereas Ferdinand had been born and brought up in Spain. Removed from the Spanish scene as a dangerous potential rival, the younger man had been sent to Vienna, where he was now firmly established as head of the Austrian branch of the family, and, what is more, had been elected 'King of the Romans', the title given to the Holy Roman Emperor's official heir-apparent.

Already the notion of a hereditary Habsburg succession to the purple was in the minds of both brothers. But hereditary in which branch? Ferdinand too had a son, the Archduke Maximilian, now acting, as we have seen, as Regent of Spain in Philip's absence and married to his sister, Maria. Must Ferdinand succeed as Emperor, with Maximilian as King of the Romans and designated Emperor in turn? This ran counter to the laws of primogeniture. That Philip should displace Ferdinand on the imperial ladder was never feasible, given the prestige that Ferdinand already enjoyed as King of the Romans. But that Philip should take precedence ahead of Ferdinand's son, Maximilian, seemed on the face of it both logical and just. Why should the crown not alternate between the Spanish and Austrian branches of the family? Why should Charles, having promoted the succession of his younger brother, stand aside and allow Maximilian, that younger brother's son, to find a place ahead of Philip, as he probably would if everything were left to the Electors?

At Augsburg in the closing months of 1550 all these points were thrashed out in a family conclave attended also by Maximilian, who had been secretly re-called from Spain by his father for the occasion, and Mary, Regent of the Netherlands, the Emperor's invaluable ally and adviser. From the discussions emerged the so-called 'Family Compact' of 9th March 1551.

Ferdinand would succeed Charles. There had never been any doubt of it. But Ferdinand now pledged that after his coronation he would urge the Electors to make Philip King of the Romans, provided Philip would promote Maximilian as *his* successor instead of his own son, Don Carlos. Thus the see-saw between the two branches would be kept in motion.

It was the purest fantasy. The Electors, being German bishops and princes, would never prefer a foreigner such as Philip to Maximilian, one of themselves. Intent in defence of their own local interests to limit, not aggrandize, the

Left: Philip's cousin, the Archduke Maximilian, painted by Moro.
Courtesy the Prado, Madrid.
Right: Maria of Austria, Maximilian's wife and Philip's sister, and mother of Philip's fourth wife, Anne; painted by Moro.
Courtesy the Prado, Madrid.

powers of a Holy Roman Emperor, they would not elect a man who was already heir to half the world. The Family Compact was never signed; Ferdinand merely expressed his verbal agreement to a deal which he well knew would not be implemented. The military disasters that were to befall the Emperor in 1552 at the hands of the Lutheran princes and the French reduced Charles's power to influence events and made the whole concept an absurdity. Nothing more was ever heard of it.

Yet from this tangled skein one small strand of family union had emerged. As Philip, buoyed up with an illusory sense of triumph, hurried homewards from Genoa to Spain, there was already in existence a niece just born to his sister Maria and Maximilian. The child was baptized Anne and was to become his fourth and last wife. This was the queen through whom the Spanish male line was to continue for three more generations. She was to become the great-grandmother of the semi-imbecile Charles II of Spain and of Louis XIV of France. The armies called into being by her descendants on either side of the Pyrenees were to help tear Europe apart in the terrible carnage of the Thirty Years' War.

Chapter 2

The English Marriage

The course taken by Philip's affairs in Spain over the years that followed was in sharp contrast to his father's experiences in Germany over the same period. Well governed and with an empire in the Indies growing to wealth and power, Spain was becoming the strongest of European states. In Germany, Charles was sinking from the heights he had reached after his victory at Mühlberg over the Protestant princes to the depths of impotence, culminating in his flight over the Alps from the armies of Maurice of Saxony and his humiliating failure to re-take the city of Metz which the Lutherans had ceded to the French king in return for his support. The power balance in Europe was shifting towards the maritime nations of the west at the expense of a central Europe torn by the religious feuds unleashed by the Reformation and by the advance of the Turks into Hungary. While the Holy Roman Empire was declining, Spain was founding a New World. It was the end of an era and the beginning of another in which the man whom admiring contemporaries had called 'Caesar' had only a few brief farewell scenes to play.

Charles had only managed to survive at all by grace of his enemies who, in Maurice of Saxony's words, had not a cage large enough to hold him. The Emperor's retirement after his defeats to Brussels, to the still nominally faithful Netherlands, was in a sense another Elba, from which he longed as fervently as Bonaparte to escape. But where the Corsican was to dream only of other triumphs, Charles, already a sick and prematurely ageing man, was consumed only with despair. Fortune, he remarked, was a strumpet who reserved her favours for the young; and for days on end he would remain sunk in apathy, from which even his closest confidants found it impossible to rouse him. Two thoughts however continued to intrude into this morbid, almost pathological withdrawal: he needed money and he had a son. His sister the Regent had urged him to send at once for Philip to return to Brussels if the Netherlands were not to go the way of Germany in the face of heresy and the French; and in the spring of 1553 Charles gave effect to this excellent advice in a letter which

34

was both a call to filial duty and a demand for quantities of hard cash. Then he turned to other dynastic matters:

> It is now a long time since the death of the Princess (whom God receive in His glory); and it seems to me suitable and necessary that you should marry again, because of your age, and because of the progeny which I hope God may grant you.

Maria of Portugal had been dead nearly eight years. And now it was another Portuguese – indeed another Maria – whom the Emperor had in mind for his son. He understood that he 'inclined towards her', as he put it; and this was true, for the Prince had been negotiating with Portugal almost to the point where a marriage contract was in the offing. The only real dispute was over the size of the dowry the bride would bring with her. If the Portuguese marriage failed to materialize, Charles could see no alternative among the princesses of Europe except perhaps a sister of the King of France.

Evidently no one at this stage had thought of England as likely to provide a suitable wife for the Prince. For England was in the toils of a Protestant dictatorship and its king a youthful nonentity. If the boy were to die soon, as seemed likely, it was the Emperor's view that the best diplomatic move would be to support the claim of the rightful heir, the Princess Mary, Henry VIII's daughter by Catherine of Aragon, but not to the point of making it appear that the Spanish were meddling in English affairs. The game must be played delicately, as Charles instructed his special representative in England, Simon Renard. Perhaps the best that could be hoped for was to see her married off to some Englishman who was not actively anti-Spanish – say Courtenay, Earl of Devon, a sprig of the old royal line.

No one in the Emperor's circle had very much hope of even this limited success. Spanish diplomatic efforts in England were faced with a powerful clique of Protestant noblemen who would stick at nothing to bar the papist Mary from the throne. Only when the thing happened – when the young king died, the Jane Grey usurpation failed, and by her courage in the crisis Mary came to be accepted by the nation as its rightful Queen – only then did the possibilities suddenly break in on the cautious, anxious diplomatists at the imperial court. For a pro-French, Protestant King, England had exchanged a Queen whose mother had been Spanish and who was herself the Emperor's first cousin.

This unexpected bonus acted like a tonic. From apathy the Emperor leapt into action. He became once more the able, experienced statesman of his early middle age when kings and peoples had trembled at his bidding. Yet now, as then, he was no fanatic: he calculated the odds. From his own early experiences with King Henry VIII he knew what an unpredictable ally England could be. Mary was now Queen. This was a great gain for his policy and it must not be compromised by haste on anyone's part. 'For God's sake', he wrote to his representative in England, 'let her moderate the lust for vengeance that probably burns in her supporters . . . !' As to marriage, she would obviously have to marry somebody, virgin queens being as yet unheard of. Any reasonable match would do. But as England settled down under the new régime, a new notion

An anonymous portrait of Mary Tudor; the painting is now in the Musée des Arts Décoratifs in Paris.
Photograph, Giraudon, Paris.

occurred to the Emperor's fertile mind. He recognized that the English would be likely to do all in their power to prevent their Queen marrying a foreigner. However, 'directly or indirectly', might not the Queen and her people be brought to look with favour on a match which had been talked of 'many years ago'?

For by a now-almost-forgotten treaty of 1522 Charles himself had been engaged to Mary Tudor, who had been an infant of six at the time. Nothing had come of it: instead he had married a Portuguese bride. Now widowed, ageing, tired and gouty, he no longer had any heart to marry anyone. But suppose his share in the contract could be transferred to Philip! The advantages were obvious. Englishmen could once more figure on the diplomatic and military stage as allies against France. They could be offered all sorts of inducements – even the prospect of recovering French territories which they had lost during the Hundred Years' War in the time of Joan of Arc. In fact the Emperor could see only one real objection: that perhaps Philip's negotiations for his Portuguese bride might have gone too far to be halted.

Fortunately for the planners of the new policy no such thing had happened, as Philip made clear in his reply:

> I will first of all kiss your Majesty's hands for what you say to me, for I very well see the advantages that might accrue from the successful conclusion of this affair. Your letter arrived at just the right moment, for I had decided to break off the Portuguese business. . . .

The Portuguese had been too niggardly over the dowry. Then came the Prince's contribution to the debate. If Queen Mary wanted a Spanish match, and if Charles himself was prepared to go through with it, would not the implementation of the 1522 treaty be the best possible result? Nevertheless if the Emperor was reluctant to play the bridegroom, and if Mary would accept a substitute, then he, Philip, would answer the call to the altar like a dutiful and loving son.

Armed with this acquiescence, Charles now turned to the problem of winning the lady in a stream of letters to his trusted Simon Renard at the English court. He excused his own reluctance in poignant, almost comical terms:

> We ourself, who esteem her and her virtue and gentleness . . . were we of a suitable age and disposition . . . would prefer no other alliance in the world to hers . . . But our health and age are such that we should consider ourselves to be doing but little for her in offering our person; nor do we see that we could in any way further her interests.

Charles then discloses a radiant prospect:

> But we could not propose to her anyone more dear to us than our own son the Prince, whose alliance would be much better suited to her, both because she could hope more surely to have children and for other reasons. We desire that the proposal may be made to her if she thinks it can be accomplished.

Poor Mary! She deserves more sympathetic treatment than she usually gets in the history books. She was brave, she was modest, she loved her country and her religion, perhaps too well. She was no dupe. She was not dazzled by the proposal. Given the choice, she would certainly have preferred the Emperor, an old friend, gentle, considerate, above all *mature*. Faced with the alternative of Philip, she timorously drew back. She had heard, she told Renard, that the Prince was not as wise as his father, and was he not very young? If he was disposed to be amorous, such was not her desire: she had, she added touchingly, never had thoughts of love. To this Renard replied in the true language of diplomacy, that the bridegroom was in fact so virtuous, prudent and modest as to appear 'too wonderful to be human', which was really to minimize his qualities. A superbly tactful and sensitive man, Renard went on to reassure the old maid that Philip at twenty-six was of so staid and settled a character as to be 'no longer young' – men were becoming as old now at thirty as they had once been at forty.

The Queen was captivated but not wholly convinced. Was all this about Philip really *true*? Was he really of such even temper and balanced judgment? Was he, she anxiously enquired of Renard, *well conditioned*? And when the ambassador assured her that it was so, she pressed his hand, saying: 'That is well.' Though she asked for an opportunity of seeing this paragon of a bridegroom, her decision was already made, and at a meeting of her Council she whispered to Renard out of earshot of the rest that she believed she would agree to the Emperor's proposal for the match.

Meanwhile from all over Europe offers were arriving for the bride – almost everyone wanted to marry her. Always adverse to foreign entanglements, the Queen's advisers were pressing her to stick to an Englishman and marry her distant kinsman, Courtenay, or Cardinal Reginald Pole, who also had royal blood in his veins. Pole himself, a true friend from her mother's time, advised her not to marry at all – it was the only good advice she was ever to receive on the subject. But Mary was her father's daughter, a true Tudor with the imperious temper of her race, and though she shrank from the very idea of matrimony, she had come to feel that it was her duty to her people. As to the husband of her choice, she would be guided by her cousin the Emperor; she would not be bullied or put upon by intriguing and self-seeking councillors. Small and ill-formed she might be; but her spirit, noted the Venetian ambassador Micheli, was lofty and undaunted by danger. A deep vein of fanaticism underlay her nature, partly hereditary, partly the result of her early sufferings, when she had had to live through her mother's divorce, the attacks on her religion and her own rejection by her father. At all events her mind was made up, and in Renard's presence she sank to her knees in her oratory and solemnly promised that she would wed the Prince of Spain, always provided, she added as an after-thought, that Philip was still free and not betrothed to the Portuguese princess.

During the next few months Charles's ambassadors were engaged in working out the details of a marriage contract that would satisfy English susceptibilities and calm English fears. The underlying aim was to attach England to the Spanish camp in the duel with France, but to do it with silken strings. Many of the provisions of the treaty were wise and salutary: Charles hoped through the issue of the marriage to shed some of the intolerable burden that he himself had suffered in governing both Spain and the Burgundian possessions divided from one another by half the width of Europe. If Philip and Mary had a son, that son would inherit England, also the Habsburg territories of the Netherlands and the Franche Comté. All the rest of Philip's inheritance – that is to say Spain, Naples, Sicily, Milan, the Indies and the Islands – would ultimately go to Don Carlos, Philip's son by his dead Portuguese wife. If this division had come about the whole course of history might have been changed: there might have been

Opposite: Mary Tudor painted by Hans Eworth in 1554, the year of her marriage to Philip. Courtesy of the National Portrait Gallery, London.

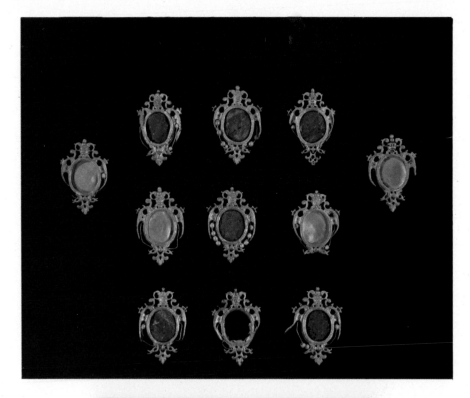

This life-size sculpture of Philip II in bronze is by Leone Leoni and was completed in the year before Philip's marriage to Mary. The prince is wearing half-armour richly embossed in the classical manner. The Assumption of the Virgin is depicted in high relief on the breast-plate.
Courtesy the Prado, Madrid.

no rebellion in the Netherlands and no Armada. Even the provisions affecting England look eminently sensible. Philip promised not to interfere in English affairs or to drag the country into continental wars: his connexion as sovereign would end with his wife's death. We can see that everyone in Charles's circle

Opposite: The portrait cameos illustrated here represent Roman Emperors. The frames are gold set with pearls, the portraits are carved lapis lazuli. These are typical of Renaissance jewellery. Courtesy of the Ulster Museum, Belfast.

had struggled to appease the English with concessions of a far-reaching kind. Yet so hated was Spain and so xenophobic and suspicious were the islanders,* that the direct result of the marriage treaty was Wyatt's rebellion which came within an ace of costing Mary her throne – only her courageous appeal to the Londoners saved her from humiliating capture and probably death.

What a country to govern! What a nation to marry into! The Queen herself remained undaunted, and in a solemn ceremony in the presence of her Council in the spring of 1554 knelt to ask God's blessing on her coming union, which she called on her people to support. But in Brussels there was less resolution. The Emperor, always a great worrier, had for months been pestering his representatives in England to tell him if it was really safe for Philip to venture there. At the same time he besought his son to give no offence by word or deed to these prickly islanders. Almost everyone in the Prince's circle found himself bombarded with similar appeals. 'Duke,' wrote the Emperor to the magnificent Alva, 'for the love of God see to it that my son behaves in the right manner; for otherwise I tell you I would rather never have taken the matter in hand at all.' Once in England the Prince must show himself loving to the Queen, must be cordial to all Englishmen, and must see to it that the Spaniards in his suite behaved with moderation and refrained from throwing their money about and bankrupting themselves. From far off in Rome came an appeal to Philip of rare poignancy from the Emperor's ambassador: 'For the love of God, appear to be pleased!'

And what of Philip himself, whose marriage had been arranged for him with a woman eleven years his senior in a country he had never visited? People have judged his conduct at this time as cold and repellent. Certainly he wasted no endearments and only at a very late stage of the proceedings sent his future wife even the token of a ring. But then the truth was, that for all his compliance with the Emperor's wishes, he felt a deep personal repugnance to the match. Early in 1554 in a secret document signed at Valladolid in the presence of the Duke of Alva and of his favourite, Ruy Gomez, Philip had protested that he had signed the marriage terms against his own will and would not bind himself or his heirs to observe them. For the rest, he probably averted his mind as far as possible from coming events in a strange land. In no way however could he dodge the stream of advice that continued to descend on him from the Emperor:

> My son: by all you hope to achieve by means of this match, I beg you to act in conformity with the instructions I sent you . . . They now tell me that married women are going to accompany their husbands in your suite. I believe even soldiers would be more likely to get on well with the English, so think whether it is meet to allow these women to follow you until things are more settled in that quarter.

Needless to say, the Emperor's confidential adviser and ambassador on the spot, Simon Renard, was not backward with suggestions of his own:

> Item, when his Highness enters the Kingdom, he will be well advised to caress the nobility and be affable. . . .

---

* And rightly. At the very first opportunity Philip embroiled England in war with France. It cost the nation Calais.

> Item, it will be well to show a benign countenance to the people and lead them to look for kindness, justice and liberty.

Philip would be well advised also to take the nobles out hunting. Above all, no women and no soldiers to be brought. A text-book for conduct in a foreign land.

Philip however was in no hurry to leave Spain. Throughout January and February 1554 he had been urged on by shrill cries from the Emperor to set out at once and not lose a moment. If he had obeyed his father in this, he would probably have been either shipwrecked in a winter storm in the Channel or murdered during Wyatt's rebellion. Evidently there were advantages to be gained by going slowly – a lesson he was to remember all his life. When he bothered to reply to the Emperor at all – and the gaps in his correspondence at this time caused constant anguish at the imperial court – his tone was cool, impersonal. One writer, Sandoval, was later to remark that Philip had sacrificed himself on the altar of filial duty 'like another Isaac', and no doubt this was largely true. His placid, orderly life was being brutally uprooted, for the English marriage meant the dismissal of his mistress, Doña Ana de Osorio, with whom he had lived for ten years.

At Corunna a fleet of over a hundred sail had assembled to take the Prince to England to claim his bride. He himself thought of the journey as a Crusade, and he acted out the preliminaries in a style suitable to the occasion. Having handed over the Regency to his younger sister Juana, widow of the King of Portugal, he set off for the north and at Benavente had a ceremonial meeting with his son, Don Carlos, in whose company he went hunting and watched a bullfight. At Santiago de Compostella, the shrine of Spain's patron saint, St. James, he knelt bareheaded on the stone floor of the sanctuary to pray for divine intercession for his journey; then embarked at Corunna on his flagship, the *Espiritu Santo* which flew his standard at its masthead, a vast thirty-foot-long crimson banner inscribed with his arms. It was Friday 13th June. The journey to Southampton was made in boisterous weather, and Philip's lifelong friend, Ruy Gomez, was to write that he (Gomez) had nearly died of seasickness on the way. But no thunderbolts fell. The omens seemed good. On 19th June the fleet was anchored safely at its destination.

The Prince dined and slept on board the *Espiritu Santo* that night, and after accepting the insignia of the Garter from the Queen's emissary, the Earl of Arundel, landed next day to a salvo of guns from the town and the respectful salutes of a welcoming delegation of the English Catholic nobility. The Spaniards of Philip's suite were headed by a phalanx of grandees and the wives whom Renard had besought them not to bring: the Dukes of Alva and Medina Celi, the Admiral of Castile, the marquesses of Pescara, de Valle, Aguilar and de las Nevas, the counts of Feria and Chinchon, the Bishop of Cuenca – a roll call of famous names whom we shall encounter again and again in the great events ahead. Solemn rejoicing was the order of the day, as, mounted on an Andalusian cross-bred specially selected by the Queen, he rode to the church of the Holy Rood to hear Mass, and then at his lodgings, sitting on a dais in a state chair upholstered in crimson velvet, addressed his hosts in Latin, assuring them that he came among them not as a stranger but as an Englishman. And in fact there was just an element of truth in this, since on both sides of his family he was distantly descended from the old royal line and had Plantagenet blood in his veins. To better prove it, he downed a flagon of English ale.

On the morning of 23rd June the Earl of Pembroke arrived with a company of gentlemen in black velvet and archers in the yellow and crimson livery of Aragon to escort Philip to Winchester and his bride. Of course it was raining, and long before the cavalcade entered the old Norman capital the bridegroom and his suite were soaked to the skin. Undaunted, after a quick change of clothes, Philip proceeded to the cathedral, to kneel at the altar while a *Te Deum* was sung after which he was taken in torchlight procession to the Dean's house for supper.

All this time the Queen had been preparing herself for martyrdom. She had not really sought a husband and part of her nature shrank from the ordeal. But now at Winchester with her bridegroom so close, her womanly curiosity overcame everything else – patience, protocol, decorum. Perhaps she had not been wholly convinced by Renard's many reassurances; at all events, at ten o'clock at night, she sent a message to the Prince, bidding him come with a small body of attendants through the gardens and up the back stairs to the long gallery in the Bishop's palace.

There at last the parties met and Philip first set eyes on his bride, a faded spinster of thirty-eight, small, thin, erect, determined, with reddish hair, no eyebrows, and a disconcertingly mannish voice. Though she had dressed gorgeously for the occasion in a black velvet gown with a silver petticoat and jewelled girdle and collar, and though the Venetian envoy thought she might have been called 'handsome rather than the contrary' if only her age had not been 'on the decline', she must have been something of a disappointment for an experienced widower of twenty-seven, trimly built, bearded, fair-haired, blue eyed, hardly the ageing valetudinarian pictured by Renard. The embarrassment was mutual: then the Prince advanced and they exchanged the ceremonial embraces of Spain, after which in the English fashion he kissed her on the mouth. Almost certainly from that moment she loved him, an emotion that was to last till her death.

Two days later they were married in Winchester Cathedral by Bishop Gardiner in a ceremony of great splendour: a marriage between equals in rank, for Charles had resigned the throne of Naples to his son for the occasion. It was St. James's Day, the day of Spain's patron saint, whose good offices were needed, for the Spanish gentlemen had much to endure before the night was out. The Queen for a start kept her lover waiting for half an hour at the cathedral door. When she appeared it was in finery almost outshining his – white satin with pearls and diamonds, a black cloak, red slippers. Such details have a worldly sound; but a Spanish observer of the Queen as she knelt at the altar saw that her eyes were fixed on the sacrament throughout. 'She is a saintly woman,' he added with reluctant respect.

After the ceremony in the cathedral there was a banquet, each course announced by blasts on the trumpet. The Queen was served on gold plate, Philip on silver – the English were determined to impress his inferior status on

Two medals depicting Philip (left) and Mary (right) issued in 1555; both are by Jacopo da Trezzo.

Courtesy National Portrait Gallery, London.

the man from the start. Later there was dancing, during which the bridal pair stepped out to a German measure. Naturally no Spaniard had a good word to say for the occasion. Few of the Queen's ladies seemed beautiful to those jaundiced eyes, though admittedly 'some were better than others'. They dressed their hair in the French fashion. Such a pity! If only they had imitated the coiffure of unmarried Spanish ladies it would have suited them so much better. As for the Queen, Ruy Gomez found her 'a good creature', though rather older than they had been told in Spain. Later, in this sanctimonious country, the bishops were brought in to bless the bridal bed before the royal couple retired from view. 'And here ceases all that I can tell your Majesty of what happened that day,' coyly reported another of the Emperor's spies on the spot.

Next morning Philip was up at seven. The Queen was secluded with her ladies. If, as some historians hold, conscience, not inclination, had driven her to wed, all that had been changed. Already she loved, adored, her husband – one has only to read her letters to her new father-in-law, the Emperor, full of impassioned gratitude and references on almost every other line to 'my lord and husband', as naive as from any young girl in the first pride of matrimony, of possession.

Through the eyes of members of Philip's staff we catch the other side of the picture, often in sharp and devastating detail. Writing to a friend in Spain, one of his gentlemen sees the bride with eyes unclouded by illusion: 'The Queen is not at all beautiful: small, and rather flabby than fat. . . . She is a perfect saint, and dresses badly.' With this judgment Ruy Gomez agreed: 'The King is well. . . . He treats the Queen very kindly, and well knows how to pass over the fact that she is no good from the point of view of fleshly sensuality.'

Yet everyone united in praising the kindliness with which Philip treated this unwanted bride; and if most of the tributes come from Spaniards whose interest it was to admire his benevolence, the Queen's own devotion to her husband is at least strong evidence that the tributes were true. On the ride to London he was noted as being always at her side, helping her to mount and dismount her horse. At court he showed her a charming deference. The Venetian ambassador praised him as the best of husbands, tenderly attached to her, and the evidence on the whole does seem to point, at least during the early months, to a fairly harmonious marriage between two people who shared the same political and religious hopes and depended on one another in the dangerous climate of the times. They had a language in common. Philip was a poor linguist, with no English and little French, but the Queen had as a girl been proficient in Castilian, her mother's tongue, and under the spur of marriage re-learned it very quickly. Both were of a retiring nature and found a haven in the quiet gardens and galleries of Hampton Court. Occasionally we get a glimpse of them in a wider setting, as in the report of the Duke of Savoy's travelling ambassador, who saw them in procession on the way to Mass at Westminster, the Queen in her litter, Philip riding companiably close beside her, amidst acclamations from the public.

The Duke of Savoy and his ambassador were clients of Charles and Philip and we may make some allowances for what they chose to see and hear. But that Philip came gradually to be accepted by at least some Englishmen is no more than the sober truth. After all, he had spent a fair amount of money in bribing the more biddable grandees with what were euphemistically called 'pensions', and there had been a good distribution of gold collars to the deserving. This was not without effect. Philip's presence, and even his advice, came to be accepted in the Privy Council; within two months of the wedding we find him telling his sister, the Regent of Spain, that for some days past he has been busying himself with affairs of state and has made a fair beginning. All well and good. Yet the real duty expected of him was not advice in Council but activity in bed, and by mid-November he seemed to have succeeded even in this, for rumours had begun to circulate that the Queen was pregnant.

Now in the very first days of the marriage one of Philip's gentlemen, after complaining of the immodest way the English court ladies dressed and of the phenomenal amount of beer drunk in England, which would fill the river at Valladolid, commented cattily: 'This match will be a fine business if the Queen does not have a child, and I am sure she will not.' But a great many hopes had been invested. Even Renard, normally one of the shrewdest of men, allowed himself to be deceived by what he heard and what he thought he saw. In November he was writing that there was *no doubt* that Mary was with child, for her stomach clearly showed it and her dresses no longer fitted her. By the end of the month he had the babe actually moving in the womb and recognized unmistakable signs 'at the breasts and elsewhere'. Ruy Gomez too was quite certain that the Queen was pregnant. And so was Philip himself, for in a letter in November to the Emperor's Spanish Secretary, Eraso, he opens up confidently: 'Now that the Queen is with child. . . .'

It was the onset of dropsy, perhaps complicated by an ovarian tumour. Fate could have played no more macabre game with anyone than with the poor deluded, passionate woman who was the Queen of England. On one occasion the actual birth of a Prince was rumoured and the bells began to ring throughout the country. Certainly in late November it really seemed that everything had combined to crown her joy, for to private happiness was joined the triumphant vindication of her faith, with the arrival of the papal Legate, Cardinal Pole, to reconcile England to Rome and receive the nation back into the arms of the Church.

This was the high-water-mark of the reign. As, with her husband beside her in the presence of the assembled Lords and Commons and her Privy Councillors, she heard the papal Absolution pronounced and joined in the singing of the triumphant *Te Deum* that followed it, she must have felt the certainty of God's blessing after the long tribulations of her life. Yet by a sad irony the victory of Catholicism, for which she and her husband had worked, was to prove the chief agent of her downfall. Parliament, bishops, councillors, all had tacked sharply with the changing wind to Rome, and hardly had reconciliation between nation and Pope been reached than the executions of heretics began.

On 1st February 1555 John Rogers was burnt at the stake. One of the distinguished translators of the so-called *Matthew's Bible* and ornament of the Reformed Religion, he had had the temerity to marry and then to preach

Five English protestants being burned at the stake in 1555.
Mary Evans Picture Library, London.

Engrav'd for Fox's Book of Martyrs.

The Martyrdom of G.Catmer, R.Streater, A.Burward, G.Brodbridg, *and* I.Tutty, *at* CANTERBURY.

against Popery at St. Paul's Cross soon after Mary's accession, the first of a long line of Protestant martyrs that was to include Latimer and Ridley and Archbishop Cranmer. Simon Renard had taken alarm at once and hastened to advise Philip that such cruelties were repugnant to the nation and should be stopped. In fact Philip, like his father, was sensitive to the political disadvantages that might result from too rigorous an application of the new laws against heresy and did at least do something to restrain the fanaticism of the Queen and her more bloodthirsty bishops, to the point of permitting his own chaplain to preach against the executions. All the same, his correspondence shows that he was not altogether averse to roasting an English Protestant or two, for in the early days of the persecution, in March 1555, we find him writing cheerfully enough: 'Things have been going better and better. Some heretics have been punished.' This was a misjudgment. The fires of Smithfield had been lit, in whose flames perished not only the victims immortalized by their sufferings, but also the Catholic ascendancy in England and the policy of alliance with Spain.

On 27th March, Renard wrote to the Emperor that there was much disaffection in England and that the executions had hardened many hearts, and this at a time when rumours were abroad that the Queen's pregnancy was a false one. A month later he seemed to have changed his tune, for he had a date to offer – 9th May, which was actually three days after talk of a birth had swept the country. By 22nd May Ruy Gomez, the best informed of Philip's entourage, had begun to develop doubts, after seeing the expectant mother stepping out so briskly in the Hampton Court gardens that all hope for a birth that month

A passport issued for Lord Howard of Effingham, High Admiral of England, at the end of May 1555. The intention was that he should go to Charles V to announce Mary's safe delivery of an heir, but there was never any need. Philip and Mary's signatures can be seen at the top of the document.

had obviously been abandoned. On 1st June Mary was reported as feeling the first pains. So deluded were the authorities, that a series of letters announcing the child's arrival (with only the date and sex left blank) had already been prepared for despatch by courier to a waiting Europe. On 8th June Ruy Gomez reported that the calculations of the doctors and of Mary's ladies had apparently got mixed up, and he added percipiently: 'All this makes me doubt whether she is with child at all. . . .'

It was one of the most grotesque and pitiful episodes of an unhappy reign. Only the Queen continued to believe for a few weeks more. The worldly Philip cannot have entertained such hopes for long. In August the Venetian ambassador was reporting that the comedy was over and that no one talked or thought of pregnancy any more; by the 18th of that month he had divined that the husband was about to bolt.

Only a pretext was wanted. Philip had been trapped in a position where he had not only to suffer the sneers and pasquinades of English enemies with their imputations on his virility – libels which led two of the most malignant of them to the tower – but even worse, he had to endure the official congratulations offered by the ambassador of a foreign power (Poland) on the actual birth of an heir.

Such a situation could obviously not be allowed to last for ever, particularly when the victim was a man of fanatical pride. As the months had gone by, Philip had become increasingly disenchanted with his actual powers to rule or even to influence the English. The Spaniards in his suite were in a semi-mutinous state. They complained about the weather, about English women, English dancing, about the insults they had to suffer, the denials of justice in the courts, the over-charging, the robberies and violence. Small wonder that as the Queen's pregnancy was revealed as an illusion, he should have begun to look around for some way out of the impasse. The Emperor's determination to abdicate his thrones, commencing that autumn with the sovereignty of the Netherlands, provided the perfect excuse for Philip. He was needed in Brussels.

Late in August he wrote in his own hand: 'I intend to leave this place within four or five days. It is no season to delay further.' The English venture was all but over. It had yielded very little. After a long period of indecision he had made up his mind. On 29th August, after punctiliously kissing the assembled maids of honour and suffering the embraces of his wife, he embarked for Flanders from the watergate at Greenwich. The Queen bore herself bravely. Only when he had gone downstream out of sight of her, as she watched from a window overlooking the river, did she give way to a paroxysm of weeping.

Chapter 3

Philip's Accession : War with France

On 8th September 1555 Philip rode into Brussels and was re-united with the father he had not seen for four years.

The Emperor was only fifty-five but already failing, and his public tears and embraces for his own son were certainly not feigned: he was finding other shoulders on which to lay the appalling burdens that weighed him down – heresy; war with France; unrest in the Low Countries; quarrels with the Papacy; the threat of bankruptcy and a staggering debt of twenty million ducats.

Given all this and the broken state of his own health, his abdication seems unsurprising. Yet that was not how it struck contemporaries. Emperors like other mortals died – on the battlefield, in bed, by poison, womanizing, disease, assassination or the activities of their physicians; they were sometimes deposed. But not since Diocletian in the days of Imperial Rome had anyone actually resigned. Such an act demanded explanation, and with a wealth of pageantry, to a bewildered and sceptical world.

So it happened that the abdication ceremony which took place on 25th October 1555 in the palace of the dukes of Brabant in Brussels was intended by its sponsor – and understood by everyone present – to be a cataclysmic event. And so in retrospect it was. On that autumn day the Emperor abdicated none of his crowns, only his rights as duke, count or lord of seventeen Nether-lands provinces and the Franche Comté, which in size, if not in wealth and power, formed only a minute part of his inheritance. He did not resign Castile or Aragon or the Indies, which were made over to Philip some days later at a private session of the Council. Nor did he abdicate the imperial crown, whose transfer his brother Ferdinand had asked him for political reasons to postpone for a while. Yet these were formalities, and at Brussels it was already clear that with Charles's departure something of the utmost importance had occurred – the collapse both of the medieval dream of one unitary Christian world under Pope and Emperor and of the union under one hand of Germany and Spain which had come about through the dynastic accidents of Charles's birth and accession. Normality was re-appearing with the division of the house of Habsburg into its Austrian and Iberian wings. Only in the continued Spanish rule over the Netherlands, on the northern fringe of the Germanic empire, was the unnatural union to be maintained – with fateful consequences for everyone – till the final divorce after eighty years of almost continuous war.

The choice of Brussels for the great ceremony marked Charles's own appreciation of what was happening. He could hardly have held it in his old imperial capital of Augsburg, in a Germany from which he was a fugitive, but probably in any event he would have chosen somewhere in his native Low Countries. By this formal handing-over of the patrimonial territories to his son, he was warning off not only the French, but also his own brother in Vienna and the North German princes who at one time or another had believed – or affected to believe – that the Netherlands were part of the Holy Roman Empire. By abdicating the provinces quite separately from that Empire and with maximum solemnity, Charles was asserting on the contrary that the Netherlands were tied not to Germany but to *Spain*. Buried under the rubble of failed hopes lay his earlier plan to unite the provinces and England under one crown, allied to, but independent of, Spain – the solution which might have averted the wars that were to follow but which had failed when Mary Tudor proved barren. Seen in this light there was a certain element of bravado, of whistling in the dark, about the performance in Brussels which can all too easily be missed.

This allegorical representation of the abdication of Charles V in 1555 in favour of his son Philip and (later) his brother Ferdinand was painted by Frans Francken.
Courtesy the Rijksmuseum, Amsterdam.

The deed of abdication of Castile and Leon. Charles made these provinces and others over to Philip II some days after the official abdication ceremony in Brussels.
Courtesy Simancas Archive, Valladolid. Photograph MAS, Barcelona.

As usual when in his homeland the Emperor was at his best and most relaxed – a benevolent father figure dressed soberly in black relieved only by the gleaming collar of the Golden Fleece, and leaning, as he entered the assembly, on the shoulder of a young grandee of eighteen: William, Prince of Orange.

Charles was unquestionably an artist in effects. After a brief statement of intent had been read by an official he rose to address the audience, describing his endless round of journeys up and down Europe and across the seas to Africa in defence of his peoples and the Christian faith, and begged forgiveness for any wrongs he might unintentionally have done. The whole assembly began to weep 'at the dolefulness of the matter', to quote the words of an English observer of the scene. Most of the audience were courtiers to whom tears – or any other emotion to order – came as naturally as breathing; yet there is no reason to doubt that Charles had moved them as deeply as he was moved himself. 'God bless you! God bless you!' he exclaimed as he sank back exhausted after his formal valediction to his heir: 'Fear God; live justly; respect the laws; above all, cherish the interests of religion; and may the Almighty bless you with a son to whom . . . you may be able to resign your kingdom with the same goodwill with which I now resign mine to you.'

It was then Philip's turn to take the centre of the stage. He was spared the knowledge that the young man on whose shoulder the Emperor had leaned was destined to shake Spanish rule in the Low Countries to its foundations and tear seven provinces from his grasp. But his task was anyway thankless enough. The Emperor had spoken in French, the language of the Burgundian court. Philip himself had only Spanish. The few halting words in French he managed to utter were mostly apologies, introductory to the speech by proxy from the throne which was about to be made for him by the glib and eloquent Bishop of Arras, the future Cardinal Granvelle.

Looking back on it, we can see that the choice of Orange, the choice of Arras (by birth a Burgundian, but from the Franche Comté), and Philip's own performance, were all prophetic. Even the chosen spokesman was a foreigner. The new ruler had been made to look a stranger in the Netherlands – and a stranger he was to remain.

Successive Venetian ambassadors kept a watchful eye on Philip during this formative period of the reign. Federigo Badovaro, reporting in 1557, gives us a portrait:

> He is small of stature and his limbs are mean. He has a fine large forehead, his eyes are large and blue, his eyebrows are thick and close together, the nose well proportioned; his mouth is big and the lower lip protuberant; this last is rather unbecoming. His beard is short and pointed. His skin is white and his hair is fair, which makes him look a Fleming; but his air is haughty, for he has the manners of a Spaniard. His disposition is phlegmatic and melancholic; he gets cramps in the stomach and bowels . . . As far as one can judge he is religious . . . By nature he seems to be inclined towards the good. . . . Just as his disposition is feeble, his is a somewhat timid spirit. . . . He is more inclined to mildness than to anger. . . .

Badovaro went on to underline this point by remarking that though very attentive to all that was said to him, Philip seldom looked directly at anyone but kept his eyes lowered, raising them only to 'glance here and there'; which is most surprising, since there is evidence from a somewhat later time that that dauntless woman St. Teresa found herself over-awed by what she called his 'piercing glance', while his secretary Antonio Perez, who perhaps came to know him better than anyone, spoke of his smile 'that cut like a sword'. Of course Badovaro was writing of the apprentice king, not the accomplished ruler whom St. Teresa and Perez knew. He went on in the same vein to add that Philip's 'good head' and capacity to deal with great affairs were incontestable, but that he lacked the energy the times demanded: 'To sum up, he is a prince who possesses many praiseworthy qualities' – a tepid judgment indeed.

Michele Suriano, who succeeded Badovaro at court, does not seem to have been greatly prejudiced in Philip's favour, for it was he who remarked on the bad effect the young man had made on his first tour of central Europe during the Emperor's reign and on the stern and unbending nature of his upbringing.

Yet Suriano had noticed a change in life style, a mellowing of temper and judgment. Physically, he wrote, Philip was small but well made, and he dressed in good taste. He was particular to the point of fussiness about his food; slept a lot; took little exercise. 'His policy', the envoy added, 'is directed towards keeping the peace' – a quietism which Venetian ambassadors continued to report throughout the years of war that followed. Were they grotesquely wrong? Was Suriano in particular being simply naive when he remarked that where the Emperor had sought out great enterprises, his son avoided them. It sounds on the face of it a sorry misjudgment on the king whose armies won St. Quentin and who was to preside over the victory of Lepanto, the seizure of Portugal and the Armada of '88; yet perhaps Suriano had seen more deeply than others before or since into the heart of the real man inside the shell: the orphaned child, the widower, the unfortunate father of Don Carlos. Who can tell? The most cynical if not the most illuminating report from the long line of diplomats sent by the *Serenissima* was made in 1559 by Marc Antonio da Mula, who wrote that it was hard to assess Philip's character, since kings had a thousand inaccessible grottoes and caverns in their hearts where only God could penetrate. Taking it all in all, though, the picture seems clear enough: a shy, reserved, sluggish man, a little below par physically, a fish out of water in the alien environment of the Netherlands; the man in the armour never worn in battle shown in Titian's famous portrait of about this time.

One strange note intrudes, for almost in the same breath as accusing the new ruler of feebleness and timidity Badovaro levels another kind of accusation: that he was a Don Juan who went masked by night 'even in the midst of the most important affairs' – to 'indulge himself in the common haunts of vice', adds the censorious historian Motley in his *Rise of the Dutch Republic*, where Philip is described as being 'grossly licentious'.

Licentious perhaps – it was that kind of age, where no one thought worse of an emperor for having bastards. But gross is not a word that goes comfortably with Philip. These night escapades took place, but before judging him too harshly it might be fair to remember that though King of Castile, Aragon, Sicily, Naples and the Indies, Duke of Burgundy and Milan, Dominator of Asia and Africa, titular king of England and Jerusalem, he was also a young man of twenty-eight just freed from the shackles of a carping English Privy Council, an ailing wife and an imperious father. Such a sudden rise to power and the freedom to do as he liked after a lifetime of self-discipline would have turned much wiser and older heads. He found himself surrounded by adulation, by a round of tournaments and pageants staged for him by a people famed for their extravagance and recklessness – a dozen men died in Antwerp in accidents with fireworks during just one of these displays, and heaven knows how many from drink and the pox.

Rumours of these goings-on soon reached England and the ears of the Queen. They all but prostrated her. She was sensible enough, however, not to complain directly to her errant husband. Charles (who had not yet resigned the Empire) was still in the Netherlands, and it was to him, her old friend and suitor, that she wrote in the spring of 1556, imploring him 'most humbly and for the love of God' to do all that was possible to hasten Philip's return to England now that the abdication ceremonies were over. 'I beg your Majesty to forgive my boldness,' she added touchingly, 'and to remember the unspeakable sadness I experience because of the absence of the King.'

On his accession to his clutch of thrones, dukedoms and counties, Philip had written to his wife assuring her that she was now as much mistress of each and every one of them as she was of England; but that was about the only satisfaction she got; and in May 1556 she was once again importuning the Emperor: 'I cannot but deeply feel the solitude in which the King's absence leaves me. As your Majesty knows, he is the chief joy and comfort I have in this world.' Charles himself, preoccupied with family matters and preparations for his retirement to Spain, was not helpful, and in July she gave way for the first time to bitterness, complaining that he had broken his solemn word to send Philip back to England once the formalities of the transfer of power had been completed. 'I must perforce be satisfied,' she wrote, 'although to my unspeakable regret.'

This was not altogether without effect – that summer from Ghent the Queen received a communication from her husband addressed 'Most Serene Queen, Our Most Beloved Spouse.' It concerned the payment of a debt.

The end of the relationship had not yet come, however, for Philip was to have further need of Mary, just as Charles had needed her at the time of the marriage negotiations.

The need of course arose from politico-military considerations that had nothing whatever to do with the Queen's or English interests but were concerned with the source of most of the ills of the time: the rivalry between France and Spain, with Flanders and Italy as the prize, which had begun with the French invasion of Naples in 1495 and had taken on a new tone of dynastic rivalry between Habsburg and Valois with Francis I's candidacy for the imperial throne and his incursion into the Milanese in Charles's time.

Soon after his accession Philip had agreed a five year truce with his French rival, Henry II. It was sufficiently necessary, since both sides were on the verge of bankruptcy, and it might even have lasted if in Rome, in the chair of St. Peter, there had been any other Pope than the Neapolitan Paul IV, who spoke openly of Spaniards as 'a race accursed of God, the spawn of Jews and Moors'.

Paul's hatred of Philip and the Emperor was partly personal, the result of slights and injustices suffered in his career, but sprang also from his love of Italy, which he saw polluted by the Spanish presence in Naples, Sicily and Milan. As ruler of the Papal States he had good reason for wanting the Spaniards out. That the French in that case would move in to fill the vacuum troubled him not at all – indeed he was prepared to welcome a French prince on the throne of Naples, a French alliance, and even help from the Ottoman Sultan, 'the Grand Turk', if he could only rid himself of the hated presence. And naturally Henry II was tempted to fish in these troubled waters like his father before him.

A similar grouping of a grasping adventurer in Paris and ambitious and reckless forces in Italy had threatened the basis of Spanish rule in that peninsula early in the Emperor's reign during Francis I's invasion which had ended so ingloriously for the French at Pavia. But where Charles had faced war on one front, Philip had to reckon with two; for while a French army under the Duke of Guise, loudly proclaiming its innocence of truce breaking, was marching southwards to the aid of the papal troops, other French forces under the Constable, Montmorency, were concentrating in Picardy opposite the frontiers of the Netherlands.

It was a severe test for a man whose talents were not warlike and whose life-long mentor had just left his side. Fortunately he found himself well supported by his Viceroy in Naples, the Duke of Alva, who easily checkmated every enemy move till Guise's Frenchmen had retreated across the Alps, and the Pope, abandoned by his allies, had sulkily consented to allow his even sulkier conqueror to ask forgiveness for the victory and kneel to kiss the papal toe. From this war, not of his making, Philip had gained nothing except peace in Italy and confirmation of his title of Most Catholic King. Nonetheless, by means of Alva he had tamed the Pope. And where the front in Picardy was concerned, the part he played in preparing for the eventual victory was central to it, even if in the process he was to miss the two great battles that crowned it and earn eternal obloquy in English eyes for the loss of Calais.

Of the choices open to him, a defensive campaign behind the screen of towns that lined the Netherlands frontier with France might have seemed the more congenial. But his army commander, his friend and boon companion Emmanuel Philibert of Piedmont, titular Duke of Savoy, had been driven from his duchy by the French and had never ceased bothering his Spanish allies for a chance to restore himself to power in Turin by some shattering victory over his supplanters. A spring at France's throat in Picardy was therefore likely from the start.

Defensive or offensive – in either case Philip needed men and money before taking on the enemy that had humiliated the Emperor at Metz. The nearest available allies were the English; and in March 1557 he gave his personal attention to the problem by crossing over to London and his still doting Queen.

It is not the pleasantest chapter in Philip's life. His object was simply to use Mary and the more biddable members of her Privy Council to embroil England in war with France and to raise a contingent of English troops for Flanders.

As though intent on helping him, an English traitor in French pay chose this moment to attack Scarborough Castle, arousing the slumbering hatred most Englishmen still felt for the ancient foe of Crécy and Agincourt. A declaration of war followed, and after ten weeks Philip returned well pleased to Brussels, pursued by fresh rumours of his wife's pregnancy.

His treatment of the money problem was equally sure. With the rather grudging help of the Emperor, now far off in Spain in his retreat at the monastery of Yuste in the hills of Estremadura, approaches were made to the fabulously wealthy Spanish Church, which responded handsomely. The Archbishop of Toledo, Primate of Spain, provided half a million ducats; even the Grand Inquisitor, a notorious miser, was induced to part with 40,000; and for once in a while there was actually cash in hand in the Spanish treasury, if one forgot the backlog of debts.

This was the day of professional armies. Townsmen could sometimes be driven to defend their walls but in the open field they could expect to be

This suit of armour was made in Pamplona and presented by the city to Philip II.
Courtesy Palacio Real, Madrid. Photograph MAS, Barcelona.

massacred. No ruler could hope to make war without mercenaries. Certain nationalities and groups were recognized as being quality material: the Turkish Janissaries; the Swiss; the German pikemen (*Landsknechts*) and mounted pistoleers (*Reiters*); French light horse and Spanish infantry, the famous *tercios** who were to dominate the battlefield for most of the next century. The paymaster with money or the prospect of a few fat towns to sack could take his pick of the market, but he could be sure of one thing – his men would all melt away or mutiny the moment the funds ran out.

* A *tercio* at full strength was an infantry unit of 3,000 men (all long-serving and Spanish) divided into twelve companies, armed with pikes, javelins and arquebuses (later, muskets). Like the Roman legions, *tercios* were permanently stationed abroad and were named after their place of garrison.

Opposite, above: Hieronymous Bosch was a painter particularly favoured by Philip; he is thought to have owned as many as thirty-six of the artist's paintings. This picture, The Epiphany Triptych, *was confiscated from Jean de Casembroot, a rebellious Netherlander, in 1567 and sent to the Escorial in 1574.*

Below: Charles V was Titian's greatest patron; his son followed his lead and collected at least twenty-two paintings by the artist. Philip ordered this painting, Venus and Adonis, *at the age of twenty-six and it was sent to London on the occasion of his marriage to Mary Tudor. Adonis was thought to bear a striking resemblance to Philip II.* Both Courtesy of the Prado, Madrid.

For his army in Flanders Philip had recruited some 35,000 foot, 12,000 horse and an artillery train, mostly from Germany and Spain but with a leavening of Netherlands cavalry and an English contingent of 8,000 under the Earl of Pembroke. The difficulties of commanding and supplying so motley a force need no underlining – the language problem alone would be acute, and any slight to national pride had to be carefully avoided. But given regular pay, a surprising loyalty could be evoked by a commander-in-chief who understood his trade and the strengths and weaknesses of his men. The Duke of Savoy was an efficient exponent of this kind of warfare. In the summer of 1557 he set his whole force in motion and, after a series of diversionary moves to confuse the enemy, concentrated against the town of St. Quentin in the valley of the Somme.

No one, least of all the French, should have been surprised, for this was the only place of any strength between the Low Countries and Paris. Its fortifications had been allowed to fall into a sad state of disrepair, a fact surely known to the French high command. Yet only at the last moment did one of the senior officers, Admiral Coligny, throw himself into the town and set his men feverishly at work to strengthen it.

Even so, the threat to the city remained acute, and the Constable of France, Montmorency, decided that he and his field army must cover the introduction of fresh reinforcements, to be ferried across the river in full view of the besieging Spanish army. Few of them actually reached the town; many were drowned; others lost their way in the swamps. When the Constable himself with the main body turned to retreat he found that the Netherlands cavalry under Count Egmont had occupied the high ground above the defile through which his army would have to march to reach its base in La Fère. In his perplexity the Constable is said to have asked one of his commanders what he should do. 'If you had asked me two hours ago I could have told you' was the reply. In fact it

A saddle made for Philip II in Augsburg, Germany. It is interesting to note the relief decorations which are also used on the armour on page 41.
Courtesy Palacio Real, Madrid. Photograph MAS, Barcelona.

This painting of the Battle of St. Quentin is one of a series painted by Jordan to form a frieze on the stairs at the Escorial.
Courtesy the Prado, Madrid.

was already too late. Egmont's cavalry charge swept away the French vanguard like chaff in a matter of minutes, and the arrival of Savoy's infantry completed the destruction of the remaining formations in the field. Perhaps as many as ten thousand of the beaten army were killed or wounded and the majority of their commanders, including Montmorency himself, were taken. For France it was a disaster greater than Pavia, which at least had happened on foreign soil; perhaps as great as Agincourt. Only Coligny and his remnant in the citadel and the fugitives who managed to reach La Fère remained as combatants.

The battle of St. Quentin, fought on 10th August 1557, St. Lawrence's Day, was one of the climaxes of the reign. According to one story, when Charles heard the news at Yuste he looked to the fall of Paris within a few days and could hardly conceal his rage and disappointment as the weeks went by without this supreme triumph. He must have forgotten that after his own defeat in Germany at Protestant hands he had been allowed to escape across the Alps because not even his bitterest enemies could envisage so final a result as the capture of an Emperor. The taking of Paris would solve nothing either – as the future was to show many years later in the 1590s when Spanish troops were for a while inside the town. Philip's generals at the council of war that followed the victory of 10th August might boast and argue, but at heart they knew better than to drive much deeper into a country of the size and power of France without the support of some party or faction inside it. There were English, and indeed Burgundian, precedents from the time of Henry V and Henry VI to remind them of some of the dangers. In any case there was not enough money to keep an invading army in being so far from its base. The most that could be attempted was the capture of St. Quentin itself, which fell seventeen days after the battle amid scenes of horror which even the hard-bitten English regretted. The burning of the town lost them some of their share of the loot.

Philip had not been present at the battle and it was not till the following day that he came dressed cap-à-pie in inlaid silver armour to the camp to inspect the captured prisoners and flags. But he was with the army at the storming of the town – his first taste of warfare, apart from his nominal command of an expedition against an invading French force in Roussillon when he had been sixteen – and he found the holocaust of blood, rape and fire distressing. Of course there was little he could do about it – few sixteenth-century commanders could hope to control the maddened mob of soldiery at the sack of a town – but at least he managed to save some of the women and children and the bones of the local saint, Quentin himself, which he housed in his tent, to the scorn of the historian Motley when he came to write of the scene three

A letter from Philip to his father telling him of the victory at St. Quentin.
Courtesy Simancas Archiva, Valladolid, Photograph MAS, Barcelona.

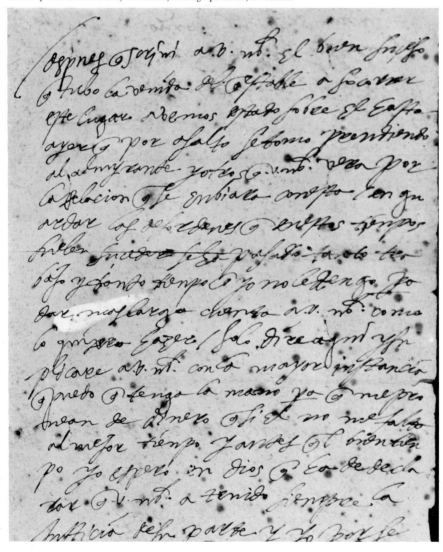

hundred years later. The King should surely be allowed some credit for his humanity.

That the English had distinguished themselves during the siege and had been the first troops over the walls had been freely reported in London, and great was to be the dismay of Queen Mary some weeks later when Philip's tactless envoy, the Count of Feria, denied that this had actually been the case. By then even worse things had happened to distress the islanders. For over two hundred years, last survivor of the conquests of Edward III at the start of the Hundred Years' War, the town of Calais had belonged to England, a splendid sallyport into France for English armies and English trade. Late in December 1557 the Duke of Guise, returning from his discomfiture at Alva's hands in Italy, concentrated an army in Artois and moved against the fortress in overwhelming strength.

On the last day of the old year, as the French closed in, the commander of the garrison, the Earl of Wentworth, sent a desperate call for help to the King. On 2nd January Philip sent him in return a last minute warning of French intentions: this was the day the siege began. On his second visit to England in the previous year he had passed through Calais and had drawn the attention of his wife's Councillors to the poor state of its defences. He had even offered reinforcements of Spanish troops but these had been declined: the English were too suspicious of his motives to allow any of his troops inside the town. But they had done nothing to strengthen the place, and on the 3rd January Wentworth wrote to Philip that there was little hope unless relief was sent at once. This was the last appeal from the town which fell four days later.

The furore and shock in London were tremendous. The nation's most prized possession had been snatched away. This was what came of the hated and unnatural alliance with foreigners! Even Philip, who seldom excused or explained, felt the need to exculpate himself, and in a letter to the Privy Council asserted that the aid he had provided would have been sufficient if those in command of Calais had done the minimum to help themselves.

This disaster, soon followed by other reverses for English arms at Guisnes and Hammes, probably hastened the mortal illness of the Queen, alone and deserted by almost everyone. She felt disgraced before her own people, surrounded by troubles on every side. Even Feria, not normally a man of very sensitive feeling, advised his master, if he could not come to London, at least to write to his wife. The poor woman still clung desperately to the belief that she was pregnant – her only solace through nights of sleeplessness filled with fears (as Feria told the King) that the reign had come to nothing.

Immersed in the problems of war and peace in Flanders and the spread of heresy, which had gained a foothold even in Spain itself, Philip had neither the time nor the inclination to bother himself about an ailing wife. The most charitable explanation of his silence is that he failed to appreciate that she was dying. On the 22nd October he wrote to the English Privy Council that having learnt of her illness, he was sending 'a person' – the Count of Feria again – to attend to certain business with her and 'excuse' his absence.

When he reached London Feria found the Queen far gone. She had been unconscious most of the time, he reported, but in her waking moments was always in fear of God and love of Christianity. The great matter at stake was the succession to the throne. During the troubles that had arisen from Henry VIII's matrimonial entanglements his daughter by Anne Boleyn, the Princess Elizabeth, had at one stage been declared a bastard and had long been an object of suspicion at her half-sister's court, but few Englishmen, or for that matter Spaniards, doubted that she was the rightful heir who must inherit on Mary's death: this was the course Feria had been sent to press on the Queen, and to it she wearily assented.

Feria went on to Hatfield to sup with the rising sun, carrying messages of good-will from his master. On all sides great events were pending, for a peace conference had been convened near Cambrai to put an end to the long feud between France and Spain, and it was Mary's fate to be ignored in death as during most of her tragic and pitiful life. Even the news of her passing was overtaken by despatches from Yuste announcing the death of the Emperor Charles. Under this greater bereavement Philip's reactions to the loss of a wife were sufficiently controlled. In December he wrote to his sister Juana, Regent of Spain, regretting that the question of the peaceful recovery of Calais could not be settled quite so easily now that the Queen of England was dead. She had had some uses. 'May God have received her in His glory', he added, using the usual formula for such events. 'I felt a reasonable regret for her death. I shall miss her even on this account.'

Chapter 4

After Mary's Death: Philip and the Netherlands

The peace negotiations had in fact broken down on this question of Calais, which with Mary's death no longer directly concerned the King of Spain. The French were willing to cede the very substantial conquests they had made in the Emperor's time in return for the more modest Spanish gains in the recent war, but where Calais was concerned they were adamant: they utterly refused to give it up. The English insisted just as strongly on recovering it. Were the prospects of peace to be thrown away to preserve the illusions of grandeur of a small nation which had lost a town through its own fault?

No one in England then or since has ever given much credit to the position which Philip honourably chose to take up. Faced with the chance of a military and diplomatic triumph as great as anything his father had achieved, he still refused to buy peace at his ally's expense. If he had acted badly in dragging England into a war that did not concern her, at least he stood by the consequences. But with Mary's death a new factor had appeared on the scene: the Princess, now Queen, Elizabeth.

What could be done with her? What could be done with her country, all too dangerously poised on the brink of heresy? In his dilemma Philip had one guide-line – his father's last political testament:

> Preserve peace with France as well as you can, but never lose the friendship of England.

Did he remember that advice in the years of misunderstanding and rivalry that followed till the day when the Armada put out of Lisbon? In 1558, in the immediate aftermath of Charles's death, one solution that fully accorded with the Emperor's words presented itself – why should he not marry his dead wife's half-sister and continue as titular King of England, perhaps with the added dignity of the Crown Matrimonial which the English had contrived to block? Once in this position he could face the French with the threat of a re-invigorated Anglo-Spanish alliance and of a joint march on Paris if Calais were not restored.

In London the Count of Feria, who himself had married an Englishwoman, was doing his best to judge the prospects for the new reign. A blunt, forthright man, he found the excuses, blandishments and double-talk exasperating. 'Really this country is more fit to be dealt with sword in hand than by cajolery', he reported back to his master shortly after Mary's death. But in spite of himself he found the young Queen impressive. 'She seems to me', he wrote that December, 'incomparably more feared than her sister and gives her orders and has her way as absolutely as her father did.' No one ever read Elizabeth better than Feria, even down to the quirks of her devious, many-sided nature: 'She is very fond of having things given her and her one theme is how poor she is', he noted of her parsimoniousness, to become world famous. Less happily inspired, he told his master of a prophecy that she would reign only a short time and that thereafter Philip himself would return to rule in England. He could hardly have believed it.

Early in the new year of 1559 Philip began to brief Feria on the line to be taken with the Queen and her Council. He could already, he remarked, have signed peace with France and have left them in the lurch. The fate of the negotiations largely depended on what England was prepared to do. Would she accept the French draft treaty and the loss of Calais? Or would she reject it? – in which case she must play her full part alongside Spain in the renewal of the war that must follow. 'If they do not decide soon in London,' he wrote, uttering one of his delicate diplomatic threats, 'I am not sure that I shall not have to resolve as suits me, it being needful for my affairs.'

Along with this reminder, however, went the offer of a marriage – on terms. In his instructions to Feria, Philip led off by saying that it would not look well for him to be united with Elizabeth, who was far from sound on religion. He was still prepared in the interests of Christianity to forget such a 'disadvantage' and make an offer for her hand, with this proviso, that the bride must make her formal submission to Rome and swear to uphold Catholicism in England. Furthermore, any child of the union would not (as under the marriage treaty with Mary) inherit the Spanish Netherlands, which would go to Don Carlos. This was Philip's first break with the policy of Charles V which had aimed at detaching the Netherlands from Spain; he was only to revert to it at the end of his life.

How seriously was all this meant? On the face of it few more grudging or perfunctory proposals of marriage have ever been made, almost as though he was inviting a refusal or testing out a line he doubted would come to anything. On the other hand in his wife's lifetime he had managed to make her very jealous by the attentions he had paid the princess. Feria, having personally witnessed much of this, suggested that the warmth of these attentions should be used as arguments for the strength of the King's attachment *now* – an approach which Philip vetoed immediately out of a sense of Castilian punctilio. Yet the marriage as an extension of his father's policy towards England would have suited him politically, and the twenty-five-year-old Elizabeth, high-spirited, passionate and by no means unalluring, must have seemed a decided improvement on Mary Tudor in the eyes of a widower of thirty-two. From his standpoint the only real question mark hung over the matter of religion, and to it he returned in February in instructions to his ambassador to approach the Queen with

earnest exhortations not to change her country's allegiance to the Pope –
rumours of which change were already rife in Europe. If she persisted in such
heretical ways Feria must consider whether or not to withdraw the marriage
offer: a truly astonishing communication from a bridegroom to his agent and
early proof of the man's fundamental inability to make up his own mind.

In London, like so many ambassadors after him, Feria was in the coils of
Elizabethan diplomacy. At an audience in February the Queen had told him
that she had no wish to marry anyone. What hopes she entertained in her secret
heart of making the already married Robert Dudley her husband remains a
mystery, but with the example of her half-sister's fate before her it is certain
that never for one moment did she seriously think of marrying the King of
Spain. He had to be humoured however, since he was one of the arbiters of the
fate of Calais, besides being a powerful neighbour whom it would be unwise to
offend at this early stage in her fortunes. There was of course no one whom she
would prefer as a suitor and husband, she said demurely when pressed for an
answer, but marriage was not to her taste. Also the King of Spain was her
brother-in-law and such a marriage offended against the laws of God. Somewhat later she added that in any case she could not marry Philip because she
happened to be a heretic.

*This portrait of Robert Dudley, Earl of Leicester, as a young man, is attributed to
Steven van der Meublen.*
Courtesy the Trustees of the Wallace Collection, London.

Under this treatment the Count of Feria had become first bewildered and then more and more enraged. He was inclined to blame a good deal on the Queen's advisers, particularly Cecil, 'a pestilent knave'. But the Queen herself was not much better – the daughter of the Devil, he concluded. As some compensation for the hard news he was transmitting to his master, he had already correctly guessed that she would not bear children.

For his part, Philip accepted the rebuff to his proposal with good grace. He did not even allow himself to be too shocked by the rumours flying about Europe of Elizabeth's liaison with Dudley, whom she had created Earl of Leicester. He took steps with the Papacy to prevent her being publicly declared a bastard, his aim now being to marry her off to one of his Austrian relations, the Archduke Charles, and so hold her in the Catholic camp. Even at this stage in the duel that was to engage the pair of them for their lifetimes he had acquired a respect for that devious and protean woman, a doubt as to how far he could curb and contain her. As the future was to show, his was the more tentative spirit: it was almost always he who worked the harder to propitiate and explain. Yet at this first encounter, his was the diplomatic victory, if not in the bed-chamber, at least in the conference room at Cateau-Cambrésis, where of the three treaty-making powers it was England that was the loser. Spain won back territories for herself and her allies. France recovered a few towns. Elizabeth was forced to accept a face-saving formula for the eventual return of Calais which everyone knew would never take place. Also as part of the peace settlement Philip engaged to marry her namesake, Elizabeth of Valois, the daughter of the French king. She made Feria a terrible scene about it.

'According to the news I receive, the King of France is no less hard up than I am,' Philip had written to his sister Juana soon after the fall of Calais. This was putting it mildly, for these two crowned comrades in misfortune were actually bankrupt and Philip for one had felt the need for peace so acutely that if his opponent had not sued for it he would have sued for it himself – or so at least he was later to tell the Venetian envoy Suriano. Exhaustion of credit was thus one of the main reasons for the Cateau-Cambrésis treaty. Another was the realization of the combatants that they had as much to fear from internal enemies as from each other. For heresy had been spreading rapidly among sections of the French nobility and had begun to seep into the Netherlands in both its Lutheran and Calvinist forms.

For a brief moment after the signing, the possibility of joint action by the 'Most Christian' and 'Most Catholic' kings in defence of the old religion was in the air, and one of the tokens of it was Philip's marriage by proxy with the princess who had originally been intended for his son, Don Carlos. But during the celebrations which followed, the bride's father, Henry II, was mortally wounded in an accident in the lists; and France, under the rule of his widow and three degenerate sons, became the scene of thirty years of intermittent religious war between Catholic and Huguenot.*

* The word 'Huguenot' derives from *Eigenot*, or German *Eidgenosse*, meaning a citizen of Geneva, the citadel of Calvinism.

68

By this marriage and death Philip was freed for the time being from one of the major problems that had plagued his father throughout his life and in the end had brought him down. It was pure gain, for however hostile to Calvinism Henry II might have been, a strong French king would have been tempted to take advantage of a Protestant rising in the Netherlands, and sooner or later French intervention would have occurred along the lines that had been followed in support of the German Lutherans in Charles V's day. Philip was spared a repetition for the moment. But the very impotence of the French monarchy after Henry's death had its dangers, since it encouraged Huguenot militancy and recourse to civil war – a brushfire war all too close to the frontiers of the Netherlands for Spanish comfort.

The Spanish Netherlands

In France, from beginning to end, Catholicism was the popular religion except in parts of the south and in the sea-ports of the north-west. And broadly the same was true of the Netherlands, where Catholics were long to remain in the majority, even in the provinces whose leaders embraced Calvinism. At Philip's accession a majority everywhere undoubtedly recognized his rule. But they recognized him as hereditary duke, count or lord of their particular province, not as their king from Spain. And certainly, almost to a man, they detested the Spanish troops stationed on their soil and Philip's Spanish favourites and advisers.

These were about the only things they did agree on, for the seventeen provinces of the Netherlands differed widely from one another in race and social structure. Some, like Artois, Hainault, Holland, Flanders and Brabant, were among the richest communities in Europe and included in Antwerp Christendom's greatest port and commercial centre after Seville. Some were poor, comprising a few mud-flats lost in the wastes of desolate lagoons. Some were industrial, some agricultural. There was no common language. North of a line running from just above Liège through Tournai to the sea near Dunkirk people spoke a Low German dialect; south of it, and in the linguistic island of Brussels, French. The division has survived into our own times. The present kingdom of the Netherlands, popularly known as Holland, falls squarely into the northern sector, with some rather baffling side-results, for we must remember that in Philip's day the term 'Netherlands' meant all seventeen states, while 'Holland' was just one of them. Modern Belgium includes the old provinces of Flanders and Brabant and their Walloon cousins of Namur, Tournai and Hainault, with the language line still dividing them. The old archbishopric of Liège has been incorporated in the modern kingdom, but most of Artois is now in France. Luxemburg stands much as it was. Today's divisions are however noticeably fewer than they were in Charles's and Philip's time when the seventeen had no semblance of unity. Each province had its own laws, its own customs. There was a body called the States General that was supposed to represent the whole, but it had far less tradition behind it than the English parliament and had barely begun to find its voice. Even the local organization of the Catholic Church within the territories was rudimentary. There were only three resident bishops: at Tournai, Arras and Utrecht. Utrecht was responsible for over a thousand churches and two hundred townships. Luxemburg was shared between three bishops and as many archbishops, none of whom lived within its borders. The hierarchy that governed the spiritual welfare of every Netherlander was foreign-based – men looked to Rheims and Cologne.

For well over a century Philip's Burgundian ancestors had tried to cobble some kind of governable and more logical unit out of this hotch-potch of jealous parochialism. To give the provinces a centralized administrative and legal system had been the aim of the Emperor Charles, and to some extent he had succeeded. Even the existence of the States General was the result of a royal initiative – not entirely an unselfish one, since it was also the means of making tax collection simpler for the ruler. It was Philip's hope to do the same for the Netherlands Church, by replacing its pitifully small establishment with

The first of a series of four engravings (executed in 1572) showing the conflicting parties in the Netherlands unrest: Philip is here standing between the Inquisitor and the Bishop while at his feet two monks complain that they are being driven out of their churches.
Courtesy Atlas van Stolk, Rotterdam.

a grand structure of three archbishoprics and fourteen bishoprics to match the wealth and dignity of the country.

Some such reform was certainly needed – on paper – and in Charles's time it could probably have been carried out without much difficulty. The Emperor had meditated the step but significantly had stopped short of performance, for he had a very acute sense of what could and could not be done in the land of his birth. Philip's plan was no more than an extension of his father's. He was more an inheritor than an initiator. Most of the draconic edicts against heresy, prescribing death for anyone who bought, sold or handled heretical books, who made or sold libellous cartoons of the Virgin or Saints, who defaced images or took part in illegal preachings on the Scriptures, had been enacted by his father, long before his accession. So had the savage edicts against the Anabaptists, who were to be executed for their beliefs even if repentant, and if unrepentant were to be burnt alive. The activation of the Papal Inquisition in the Netherlands had also been Charles's work. None of this had come from Philip's brain. However, it was his misfortune that he tried to implement it at a time when social and religious unrest was rising, and then remained blind to the dangers till too late.

There were arguments for a forward policy on his part. To have sat idly by and watched the unreformed Netherlands Church sink deeper into apathy and impotence might have paved the road to heresy just as quickly. There were risks either way, and in making his choice Philip had not acted without reason. Though he lacked his father's mastery in Netherlands affairs, he had taken steps to conciliate public opinion by the appointment to the Regency of his own half-sister, Duchess Margaret of Parma, one of the Emperor's bastards but a highly regarded one, and to gratify the high nobility by appointing them his royal governors (Stadholders) in the provinces, singling out the most influential and potentially dangerous among them, Egmont and the Prince of Orange, to hold a whole clutch of these important offices. He had allowed for a certain restiveness in a land which even his father had not always ruled in peace. But when deep-rooted opposition to his rumoured church reforms began to spread, reaching its peak in the general hostility shown him at a meeting of the States General in Ghent in the late summer of 1559, the situation still came as a most unwelcome surprise.

All he had wanted from the States General was a grant of money, surely due to him after all he had done to bring peace to the nation after years of ruinous war. Yet the grant was accompanied by sour and pointed reminders that no foreigner should by Netherlands law be appointed to office there: a palpable hit at the man who had become his chief adviser on local affairs, the Bishop of Arras, soon to become better known as Cardinal Granvelle, Archbishop of Mechlin. For a moment Philip's urbane façade collapsed. As a Spaniard, must he too resign all authority there? he burst out passionately. It was not the only insult he had to bear, for the States were demanding also the recall of the four thousand Spanish troops of the army which had won St. Quentin. Recovering himself, the King agreed to this demand, in the evident hope that the Regent would find some means of evading it after he himself had left the Netherlands.

And on this note of reconciliation ended Philip's final visit to that land of rich promise which Suriano had called 'the treasure of the King of Spain . . . his Indies'. For months he had been aching to be gone – 'to cure his homesickness', in Feria's contemptuous words. On 20th August he went aboard his ship at Flushing, attended by the grandees of the Burgundian order of the Golden Fleece, so many of them soon to die. There is a story that on the quayside he reproached the Prince of Orange for being the hidden hand behind the opposition which had shown itself at Ghent, and that when the Prince replied that all had been done in accordance with the usages of the States, he seized hold of him, crying angrily: 'Not the States but *you, you, you*!' It is probably apocryphal: but the anecdote neatly symbolizes the beginning of a personal duel which heralded nearly eighty years of war.

Chapter 5

Spain

Few greater physical contrasts could be imagined than that between the provinces Philip was leaving and the country where he was bound. Behind him lay the fields and meres of that watery landscape immortalized by generations of Dutch painters: ahead, beyond the green Atlantic fringe of Asturias and Galicia, the treeless windswept plains of Castile and the bleak heights of the sierra.

But if the geography was different, politically there were resemblances, for like the Netherlands, Spain was no unified monolithic state. As we have seen, through his great-grandmother, Isabella, Philip was King of Leon and Castile; through his great-grandfather, Ferdinand, he was King of Aragon, which like the Trinity was one and yet three, with separate parliaments for Valencia, Catalonia and Aragon itself. Philip told a French ambassador that their laws and customs greatly limited his royal powers. In Castile he was far more absolute, but even here Seville's *Casa de la Contratación*, which regulated the monopoly of the Indies trade, was in itself a formidable entity requiring careful handling, as did the sheepbreeders' guild of the *mesta* and the great territorial magnates whose estates and incomes were as large as kingdoms elsewhere.

If Spain had had as many sects and heresies as she had parliaments and grandees she would have been ungovernable. But the Moriscos apart, and at a cost, she was fervently and wholly Catholic. The few Lutheran cells which had grown up in the big towns, notably Seville and Valladolid, had been pounced on and eliminated in the year before Philip's return to the peninsula, and signs were not lacking that the Moriscos also would soon be brought to heel.

The cost of course was the existence of the Holy Office, the notorious Spanish Inquisition, which Ferdinand and Isabella had set up in 1480 by right of a papal bull of 1478. No individual was beyond its reach. At the moment of Philip's return to his homeland, the man he had himself made Archbishop of Toledo and Primate of Spain, the friend who had held the crucifix before the Emperor's dying eyes at Yuste, lay in one of its gaols, accused of heresy at the instigation of a nominal inferior, the Archbishop of Seville, who happened also to be Inquisitor General.

The Inquisition pronounce sentence in the Great Square in Madrid. The King and Queen sit in the balcony in the centre of the picture.
Mary Evans Picture Library, London.

A biography of Philip is no place to labour the history of a body about which volumes, libraries, have been written, but at least this much should be said. The Inquisition concerned itself with every aspect of Spanish life, from the enforcement of Catholic dogma to the censorship of books and the issue of certificates of pure blood free from any taint of Moor or Jew. Some of its activities were in the short run beneficial to Spain, for the very vigour with which it smelled out heresy spared the Spanish people much of the suffering caused by religious wars elsewhere. It was less cruel, less capricious, less un-just, than some of its critics have maintained, and in its persecutions not noticeably much worse than the English Catholic bishops under Mary and the Protestant Jesuit-hunters under Elizabeth.

But it was far more systematic, and there lay the peculiar horror of it. Under its standard, bigotry was brought to a fine art and enshrined in a code that was a travesty of justice. A man accused before the Inquisition of heresy or religious laxity in whatever form was never able to confront his accusers. He was not even told who they were. Process was secret. So was interrogation in the *Suprema's* gaols. So was torture. So was trial. Only punishment was public. This could take several forms. Only a small fraction of those accused of crimes before the Inquisition actually went to the stake, and only a tiny remnant of

Opposite: England's support of Protestantism and her acts of piracy against Spanish shipping convinced Philip that he must defeat her to ensure the safety of Spain's empire. This portrait of his arch-antagonist, Elizabeth I, is by an unidentified artist.
Courtesy of the National Maritime Museum, London.

those were burnt alive, for recantation, even at the last moment, was normally sufficient to earn the mercy of a garotting before the body was given to the flames. Most of the punishment meted out was much less severe. It could amount to no more than acts of penance to be carried out on a number of Sundays before a priest. Rising in the scale, it could be a matter of fines, imprisonment, loss of property or of civil rights, which might affect not only the deliquent but generations of his descendants.

The more heinous of these crimes and criminals were reserved for judgment at one of the great set pieces of the Inquisition's work at an *auto-de-fé* held in a town's central square. It was a gala occasion which people who wanted to keep clear of trouble felt it prudent to attend, and probably enjoyed attending. For the mixture of religious passion – the prayers and sermons and invocations to the faith – was cunningly interwoven with appeals to that lamentable human instinct to feel pleasure, or at least some comfort, in the misfortunes of others.

At the centre of the awesome display the victims stood. Penitents were absolved; though this did not necessarily spare them imprisonment or loss of property or goods. The 'unreconciled' and those whose crimes were judged too horrible to deserve God's mercy were then paraded in their yellow robes and tall conical hats like those of magicians in a pantomime, to be 'relaxed' to the

Opposite: This portrait of Philip II was painted in the mid-1550s. There are two copies, one in Naples and this one in Florence. After it was cleaned in 1964 it was generally agreed that this is the finer of the two, the result of closer involvement by Titian himself. Courtesy of the Galeria Palatina, Pitti Palace, Florence. Photograph Scala, Florence.

An auto-de-fé in Valladolid.
Courtesy Atlas van Stolk, Rotterdam.

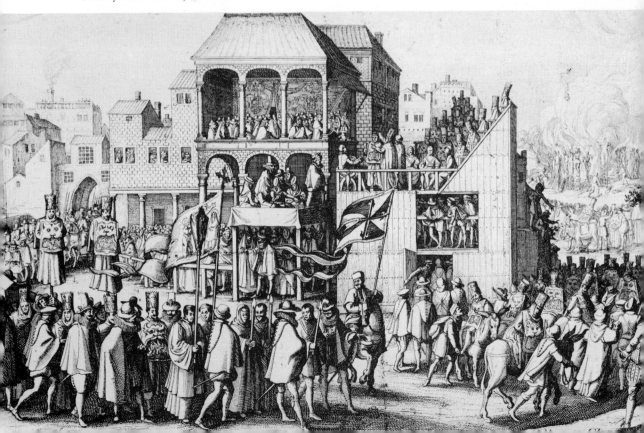

civil power for burning at the stake at a *quemadero* outside the city walls. For the Holy Office did not officially stain its hands with blood.

It was at one of these repellent ceremonies staged in his birthplace of Valladolid that Philip made his first ceremonial re-appearance in Spain. He was not naturally cruel but the bigot in his nature certainly accepted cruelty as a weapon in God's service, and his complete identification with the Holy Office and all its works cannot be doubted. He took care to keep it independent of papal control: a specifically Spanish instrument. But how far he controlled it – how far it was controllable – is another matter, for it had its own momentum. Conceivably the power that had destroyed a Primate of Spain could have destroyed its King. Certainly Philip was never tempted to thwart it, for in their zeal for the Catholic religion and the suppression of heresy he and the Inquisition were one.

Now at Valladolid, high up in the tiered galleries of the stands he sat as though in the president's box at a bullfight, attended by his son Don Carlos, his sister Juana, and the young Alexander Farnese, who in the years to come as Duke of Parma was to be one of the key figures of the reign. Proceedings opened with a sermon by the Bishop of Zamora, after which the Inquisitor General, Don Fernando Valdes, administered the oath to defend the Holy Office to the kneeling people and their King, who symbolically drew his sword in assent. Huge crowds had been drawn to the ceremony from all over Spain. Thirty prisoners were arraigned; fourteen were condemned to death, including six nuns, one of whom was already dead but whose bones and effigy went to the fire. Among the prisoners was a Florentine captain long resident in Spain, Don Carlos de Seso, of whom the Emperor had been fond, and as he passed close to Philip on his way to suffer he reproached the King for allowing him to be so misused by a pack of friars. The King is said to have replied: 'If my own son had been as wicked as you I would myself have fetched the wood to burn him.' The story could be an invention but it has the ring of truth about it, in which case Philip spoke more fatefully than he knew.

Elizabeth of Valois – Isabel, as the Spanish called her – had been little more than a child when Philip married her by his proxy, the Duke of Alva, in Paris in 1559. One authority tells us that she was still given to playing with her dolls – if so, she very quickly grew out of it. The occasion had been marked by a tremendous show of pomp and circumstance on both sides, the French being determined to impress the Spaniards with the wealth and beauty of the bride, the Spaniards the French with the power and wealth of the bridegroom. Both courts were of course bankrupt. And the wedding celebrations cost the hosts their king into the bargain: fatally wounded in a tournament.

Even a death like this could not be allowed to hold things up indefinitely, for Philip was clamouring for his bride. Late that autumn she set out by road for the south with a suite that included bevies of ladies of the bedchamber, three chaplains, two secretaries, twelve *valets de chambre*, cooks, scullions and physicians, a band of six musicians and a dwarf called Montaigne. Their numbers horrified the Spanish ambassador, Chantonnay, who had to make the arrangements for delivering them safely. The Queen, his sovereign lady, he wrote, was much troubled to know how her wardrobe and other luggage could be

Elizabeth of Valois, painted by Sanchez Coello.
Courtesy the Prado, Madrid.

conveyed over the Pyrenees. Much of it was packed in boxes too large to be carried by mule, and whole crate-loads were to go astray in the mountains, taking months before they finally reached their destination.

Snow was falling as the convoy crossed by the pass of Roncesvalles into Spanish Navarre, where frantic efforts had been made to receive the lady in fitting style. Philip himself had planned the entire programme down to the minutest detail. To the command of his escort he had appointed the Duke of Infantado, head of the great house of Mendoza, whose annual revenues were about equal to those of England. It was to be very much a Mendoza occasion, for not only had the Duke's palace at Guadalajara been chosen for the second marriage ceremony, but his brother, the Cardinal Archbishop of Burgos, was also of the party. The two brothers were at pains to upstage one another. At the grand handing-over ceremony at Roncesvalles the Duke was accompanied by forty men at arms in cloth of gold. His brother had matched him with forty pages in crimson velvet. Indeed, on the whole, the Cardinal carried off most of the honours. Even so, he had to work hard to surpass the French, whose delegation was headed by no less a person than the King of Navarre, first Prince of the Blood and claimant to all this territory between the Pyrenees and Pamplona. Navarre's royal condescension passed all bounds. Never before, he remarked, as he handed over his princess from the family of the greatest king in Christendom to present her to the most illustrious sovereign of the world, never before had Spain received so perfect a model of grace and virtue; and for once this weak and ineffective man had spoken no more than the truth.

On Sunday 4th February 1560 Elizabeth rode into the Guadalajara strong-hold of the Mendozas. Under an awning in an oak wood she received addresses of welcome. The trees were alive with linnets and nightingales – how they had been persuaded to stay there for the occasion is not recorded, though presum-ably they were caged, rather like the rabbits and fawns and other fauna tethered below them. In the patio of the palace under a gold canopy she was received by her sister-in-law Juana and other ladies of the court. Observers noted how well she graced the scene: a small dark girl with lustrous eyes and majestic carriage, already far older than her years. The King, waiting behind the doors of the grand salon as they were drawn back to reveal his bride, seems in the emotion of the moment to have forgotten his own strict sense of protocol – before she could kneel to him he had embraced her and raised her up tenderly. Nevertheless, at one stage of the proceedings, perhaps too conscious of the age gap dividing them, he is said to have caught his wife's gaze fixed on him and snappishly reproved her: 'What are you looking at Madam? To see whether my hair is grey?' At thirty-three he was twice her age and no doubt it rankled.

If this was a cloud over their relationship, it soon passed. The King made way for his wife and watched from the shadows like some Svengali as, dressed brilliantly in blue damask and lace ruff, she made her triumphal entry into Toledo in a procession which included eighty canons and minor clergy of the

An enamelled gold marten's head set with gems. Elizabeth of Valois carries a similar jewelled head in the portrait on the previous page, and bequeathed a marten's skin set with forty-one diamonds and small rubies for eyes to her daughter, the Infanta Catalina, in 1585.
Courtesy the Walters Art Gallery, Baltimore.

cathedral, seventy horsemen of the orders of Santiago, Alcantara and Cala-
trava, representatives of the Councils, of the University and the royal mint,
and a group of Inquisitors of the *Suprema*.

Shortly afterwards the new French ambassador, Fourquevaulx, found the
Queen in her private apartments dancing light-heartedly with her ladies. It
must have been a time of almost frightening excitement for so young a girl,
and it was soon interrupted by the first of the many illnesses she was to suffer
in the eight years of life left to her. By the summer she was fully recovered,
and we have a glimpse of her with her husband at a ball in Toledo, dressed in a
silver gown trimmed with gold and wearing a glittering tiara. She never wore
a dress more than once, the French ambassador reported admiringly, for the
King loved to see her in the height of fashion.

That autumn of 1560 she was struck down with smallpox and for a while her
life was despaired of. The King was not a man to parade his feelings, but at the
height of the crisis he seldom left the bedside, and in letters afterwards to her
mother, Elizabeth wrote that he had proved himself a loving husband and had
made her 'the happiest woman in the world'.

What became clear also, even in the early stages of the marriage, was that
the Queen had won not only her husband's love but his confidence, something
he gave to very few. A good judge of talent, even if he often misused it, he had
recognized in his wife a kindred spirit, wise beyond her years. He trusted
her. Was she not already – as her mother, the Queen Regent of France, was to
remark – more Spanish than French? Whatever her true loyalties, she had
certainly taken to dressing her hair severely in braids around her head in
the Spanish style. She had, says Brantôme, an air half way between gravity and
sweetness. In time the King came to rely on her so implicitly that he was prepared to send her as his representative in 1565 to that famous meeting with the
French court at Bayonne in which Protestant propagandists were later to see the
germ of the massacre of the Huguenot leaders on St. Bartholomew's Day of
1572. Though a common front against heresy between the two Catholic kingdoms did not in fact emerge from this meeting, it is clear from the comments of
the Duke of Alva, who accompanied the Queen, that she distinguished herself
in all her contacts with her wily mother by her dignity, prudence and 'discretion'.

To have such a wife was an important political asset for a King who, following a long family tradition, made great use of women of the royal house as agents
of policy. But it was in the hòpe of a new brood of children to support his
throne that he had really married her, and here for a long time things went
sadly awry. Not until August 1566, six and a half years after the marriage at
Guadalajara, could Philip rejoice in the birth of a child – and it proved to be a
daughter. It was a dynastic set-back, compounded fifteen months later when
the Queen presented him with yet another girl. Yet these two children –
the Infantas Isabella Clara Eugenia and Catalina Francesca – were in his later
years to be the chief happiness of his life. For weeks before the elder's birth at
the castle of Valsain he had made a practice of spending his leisure hours with
the Queen and of writing to her daily when he was absent in Madrid; and on the
day after the celebrations Fourquevaulx recorded a domestic picture of him

sitting by her bedside in a crimson chair in a room draped in crimson velvet. Similarly, on the birth of Catalina in October 1567, he wrote to his ambassador in France that this had given him a 'contentment' that could not possibly be increased – and behind the diplomatic, flattering words aimed at the child's French grandmother there undoubtedly lay a wealth of love that was later proved by his famous letters from Portugal to the Infantas. A model husband and family man.

Even the mistresses who varied the King's uxorious régime were kept strictly incommunicado, and not paraded as Elizabeth's own besotted father, Henry II, had paraded his soulmate, Diane de Poitiers.

The years of Philip's third marriage were thus among the happiest of his life: they were also of great importance to Spain and to Europe because they saw the beginning of that style of royal bureaucracy that was to reach its apogee in the rule of his great descendant, Louis XIV.

Much of the machinery was already there in the various Councils: of State, Castile, Aragon, Italy, the Indies, War, Finance, and Inquisition. There was a network of ambassadors and spies serving the closely knit secretariat around the King; but all required a master as painstaking and meticulous as themselves. In Philip they found him: a man who felt bound in God's service (and Spain's) to supervise the day-to-day workings of a large part of the globe and most of the people in it.

The system was a mixture of 'Conciliar' and 'Personal' government. Its responsibility to the embryo parliaments of the time was minimal, though the Cortes of the province of Aragon had a certain nuisance value and by jealous regard for its rights prevented that north-eastern part of Spain from being policed as effectively as the rest – its roads, for instance, teemed with beggars and robbers, while in Castile one could travel in perfect safety even by night.

The Councils met normally in the absence of the King, but nothing came of their debates or recommendations unless he himself endorsed them – decisions on even the most trivial matters required his counter-signature before any action could be taken. Some of the disadvantages of the system were more apparent than real, since according to the Venetian envoy Tiepolo the King normally accepted his Council's advice, confining himself to minor amendments and interpolations in the texts of minutes and despatches. He was certainly open to advice on Church matters from his confessor and the Holy Office, and in foreign affairs and war from the two most trusted of his grandees, the Duke of Alva and the Portuguese Ruy Gomez de Silva, Prince of Eboli, in another Venetian's words 'the twin pillars on which depended the government of half the world'. Alva and Eboli were usually on opposite sides: it suited the King to hold the balance between them. In military matters he turned to Alva; otherwise he leaned to Eboli, 'Roi Gomez' as the wits called him, a pliant and insinuating figure whom Philip had enriched out of an old friendship, even finding him a wife from the great Mendoza clan.

There were other men close to the King: the Count of Feria, who had been with him in London; the Bishop of Cuenca; Don Diego Espinosa, President of the Council of Castile, later Inquisitor General; and his principal secretary,

Gonzalo Perez, whom he had taken over from the Emperor. In Spain, as in England, it was the age of the new men, of whom Perez's natural son Antonio was to be an outstanding example. The great offices of state were held by members of the nobility – the Medina Sidonias, the Mendozas – but the closer one approached the inner circle around the King, the humbler the birth of the men one found there. Philip was never at ease with grandees of the Alva stamp, perhaps remembering the dangers to the throne and to the fragile unity of the state that had arisen in his ancestors' time through the rebellions of over-mighty subjects. He knew how to use them to advantage, but it was usually in viceroyalties far from Spain. For his intimates he preferred men whose careers and fortunes he had made and whose natural bent matched his own, which was really that of a Chinese mandarin.

To look forward for a moment: by the 1570s the mould had set and there was in existence that immensely detailed, ponderous and centralized rule which was to be the despair of Spanish diplomats throughout the world. 'If death came from Spain,' remarked one, 'we should all live a long time.' Nothing was worse, wrote another, than to have to negotiate with Madrid. But in the early 1560s the King had not shut himself away from his people; he still had a private life apart from his work. He had a young wife to please. When in Madrid he still played the part of a popular ruler in his father's style; he personally accepted petitions, granted audiences to ambassadors, dined in public, drove through the streets in his coach, went hunting, and sometimes attended masques and balls. He also made progresses through the country, rivalling those of Elizabeth in England: his son Don Carlos is said to have drawn up this satirical inventory of 'The Great Voyage of the King Don Philip':

> The voyage from Madrid to the Pardo, from the Pardo to the Escorial, from the Escorial to Aranjuez, from Aranjuez to Toledo, from Toledo to Valladolid, from Valladolid to Burgos, from Burgos to Madrid, from the Pardo to Aranjuez, from Aranjuez to the Escorial, from the Escorial to Madrid, etc., etc.

The story is from a French source, from that prince of gossips, Brantôme, and may or may not be true. It certainly brings out something distinctive in the King's nature. Valladolid, Toledo and Burgos were of course large towns, larger than Madrid before Philip decided to make it his capital. But the Pardo was a hunting lodge; the palace at Aranjuez lay by the banks of the Tagus, its gardens filled with the scent of flowers and the song of nightingales; the Escorial, built in honour of St. Lawrence, on whose name day the battle of St. Quentin had been won, was half monastery, half palace, built in the wilderness. There was also one other favoured place not mentioned in the 'Great Voyages': the castle of Valsain which Philip called 'The Wood of Segovia', where his elder daughter was born. Already, quite clearly, the King was most at home in the peace of the countryside: it was another form of the 'retreat' which he and his father had been in the habit of making after bereavements. At Aranjuez, at the Pardo, there were no tiresome ambassadors or grandees to be received; there were only secretaries, servants, intimate friends and members of his family. Solitude suited his temperament and the country air was good for his

The castle of Valsain, 'The Wood of Segovia'.
Courtesy the Spanish National Tourist Office, London.

health – he remarked on it himself. Away from the court he could expand both in work and leisure. It was at Valsain that some of the most crucial decisions of the reign were taken; just as it was on a hillside in the sierra west of Madrid that he spent his most relaxed hours watching the walls of the Escorial rise against the sky.

In many respects this devious man – 'a prince full of artifice, the father of dissimulation', as one enemy called him – was surprisingly simple and direct. The Venetian Antonio Tiepolo might say of him that everything about him was the reverse of what it seemed, yet apart from this quip (routine from an ambassador about the ruler to whom he was accredited) Tiepolo's own reports on Philip's appearance and character accord very closely with the favourable ones made by his predecessors and successors over forty years:

> [He is] white skinned and fair, very pleasantly built with a lip that hangs down a little . . . . He is very sluggish by nature but very dignified. He listens to people patiently . . . accompanies his answers with an amiable smile. He has a good memory and is extremely pious. . . . He loves repose and solitude, particularly in summer. . . . He is never familiar with any of his servants, even with the most senior and intimate, but always preserves a gravity fitting to his royal dignity. He knows how to pretend to ignore injuries, waiting for the right moment to avenge them. . . . He is more ambitious than anyone to amass money – and he certainly has good reason, for his revenues are pledged to thirty-five million in gold. He should therefore be acquitted of being parsimonious towards his servants. If driven to war he will show a belligerent spirit.

84

Other details were supplied from a variety of sources. Philip was small but 'majestic' and dressed simply yet elegantly in black. He was a quiet, urbane man who spoke in a low voice – so low at times that the French ambassador Fourquevaulx failed to catch a word that was said at his first audience. The King was a good sleeper. He was abstemious, rationing himself to a couple of glasses of wine at a meal – in this, as we have seen, a startling contrast with his *bon vivant* father. One strange dietary point: he avoided fish and fruit and enjoyed meat to such a degree that he had a special dispensation from the Pope allowing him to eat it on fast days, Good Friday excepted. He was imperturbable in good times and bad. He was not a man who lacked feeling or compassion – he had shown it at St. Quentin; he was to show it again in the care he lavished on his wife Elizabeth through bouts of ill-health and in his devotion to the two daughters of the marriage, the people he came to love most in the world. Yet in his nature, under the courtesy, the benevolence, the rather lymphatic style, lay a vein of pure fanaticism. No one had yet glimpsed it, but is was there. It was first to show itself in relation to the Netherlands.

Chapter 6

Rebellion in the Netherlands

In Spain Philip had seen heresy crushed at birth through the vigilance of the Church and Inquisition. With such an example to go by it was natural he should think that similar treatment would succeed in the Netherlands among a people reputedly much more docile and timid than Spaniards. Far from Brussels, too reliant (as also in English affairs) on his personal knowledge of a country and on the reports of foreigners to that country, he had misjudged a revolutionary situation. The causes of the coming war have been endlessly debated. Religious differences and the spread of heresy were obviously central to what happened. Yet even without Luther or Calvin, some kind of political and social ferment was bound to have spread through provinces so wealthy, so self-confident, and so misgoverned by strangers in the name of an absentee ruler.

Not all the seventeen States were rich, though by standards ruling elsewhere a good half dozen of them were fabulously so. In almost all of them there existed a long tradition of jealously guarded local rights which successive rulers had to guarantee. The sheer parochialism extending upwards from the peasants to the merchants and artisans of the towns and the nobility was one of the factors which made the Netherlands virtually ungovernable as one unit. This parochialism existed in Spain also. But then the King of Spain was a Spaniard. The real ruler of the Netherlands under the nominal sway of the Regent was the newly elevated Cardinal Granvelle, an interloper from the Franche Comté, whose presence would have antagonized the grandees of the State Council and the abbots and clergy of the Netherlands Church even if his name had not been associated with the hated new bishoprics and with popular fears that he had come to establish the Spanish Inquisition in the country.

Actually, as Philip himself remarked, a 'papal' Inquisition more pitiless than anything in Spain had existed in most of the provinces for years. Most of its victims, however, had been Anabaptists, whose levelling doctrines outraged everyone, and it was altogether another matter to apply such a weapon to the Lutheran and Calvinist elect. A repression which had worked well in Castile, where the social climate favoured it and where the visible power of Church and State was overwhelming, was bound to be more suspect and offensive to provinces surrounded on every side by lands that were either Protestant or, as in France, deeply infected with Protestantism. Such a nation required careful handling.

Philip had not been altogether ignorant of these dangers or of the kind of people with whom he was dealing – he had personal experience of them. Therefore he had taken care to appoint his Netherlands-born half-sister, Duchess Margaret of Parma, as his Vicereine or Regent; he had appointed native-born Stadholders to the governorship of provinces, and has staffed the 'State', 'Privy' and 'Finance' councils with a superabundance of local worthies. The Duchess, a regal, popular personality, with a woman's impulses and a man's moustache, would serve him excellently as a figurehead. He had to have someone with more subtlety and diplomatic touch to rely on, however, and in an evil hour he had committed the real government of the country to a junta, a 'Consulta', consisting of the presidents of these three councils, among whom Granvelle was the intellectually outstanding member. Since he alone had the ear of the King, he was in effect First Minister.

The Netherlands noblesse, many of them members of the great Burgundian order of the Golden Fleece, were in no mood to take orders from a foreign parvenu. Granvelle came from a good family in the Franche Comté, and his father had risen to be Charles V's chancellor. But William of Orange's family, the Nassaus, had produced a Holy Roman Emperor. There was a degree of difference here. The trouble was not however only a matter of social status or of personal antipathy between two able men. For the Cardinal like his father stood for that supra-national power of the Catholic Church which was under attack throughout northern Europe, particularly in the crucible of the seventeen provinces and their neighbour, France.

Granvelle, a very acute statesman, had seen the dangers of Protestant infection from the start. When the ill-feeling between the French Huguenots and the Catholic majority finally erupted into open war he wrote prophetically to Philip: 'None of our like-minded magnates have declared themselves as yet, but only God can preserve us . . . if they do.' He had long since identified Orange as his (and the King's) most dangerous enemy, whose professions of good-will he accepted with extreme distrust. Though the Prince pretended to be friendly, Granvelle wrote to Philip, he was full of disaffection.

This outbreak of religious war in France, the home of the 'Most Christian' King, ruled over by a Queen-Mother who was the niece of a Pope, caused the greatest alarm in Europe. The English sprang to action and began to intervene militarily on French soil, perhaps with hopes of recovering Calais. The King of Spain tried to order the Netherlands 'Bands of Ordonnance' across the frontier to the rescue of Catholicism, though these troops were strictly a defence militia and he should have known that any talk of employing them out of the country would be bound to inflame local feeling.

And so it proved. Orange and his associates, including the normally loyalist Egmont, used the crisis as a lever in their battle against the Cardinal. They made no revolutionary gestures beyond absenting themselves from the Regent's State Council and making the air loud with their complaints. The minor

William of Orange, painted by Key.
Courtesy the Rijksmuseum, Amsterdam.

nobility, with less to lose, took greater liberties and openly mocked their enemy by putting their servants into a livery of fools' caps and bells which was somehow supposed to reflect on his ostentatious life-style. Even the Regent, who had got Granvelle his red hat from Rome, became to some degree infected by these attitudes, fearing that her own popularity would suffer by any too close an association with him. Resentful of his tutelage and of the influence he enjoyed with her half-brother, she began to long for the day when she could dispense with him and become re-united with her people.

Everything therefore depended on the King. Would he support Granvelle by diplomatic means? Would he come to Brussels himself with an army, as Granvelle urged, to teach a sharper lesson? Or would he sacrifice the minister on the altar of expediency?

After long deliberation he chose the last, and there were good reasons for it. Nothing final or irreversible in the relationship between King and provinces had yet occurred: all that was being demanded was a strict adherence to customs which the King himself had sworn to uphold. In such circumstances even a minister as loyal and talented as Granvelle was expendable.

The way Philip tried to disguise what he was actually doing – by instructing Granvelle in one letter to ask the Regent's leave to visit an ageing mother in the Franche Comté (which amounted to a dismissal carefully wrapped up in subterfuge) and telling the Orangist seigniors in another that he had no intention whatsoever of dismissing the Cardinal – was a piece of window-dressing which deceived no one and harmed no one except poor Granvelle himself, who spent many months expecting his recall. The wits of Brussels were soon happily plastering the walls of the departed minister's palace with 'To Let' signs, auguries for a happier and more relaxed future.

But, under the surface appearance of *détente*, nothing basically had changed: things were still set on a collision course. For the Orangists, the removal of Granvelle had not been an end but a beginning, a first step in freeing the provinces from the Inquisition, the edicts against heresy and foreign interference. There was a social and political as well as a religious element in their thinking, and Granvelle had by no means exaggerated when he had told Philip's principal secretary, Gonzalo Perez, that they wanted to turn the country into a kind of republic where the King might only do what pleased them. Similarly the King, having made his gesture of conciliation by sending Granvelle packing, was determined to ignore all further protests aimed at upsetting the status quo or the religious laws. When shortly after Granvelle's departure the Pope confirmed the decrees of the Council of Trent against heresy, Philip wasted little time in having them published throughout the Netherlands. He remained unmoved by the protests of Orange and the seigniors or by the arrival in Spain of Count Egmont expressing the depths of revulsion felt in the provinces against religious persecution. To the gullible Egmont he returned fair words, but from his retreat at Valsain, the 'Wood of Segovia', in October 1565, came two despatches in which he sharply told his half-sister that there could be no argument; the edicts must be obeyed.

Even the local Inquisitors themselves must have trembled when this royal decision was at last made known. Two of the more squeamish of them had already written to Philip that their office had become 'odious' to everyone and that they feared for their lives. Almost universal anger and dismay was the reaction of leaders and people. Philip had alienated their affections, wrote the Regent, who was among the most despairing and troubled of all. The Stadholders of provinces charged with the execution of the decrees had told her bluntly that it was impossible to burn fifty thousand souls. In a letter to the King in March 1566 she wrote that only two possible courses were open: force, or some kind of accommodation with men on the brink of rebellion. The edicts should be modified and the Inquisition abolished; in which case she reckoned – and it is proof of how far things had deteriorated – that a majority would probably rally to the King.

These warnings were not misplaced, for militancy had begun to spread among the minor nobility, largely Calvinist in spirit. In the spring of 1566 a group of them, well over two hundred strong, rode into Brussels to present their demands in person. They were received in the very hall where eleven years earlier the Emperor Charles had abdicated amidst signs of profound respect; and retiring to an inner chamber his daughter, the Regent, wept. 'What, Madam!... Afraid of these Beggars?' one of her entourage rebuked her* – a jibe which the

* The Regent herself gave no support to this story. In a letter to Philip she told him about the confederates' adoption of this name, but added that she couldn't think why they had taken it up.

'Leaguers' speedily turned against the government by adopting the word as a rallying cry and a beggar's bowl as their insignia.

The reaction of the moderates on the State Council to this revolutionary situation was the inept one of sending another embassy to Spain in the persons of the Counts of Montigny and Berghen, neither of whom lived to make the return journey. Berghen fell sick on the way; very unwisely went on; fell sick again and died. Montigny was even less fortunate. He had been to Spain on such an errand once before and should have known better than to repeat it.

For the King, already deeply troubled by the course his Netherlands affairs were taking, received Montigny's embassy with suppressed rage. Controlling himself, he managed a complimentary word or two about the seigniors, whose activities he regarded as heretical, treasonable, and deserving of death. In the absence of the intruders, he summoned his closest advisers to the castle of Valsain, and there, with Alva and Eboli beside him, there was much plain talking. Obviously the Regent was afraid and in the mood to surrender to the demands that were constantly being pressed on her. A limited withdrawal, a tactical move to lull the enemy, seemed the appropriate response. The Regent was therefore authorized to make concessions, to go some way towards the suspension of the Inquisition, provided the new bishops were permitted to enter their sees and exercise their functions. At the same time the King summoned a notary to his chamber, and in his presence and that of Alva, swore that these concessions had been wrung from him under duress, were not binding, and

An engraving dated 1566, showing open-air Protestant ceremonies in the region surrounding Antwerp.
Bibliothèque du Protestantisme, Paris. Photograph, Giraudon, Paris.

were subject to his reserved rights to punish the guilty. He would rather lose all his States and a hundred lives, if he had them, he wrote to his ambassador in Rome, than reign as a king of heretics. He would try to settle the religious question in the Netherlands without force, but he would not shrink from using it in the last resort if he could preserve the true religion in no other way. Was this duplicity? Of course. But was it in the terms of those times worse than what was being done to him by subjects who professed obedience and were preparing rebellion?

Three years earlier the concessions which the Duchess had wrung from her reluctant half-brother would have satisfied most Netherlanders. But times had changed and even moderates like Egmont now regarded them with suspicion as 'conditional' and 'untrustworthy', as indeed they were. A group of confederates had met at St. Trond and had drawn up a 'Request' which they presented to the Regent. The demand was now for the calling of the States General, something which Philip would never concede. There had been a dramatic growth in Protestant (particularly Calvinist) feeling throughout the provinces, taking the form of public preaching outside the walls of towns – 'hedge sermons' under the protection of armed guards.

Suddenly, midway through August 1566, the religious passions boiled over into a wave of image breaking, starting in the Walloon south and spreading rapidly northwards like an incoming tide. On 20th August Antwerp, the commercial capital of the Netherlands, was taken over by the mob: thirty churches were desecrated, the cathedral was gutted, the famous black Madonna hacked to pieces. Soon it was the turn of Utrecht, Delft, Leyden, Amsterdam, Haarlem, and towns in Groningen on the borders of Germany. Some provinces, like Luxemburg, were comparatively unaffected, and Brussels itself stood firm. But elsewhere few of the Stadholders or magistrates put up any kind of fight against this heady mixture of religious and demagogic fury. Some of the broadsheets circulating in Antwerp at the time show the trend, far indeed from the disciplined creed of Calvin's Geneva: 'Wake up, Brabantines. A bastard cannot hold the least office in Brabant, yet you have allowed a bastard bitch to govern you. Chase out the whore and give her to the devil!'

The Regent despairingly tried to retreat from her capital to the safety of Mons. No one would help her. The seigniors opposed the move: they wanted to keep control of her. The citizens of Brussels closed the gates of the town in her face, and she had no choice but to make the best of it and remain. In an attempt to alarm the King who had left her without sensible orders or support, she passed on to him the horrific rumour that 30,000 volumes of the works of Calvin were being shipped in Antwerp for Spain. And to calm the social and religious ferment of the provinces she conceded toleration for Protestant preaching – she had done so, she told Philip, because otherwise every priest would have had his throat cut, but she called on God to witness that she had bowed only to duress.

When news of these happenings reached Spain the King was ill: it sent him into a fever. According to one story he plucked at his beard and swore on his father's soul that it would cost the rebels dear. Such a public display of his feelings runs counter to everything known about him. But the sense of outrage he must have felt is shown in a letter he wrote to his ambassador in Rome: 'I cannot tell you how afflicted I have been by the sack and pillaging of the Flanders' churches. No loss I could personally suffer could grieve me more then even the smallest insult shown to our Saviour or to the sacred images, since I have His service and honour at heart above all things.'

Obviously the time had come for really forceful measures. Much earlier, in July 1566, before the image breaking had even begun, he had authorized the Regent to raise troops in Germany, had made arrangements for the transport of Spanish troops from Naples, Sicily and Sardinia, mustered the Lombard light cavalry, and warned his ally the Duke of Savoy to prepare for the passage of an army through his territory. The coming storm was being signalled to the Netherlands and the rest of Europe long before he told his half-sister on the last day of the old year that he had chosen the Duke of Alva to command the forces he was sending to Brussels in advance of his own arrival.

Unknown to him, the tide in the Netherlands had already begun to turn. The image breaking and the rioting mobs had grossly offended moderate opinion in every province. Things had gone too far and too fast for those who wanted an end to the Inquisition and the edicts but otherwise clung to the old ways. And as though sensing this, the Regent had recovered courage and had begun to rally the traditionalists to her side. Early in 1567 the city of Tournai in the Walloon country had been recaptured, and in March a rebel force, which had tried to overrun the isle of Walcheren and cut communications with Spain through the port of Flushing, was caught under the walls of Antwerp and cut to pieces by loyalist troops. By April the Stadholder of Flanders, Count Egmont, who had turned his coat, was informing Philip that hedge sermons had stopped in his province, that the people had been disarmed and the preachers had fled.

All this had come too late. One of the causes of the tragedy soon to befall the Netherlands was simply the slowness of communications between Brussels and Madrid which prevented the King and his advisers from reacting to the mood and needs of the hour. The actual state of the Netherlands was always at least a month – sometimes much longer – ahead of the image as seen in Spain. This led to rigidity. There came a moment when it must have been realized in Madrid that the worst of the danger was over and that the Duchess Margaret had got the measure of the rebellion. But in the meantime a new policy of vengeance and repression had been decided on, and no one seems to have thought of varying or reversing it.

Part of this the world understood. After such outrages it was everywhere concluded that Philip himself would go to the Netherlands, which was certainly what his father would have done. Cardinal Granville had recommended it time and again as the only way of saving the provinces; and the Archbishop of Cambrai had put it more picturesquely by saying that Philip's presence in Brussels was as necessary as bread to the life of man. As preparations for the royal departure mounted and rumours spread, there was hardly a ruler in Europe that did not look for a Spanish descent either through Genoa or Flushing on the Zeeland coast. The Cortes of Castile, meeting in December 1566, obviously feared the move was imminent, for among the many petitions they

Opposite: The frontispiece from De Materia Medica *by Dioscorides translated into Catalan and dated 1555, one of the many fine books in Philip's collections. There is a Latin dedication to Philip incorporated in the frontispiece.*
Courtesy of the Biblioteca Nacional, Madrid. Photograph MAS, Barcelona.

PEDACIO DIOSCORIDES ANA

ZARBEO, ACERCA DE LA MATERIA ME-

DICINAL, Y DE LOS VENENOS MORTIFEROS,

Traduzido de lengua Griega, en la vulgar Caste-
llana, & illustrado con claras y substantiales Annotatio-
nes, y con las figuras de innumeras plantas exquisi
tas y raras, por el Doctor Andres de Laguna,
Medico de Iulio III. Pont. Max.

DIVO PHILIPPO, DIVI CAROLI. V. AVG.
FILIO HÆREDI, OPT. MAX.
DICATVM.

EN ANVERS,
En casa de Iuan Latio. Anno,
M. D. LV.

Cum Gratia & Priuilegio Imperiali.

presented to the King was one begging him not to leave them. They had no wish for another absentee ruler like the Emperor Charles. Nearly all the leading figures around Philip – Espinosa, the Count of Chinchon, the Prince of Eboli – were of the same mind, arguing that he must go at once, 'to drown heresy in its own blood', in Alva's words. The King himself had often expressed his determination to obey the call. In the same letter in which he had told the Regent of Alva's appointment as Captain-General of the army, he had assured her that he would soon follow; and to his ambassador in Rome he added an *insouciant* touch: 'Those who have said and are saying that I have no intention of leaving Spain . . . will soon see their mistake.'

Months went by and still the King did not set out. Instead, the world learnt of Alva's appointment and that he was on his way with his troops along the 'Spanish Road' through Savoy, Lorraine and the Franche Comté to the Luxemburg border. The Duchess Margaret became quite frantic about it. She could not know the secret instructions the King had given his Captain-General at Aranjuez – to proceed against all those guilty of subversion – but with her woman's instinct she had guessed the worst and knew that she was being supplanted. In April 1567 she sent a passionate letter of protest to her half-brother, complaining that she was being deprived of power and of the means of fully re-establishing affairs in the Netherlands: '[It seems as though] others are to enjoy the honours, while I alone had to bear the fatigue and the dangers.' And she asked leave to retire from the Regency, reminding him that she had been appointed for two years but had served eight.

To this letter Philip replied soothingly, six weeks later, that far from derogating from her powers, he intended to increase them. The poor woman in the meantime had re-entered Antwerp in triumph and had published a series of edicts against heresy and rebellion so severe that Torquemada himself would surely have approved them. They did no more than infuriate the King when he learnt of them, for they were in his view 'indecent' and contrary to religion, in fact 'the most pernicious' he had ever read. The historian Gachard, who centuries later was to edit the correspondence, seems to have thought that Philip had found even these tremendous and bloodthirsty threats of capital punishment insufficiently severe, but almost certainly what irritated the King was that they were badly timed and might drive the guilty to flight or even re-activate rebellion before the arrival of the Duke.

On the same day as the publication of the Antwerp edicts, 24th May, Alva had reported himself in Genoa. Naturally the Regent was well informed of all his movements. On 12th July, unable to contain herself, she wrote again to Philip, dwelling on the dire consequences that must follow the arrival of someone whom she described as so odious to the Netherlanders as to make the very name of Spaniard hated. Never, she remarked, could she have believed that he would appoint such a man without consulting her; and if she had not had his royal assurance that he himself would soon follow in the wake of the army, she would not have consented to remain in Brussels for a moment.

From this letter it appears that the Regent was prepared, with reservations,

Opposite: El Greco's interpretation of the words in Philippians, 2, 10, 'that at the name of Jesus every knee should bow, of things in heaven, and things in earth, and things under the earth.' Philip II appears among the saints before the jaws of Hell. Painted in 1580, the work is known as The Dream of Philip II.
Courtesy of the Escorial. Photograph MAS, Barcelona.

The Duke of Alva stands in the centre of this engraving, on his right are Margaret of Parma and Granvelle, on his left the Pope. The Pope hands a sword to the Duke and promises money to enable him to retain the upper hand in the Netherlands.
Courtesy Atlas van Stolk, Rotterdam.

to believe that Philip would really come in his good time. If so, she deceived herself. But the matter is still more complex, for one must go on to ask whether the King was deceiving her or was himself the victim of self-deception? Had he simply sent Alva as a replacement for his half-sister, counting on her indignant retirement from office? Or did he at one stage or another sincerely intend to follow in person once the troops were in place?

The question is still unanswered. Over a span of months Philip had repeated his determination to go to Brussels: on 22nd September 1566 in a letter to the Regent, on 27th November to Granvelle in Rome, on 31st December, again to the Regent. By that time he had decided to make Alva Captain-General. What did he tell the Duke when he gave him final instructions at Aranjuez in the spring of the following year? It may be significant that three weeks before this meeting the Regent was protesting that she had had no instructions for

96

fifty-seven days. Was his mind made up? If so, the comedy continued; for months later, after news had reached him of Alva's arrival in the Netherlands, he was still instructing his ambassador in Rome to tell the Pope that the Duke's mission was a mere preliminary to his own arrival, which had not been cancelled but merely delayed.

This particular letter of Philip's is of prime importance, both for its content and for what it reveals of his tortuous methods and what Gachard calls his 'prolix' literary style. It is enormously long, detailed and repetitive. But what it amounts to is a series of excuses meant for the ear of the Pope, who had obviously been expecting to hear of a personal arrival in Brussels.

The King begins by remarking that he knows well how necessary and even 'indispensable' his presence in the Low Countries has become, and because of this he is determined to make the journey in spite of all inconveniences and difficulties. But his ambassador must point out that the requisite force to protect the King's person from outrage must be established before he can contribute anything useful. For this reason he has sent an army ahead under 'a person of authority', a fair enough description of the Duke. However Alva has been delayed *en route*. (The Pope is not actually blamed for failing to use his influence with the Almighty in this matter, but the implication is there.) And it goes without saying that before the King can present himself in Brussels before his faithful subjects, not only must Alva have established a base there, but he must also have carried out 'certain acts' – a nice euphemism for the executions and reign of terror soon to follow. The ambassador must go on to point out that the Netherlands problem requires handling in two stages. First there must be the regrettable but necessary application of 'rigorous justice', for which the time has now come. But later there would follow a mellower age during which the people, having been punished, would be conciliated and their love gained by benevolence. This second phase would be reserved for the King in person. A convenient and 'appropriate' time to reap these golden opinions would be in the following spring – 1568. The letter ends with yet another reminder of Philip's inflexible determination to do his duty, shrink from no fatigue or danger in the months ahead, but with 'resolute spirit' to expose himself, if need be, to any hazard in the cause of the Catholic religion. Similar letters were sent to other Spanish ambassadors in Europe, and one can only commiserate with them.

Was all this pretence? The King certainly had the means for the journey, for the treasure fleet from the Indies had reached the Guadalquivir carrying five and a half million ducats in specie, a fifth of which belonged to the royal treasury, and the rest of which could be borrowed. But had he the *will*, the intention?

The evidence, though not conclusive, is rather against it. Fourquevaulx, the French ambassador in Madrid, had picked up a story that Philip, in conversation with his (French) Queen, had remarked scornfully that people should have inferred his intention not to go to Brussels from the ostentatious way he had paraded his preparations. Gachard finds a similar answer in another place. As we shall see, the King's relations with his heir, Don Carlos, had reached a crisis at about this time, and this impinged on his plans. If he made the journey alone, he would have to leave the unsatisfactory young man as Regent of Spain. If he took him with him to Brussels, he would probably have to leave him there as Regent of the Netherlands. Might it not be wiser to avoid the journey and leave the pacification to the Duke? More simply, Philip may have wished to remain in Madrid in that autumn of 1567 to be near his wife during her approaching confinement – their second daughter, Catalina, was born that October. Or again, as Granville's brother, Chantonnay, asserted from the start, he may have shrunk from going to Brussels because he knew how deeply he was hated and because indecision had become second nature to him.

As we know, he never went. The second phase, the phase of conciliation was never tried. But the Duke of Alva carried out the first part of the plan – 'rigorous justice' – to perfection. Within a few weeks of his arrival the Netherlands lay cowed and passive under his hand.

Chapter 7

Don Carlos

As the autumn of 1567 drew on, the King found himself faced with other problems besides the Netherlands, one of them central to the well-being of Spain and of his own dynasty. This was the problem of his son, Don Carlos.

The boy's birth had been followed almost at once by the death of the mother, never a very auspicious beginning to a father-son relationship, particularly when the father is little more than a youth himself.

For a long while thereafter things went better than might have been expected. As his care for his younger children was to show, Philip was an affectionate parent. Nor is there any evidence that in childhood Don Carlos was not an affectionate son. However from an early stage the reports on the boy made by the Venetian ambassadors were very unfavourable. Badovaro, writing in 1557 when the Prince was twelve, found his nature 'feeble' though inclined to cruelty; and he repeated rumours of hares being roasted alive and of a tortoise's head being bitten off when it snacked at the royal finger. 'Very proud, irascible and headstrong', noted Badovaro, who had never actually seen Don Carlos. This judgment reflects more on the writer than on the subject. Yet it was not a lone judgment. Michele Suriano, succeeding his compatriot, tended to agree with him. The Prince's inclinations, he wrote, were entirely different from the King's – he was a bold, cunning, cruel and ambitious boy. Nor was it only the Venetians who were critical, for a German witness, Baron Dietrichstein, joins in the chorus of disapproval for a 'weak and feeble prince'. Don Carlos was eighteen at the time. When he was twenty-one another Venetian – Antonio Tiepolo – added a more detailed and still more hostile criticism of the Infante. Tiepolo found him 'very immature for his age', a stooping figure who looked to be weak in the legs. Riding a horse tired him. He lost his temper easily and could be violent to the point of cruelty. Once upon a time he had lived chastely, but had since given himself up to excesses which occasioned 'strange disorders'. 'To conclude,' wrote the ambassador, 'just as the Spaniards rejoice at having a native-born prince as heir, so as great are their doubts concerning the nature of his future government.'

A thoroughly bad report in fact. Yet Tiepolo went on to say that Don Carlos

Elizabeth of Valois, Philip's third wife, was originally intended as Don Carlos's bride; this is a drawing from the Arras Book.
Photograph, Giraudon, Paris.

revered truth and was a compassionate and charitable man. There seems a contradiction here. And he added also that the Prince, anxious to play a full part in state affairs, resented the advisers with whom his father had surrounded him.

In this glimpse of a rather lonely, eager, green young man we may have come close to some understanding of Don Carlos. There are portraits of him: a thin, pale, sickly version of his father. He was slightly hunch-backed and one shoulder was higher than the other. Not a prepossessing figure. His health had always been poor; and in adolescence a fall head-first down a flight of steps during an amorous escapade (for Badovaro had judged him even at the age of twelve to be 'addicted to women') had resulted in a serious brain injury from which at one stage it was feared he would not recover. An operation for trepanning of the skull, combined with the introduction into his room of the incorrupt body of a dead Franciscan monk, had worked what had appeared to be complete recovery, but he remained delicate, a constant anxiety to the King and to his own household.

For these and perhaps for other reasons which we shall later have to consider, he was held back politically. At sixteen Philip had been Regent of Spain, at seventeen a married man. At twenty-one Don Carlos was still thought incapable of holding independent office or of marrying the Austrian archduchess whom the Emperor Maximilian was offering in letter after letter to Madrid.

There were other candidates for the hand of a youth who in spite of every disadvantage was still by far the most desirable matrimonial property in Europe. Proposals had at one time or another been afloat for him to wed the Queen of England, the Queen of Scots, the French princess Marguerite of Valois, and his own aunt Juana, who was eighteen years older than he was but whose cause was sponsored by the Castilian Cortes, in the hope, one French ambassador wrote, that his 'imbecility' might be mended by her virtues.

Not unnaturally Don Carlos hated the very idea of such a match. He had already suffered one emotional trauma when his father had married Elizabeth of Valois, the bride originally intended for *him*; and though he was fortunately spared the knowledge that his body would be hardly cold in the tomb before his father (bereaved for the third time) would repeat the pattern by marrying his Austrian archduchess, Anne, the frustrations and delays of the match-making had already taken their toll of a mind and body never robust.

Under these strains his behaviour began to worsen. Tales spread of acts of violence towards members of his household: he was said to have threatened one man with a knife and boxed the ears of another. Brantôme says he was full of '*bizarreries*', but then this goes for many of Brantôme's own stories. What everyone noticed was Carlos's growing antipathy towards his father and his father's closest intimates, to the point indeed of having the hardihood to insult the Duke of Alva. In September Fourquevaulx, the French ambassador, was reporting to his government that Don Carlos was quite unable to disguise his rancorous hatred for the King, and rumour was rife that he was about to fly the country – for Italy, the Netherlands, Vienna: anywhere to be free of parental control and the spies set on him, among whom he numbered the Prince of Eboli. 'In short,' concluded Fourquevaulx, 'if God does not interpose, all must one day end in a great calamity.'

About this time – in the summer and autumn of 1567 – persecution mania seized the Prince, not altogether without reason, for he was closely watched. He began to sleep with a pistol and a loaded arquebus within reach; also he had a French engineer make for him an ingenious contraption for locking or unlocking his door from the bedside. In his loneliness and anxiety he had turned for comfort to his uncle, the Emperor's famous bastard, Don John of Austria, who was nearly of an age with him and in whose company he had been brought up. The 'facts' of what followed are largely a matter of rumour and conjecture, but what seems likely is that Carlos tried to enlist his uncle's help in escaping from Spain, and that Don John, who was deeply ambitious and owed everything to the King, ended by betraying his nephew's plans.

This occurred at the end of December 1567, and soon another and still more alarming report reached Philip: that Carlos had confessed to a priest that there was a man he mortally hated, and then admitted to another that the 'man' was his own father.

In a letter written three weeks later Philip went out of his way to deny this inferentially by insisting that Don Carlos had never had any designs on his life. On the other hand the story is consistent with much other evidence of Carlos's extreme hatred of the King. What is most surprising is Philip's reaction to all this as shown in his movements. In December 1567 he was at the Escorial. Not till the 17th January did he return to Madrid. Yet in the political climate of the times, with heresy and rebellion loose in the Netherlands, the flight of the heir to the throne would be a matter of the utmost gravity, even if the fugitive got no further than Vienna, where the Emperor himself was thought by some to be a crypto-Protestant. The matter would have been more urgent and dangerous still if Carlos had had some kind of understanding with the Netherlands rebels or if Philip had any grounds at all for suspecting him of underground contacts. Was this inactivity of the King's in face of a pressing danger proof of his famous phlegm, or was it perhaps a matter of timing, of lulling the enemy before the sudden pounce? Some of the evidence suggests the latter, for rumours had been current for months that some decision as to how to treat the Prince had been taken by the King and the Council of State. Perhaps everyone was waiting for some overt, irrevocable act by their quarry, which came on the morning of 16th January when the Prince ordered the Director General of Posts to send a team of eight horses to the palace in Madrid that night. No horses were forthcoming from that cautious official, but his report on the transaction would have been more than enough to set in train the King's final moves.

On the 17th Philip returned to the capital. His first call on entering his palace was a visit of ceremony to his wife. Afterwards he gave audience to his half-brother, Don John, who had been closeted for some time with the Prince, and from that moment the tempo began to quicken.

The members of the State Council were sent for. Alva was far away in the Netherlands but most of the other notables were there. The next day, 18th January, was a Sunday. The King received the French ambassador, who found him his usual impassive self. Philip then went to mass in the royal chapel, attended by Don Carlos – the young man's last public appearance. Later that day the King sent for his son, who pleaded indisposition and retired to his apartments, where he supped and then took to his bed.

At eleven o'clock at night Philip summoned his intimates, including the Prince of Eboli, the Count (soon to be Duke) of Feria, and Cardinal Espinosa. At least two of these were personal enemies of the Prince, who had called Espinosa 'a petty priest'. Accompanied by two *aides-de-chambre* armed with a hammer and nails and a lieutenant with twelve guardsmen, the King's party came to the Prince's door. The French locksmith who had contrived the latch had been induced to tamper with it, and there was no difficulty in getting in. The Council members entered first and seized the Prince's pistol and arquebus. Awakening, he cried out; then, seeing the cloaked figures in the room, asked who they were. 'The Council of State', was the answer. At this point, Philip himself appeared, wearing steel armour under his cloak and with a steel helmet on his head. The young man asked if they had come to kill him.

The attendants were called in; the window was boarded up; the room was searched for weapons; and the Prince's papers were seized. One contained a list in two columns setting out his friends and his enemies. The Queen's name headed the first column, the King's the second.

At some point in these proceedings Don Carlos seems to have given up hope: he threw himself on his knees and begged them to kill him. Otherwise, he would kill himself. This was coolly received, the King merely remarking that it would be the act of a madman. At which the boy – for by temperament he was little else – broke in pathetically to say that he was not mad, only desperate.

It did him no good: his inquisitors were beyond pity. 'It is not as a father that I shall treat you in future but as a king,' Philip replied, or has been made to reply, for an air of mystery still surrounds these events of four centuries ago. But what is certain is that Don Carlos at the King's order was locked in his room, to be watched day and night by relays of guards. Two of his household were left to serve him, but they were ordered on no account to speak to him.

At this stage only a very small body of men, all of them devoted to the King, had any notion of what had happened. But on the Monday morning, the 19th, the people of Madrid awoke to find that all traffic on the roads out of the capital

Don Carlos, painted by Sanchez Coello.
Musée de Versailles. Photograph, Giraudon, Paris.

had been stopped. That same day the King sent for the Imperial ambassador, Dietrichstein, to tell him of the Prince's arrest. On the 20th he shut himself up in session with the State Council. It was decided not to convoke the Cortes, which had ceremonially accepted Don Carlos as heir and might be aggrieved and critical. Instead, a number of letters were sent out to individual members of the nobility, the bishops and representatives of the towns, explaining that in the name of Justice and for 'urgent' and 'essential' reasons of state the King had been forced to incarcerate his 'very dear and well beloved son'. Similar letters, this time in the King's own hand, went out to a number of addresses of still greater importance. To his aunt Catherine in Lisbon, who had herself as a young girl been shut up in Tordesillas castle with her mad mother Joanna, Philip wrote that Don Carlos's actions had been of such a nature that he refrained from speaking of them for fear of causing her further grief – a truly exasperating letter it must have been to read. The Emperor Maximilian and the Empress (Philip's sister) received somewhat similar communications which spoke of the young man's 'excesses'. Had it been merely a case of disobedience or lack of respect, Philip insisted, he would not have acted as he had. To the Pope, the key figure, he lamented that excesses and disorders arising from the Prince's temperament had passed all bounds and had made his confinement inevitable. A desire to make his readers' flesh creep without actually telling them anything is evident in almost every line of this extraordinary correspondence. And so it went on. To Alva, Philip explained that Don Carlos had done 'grave things'. To his new ambassador in Rome, Don Juan de Zuniga, the message (for the Pope's ear) was that the young man's way of life had become disordered. According to Fourquevaulx, Philip had told his courtiers in similar Delphic style that he knew of forty excellent reasons for having acted as he had.

Really in these letters Philip said nothing, gave nothing away, advanced no rational explanation for the extreme step he had taken in locking up his son. Only vague phrases were used – 'reasons of state', 'duty', 'the service of God', 'national security'. But one impression clearly emerges from behind this smokescreen of words, and that is that a decision had been taken to bar Don Carlos's rights of succession to the throne and to shut him away in some fortress till he died. It was nothing new in Spanish history, for Philip's great-grand-father, Ferdinand the Catholic, had done just that to his own daughter Joanna, the rightful queen of Castile after the death of his wife Isabella. The poor woman had been shut away in the castle of Tordesillas while first her father and then her son, the Emperor Charles, had ruled in her place, till the day came when her mind finally gave way and she became the raving lunatic of the legend, hunting her cats round the grim, dark rooms of the castle.

Was Don Carlos therefore, like Joanna, mad? Hints abound in the second series of letters which Philip wrote to European rulers once it became obvious that the first batch had satisfied no one. The trouble, he wrote to his brother-in-law, the Emperor Maximilian, was not a matter of rebellion, of plots against his life or of suspected heretical leanings (as Protestant propagandists were claim-ing), but rather a fatal 'defect' or flaw in Don Carlos's nature: something so deep-rooted and ineradicable that no improvement could be looked for, and consequently no end to the imprisonment. This line was supported by the evidence of several of Philip's intimates. Eboli (probably a spiteful witness) told the Venetian ambassador that for more than three years the King had known that his son was as cracked in mind as in body; that he had hoped for some change, but could hope no longer; and President Espinosa, when asked whether it was true that Don Carlos had conspired against his father's life, replied darkly that this was the smallest part of it.

These were interested, committed witnesses whose fortunes depended on backing up their master. But that does not mean that what they were saying was necessarily untrue. Some very compulsive reason or reasons must have been at work to cause a man to act so pitilessly against his first-born, whom at one time he had shown every sign of loving as dearly as a father normally loves his son. Had the King concluded that the accident on the steps at Alcala de las Henares and the serious illness that followed had affected Don Carlos's wits? Certainly from about that time date most of the stories of the boy's 'excesses'. But there is evidence also on the other side, from a time well after the illness: for Don Carlos was to make two wills, both rational, and one of them, far from indicating lunacy or derangement, bearing out Tiepolo's verdict of a generous, compassionate spirit. Similarly on his death bed Don Carlos was to win praise even from his enemies for his courage and pious humility – or was this just the conventional cover story for anyone who made a Christian end?

For clearly there were times when the young man's behaviour was outrageous. The evidence is too detailed and comes from too many sources for it to be wholly false. The heir to so much power and to so many thrones could hardly have accumulated enemies and distrust in such measure without something to warrant it. Why else had Philip held him back from marriage to the young archduchess Anne of Austria? It was a very desirable match from the Spanish point of view, and in the end the King undertook it himself. If he denied it to Don Carlos it must have been because he either knew or suspected that the boy was unfit as a man, perhaps impotent, as some of the Emperor Maximilian's enquiries in Spain suggest; or because there were *other reasons* of state or politics which made the match impossible and had turned Don Carlos into a grave liability to Spain.

One partial explanation may lie somewhere in the region of what today we might think of in terms of schizophrenia. Whether the clinical symptoms were there it is impossible to say at this distance in time, but that Don Carlos had some kind of a double personality seems clear. Violence and compassion, generosity and grasping avarice, humility and monstrous pride – the tales about the Prince hardly seem to relate to the same person.

And this continued to the end. It is harsh to pronounce against a young man subjected to close imprisonment, but Don Carlos's responses to the situation in which he found himself differed almost from day to day.

At first he despaired. And he had increasing reason for despair. His private apartments were handed over to two of the enemies who had figured high on his list, the Prince and Princess of Eboli; his stable of horses was disposed of by the King; the last friend among his warders was withdrawn. He went on hunger strike. The King remained unmoved. The Prince would eat, he said, when he was hungry, and so it proved. The fast actually benefited his health.

As Easter approached, Don Carlos turned to religion and sent for his confessor. The results were beneficial and there was even talk of reconciliation with his father, but once more Philip was unimpressed. The fact that the young man had been allowed to go to mass, he wrote to his sister the Empress, did not mean that he was fit to be released into the world. There were moments when even a disturbed mind was healthier than at other times, but it signified little in the long run.

Once more despairing, Don Carlos seems to have returned to thoughts of suicide. He began to eat enormously and to wash his food down with quantities of snow water which even in summer could be got from the sierras, and he took to putting ice in his bed and sleeping unclothed.

Such abrupt changes of mood may suggest a split personality in schizophrenic terms. But they could easily prove no more than the desperation of a backward, sickly, mis-shapen adolescent, motherless from birth, whose whole life had been spent in a struggle to free himself from his father's shadow in the face of slights and distrust. His reactions sound like those of a child in search of reassurance: he had the cruelty of a child, its vulnerability, its jealous nature, the passion to be loved. No wonder he looked for friendship in circles outside those of the King, and no wonder he preferred the company of women, particularly that of his step-mother the Queen, who had once been intended as his bride. This is ground which, Schiller's play and Verdi's opera notwithstanding, has largely been avoided by historians, but even putting aside any thought of an adulterous relationship – impossible anyway in so rigidly organized a court – it is easy to see the tensions that could arise between the protagonists, particularly when Don Carlos's hoped-for Austrian marriage was also forbidden by the King. It was all too easy for the Prince to see in this ban another slight, another reflection on his manhood, driving him into a complete estrangement from his father and into a desperate plan to try to escape from Spain. Equally it would have been easy for the King to read into these acts of juvenile rebellion proofs of mania amounting to a threat to his dynasty and the welfare of his kingdoms, even if there had been no extraneous political events to magnify every danger.

The circumstances of the Netherlands made the danger acute, and there were many rumours current at the time to connect Don Carlos directly with that rising. It was said that Egmont during his mission to Spain had won the Prince's sympathy for the 'Leaguers' cause, that Montigny had similarly worked on him, and that Carlos was in touch with Orangist agents who had penetrated the innermost circles of the Spanish court. Even the King's confidential secretary Antonio Perez was later suspected of being in Orangist pay; and some colour is lent to the story by the extreme malevolence with which Philip was to pursue both Egmont and Montigny to their deaths. The theory has been derided by most, though not all, historians, but it would have been nothing new for an heir to the throne to intrigue against his father, and there was even a direct precedent for it in the royal family of Aragon. It did not even have to be true: it would have been sufficient if Philip had come to *believe* that this mixture of rebel blandishments and the weak-mindedness of his son had created a situation so dangerous for the monarchy and Spain that nothing but the most rigorous surgery could cure it.

That in the end the King *did* come to judge everything in extreme terms is proved by the way he treated Don Carlos from the moment of the arrest. Five and a half years earlier at the time of his son's accident at Alcala he had been overcome with grief, unable to bear the vigil at the bedside of the supposedly dying boy. Now he acted with chilling and callous cruelty. Reasons of state were always paramount with him, and here no doubt he was also remembering that same mad grandmother at Tordesillas who at the time of the *Communero* rising in 1520 had been used as a figurehead by forces in arms against his father. It was an old story from before his birth but the lesson it taught was clear and inescapable. Suppose Don Carlos escaped to the Netherlands border and put himself into the hands of the insurgents? The combination of his gullibility and Orangist men and money could be very dangerous to the regime. Suppose again that some agent working for Don Carlos or even the boy himself took a dagger to the King? Seen in hindsight these were absurdities, but they may not have looked that way to a ruler with a rebellion on his hands, and perhaps they go some way to explain, though not to excuse, the implacable treatment handed out to the prisoner in his tower.

The final scenes were mercifully brief. Towards the middle of July Don Carlos seemed to cast off all restraint. One day, quite in the style of his gluttonous grandfather, the Emperor, he wolfed a whole partridge pie in spiced pastry. It gave him a raging thirst which he tried to quench with snow water, and soon afterwards he was seized with violent indigestion followed by vomiting and nausea.

Doctors were sent for. In that age it was tantamount to inviting death; indeed two of Philip's wives were to die of their attentions as much as from disease. By the nineteenth it was clear that the patient had no hope of recovery. But his mind seemed to all observers to have cleared. He confessed; made a second will; gave away his jewels – and he asked to see his father.

That even Philip's professional panegyrists have felt a need to excuse his conduct at this moment is shown by the fact that Cabrera in his monumental biography has provided us with a touching scene of the King appearing in the sick-room and making the sign of the cross over the head of his dying son. Unfortunately for Philip's reputation this is almost certainly sheer invention. Not only did he not go to the bedside, but he forbade his wife and his sister to go there either, for as one close observer of him was to write, he was a man who never forgave an injury, real or imagined.

In the small hours of the morning of 24th July Don Carlos died. He was twenty-three. The King took no part in the solemn funeral procession but watched it set out from a window in the palace. He allowed Don Carlos his dying wish to be buried in the convent of San Domingo el Real in Madrid. Some years later, however, he had the body removed to the Escorial, where it now lies.

There were rumours of poison, almost certainly unfounded, though it was a convenient and timely death. But if the King in reality had added this ultimate cruelty, it could not have made his conduct much worse.

The Queen had been a sorrowful but helpless witness of the tragedy. Don Carlos had always shown her respect and affection – it is one of the strongest arguments against his madness. And in return she had been his friend. That she felt any warmer regard for him is highly improbable, and it was only much later that these tales were put about by the King's enemies. But it would be natural that she should feel pity and sympathy for someone so near her own age and so unfortunate. For hers was a lonely life, surrounded by an etiquette so stiff and exacting that one could hardly breathe. She had felt this even in the early days and had told her mother about it: 'I must confess, Madam, that but for the kindness I receive from the company assembled here, and for the happiness I have of seeing the King every day, I should find this court the dullest in the world'. It must have been a sad change for a girl brought up among the gay and worldly Valois; and things got worse when at her husband's 'request', because of the jealousy of the Spanish maids of honour, she had to send away the French ladies who had come in her suite on the bridal journey to Guadalajara.

There had been times of happiness, of *fêtes champêtres* in the gardens at Aranjuez by the banks of the Tagus, her favourite home, if members of a court so constantly on the move could be said to have one. She planned improvements to the gardens, those woods and arbours filled with the sound of nightingales which her husband was to remember many years later in his letters to their daughters. She went out riding in her coach, unveiled, which in itself was a striking proof of the King's favour. But her health was poor, and the arrest of Don Carlos, coming so soon after the birth of her second daughter, seems to have plunged her into a deep melancholy. To the French ambassador she wrote that she felt the misfortune as though Carlos had been her own son, and she spent two whole days weeping till the King himself reproved her for this un-Spanish display of emotion with the words, 'Enough tears, Madam'. Even a visit to Aranjuez brought no real improvement, for she was pining for the Infantas who had been left behind in the supposedly healthier climate of Madrid.

As the autumn set in it became clear that her health was failing under the strain of yet another pregnancy, marked with spells of giddiness and fever which deeply alarmed her doctors. By the first day of October she had become reconciled to the idea of death, which she told Fourquevaulx she thought of without regret. Something of the defeatism which for all her spirit and beauty seems to have been part of her nature showed through almost the last of her meetings with her husband, when she told him not only of her sorrow at having to leave him but also at having failed to give him the son he needed. According to Cabrera the King himself was in tears as he replied that he had hoped that God in His mercy would have granted her health and a long life, but since because of his own sins this had been denied him, he could do no more than carry out her final wishes and always remember her.

About noon on 3rd October she gave birth to a premature female child, which survived just long enough to be baptized. The King was at her bedside when soon afterwards she died.

He later described her death as irreparable. In one sense he repaired it very quickly by marrying for a fourth time. But his affection for his young third wife was probably genuine enough. On his own death-bed, thirty years later, he gave their elder daughter the ring that Alva had placed on her mother's finger at the proxy wedding in Paris in 1559, with the injunction never to part with it.

The gardens at Aranjuez, Elizabeth of Valois's favourite home.
Courtesy the Spanish National Tourist Office, London.

Chapter 8

Alva in the Netherlands: the English Problem

These personal misfortunes which marked the end of the first decade of Philip's reign were the prelude to the infinitely greater tragedy of the Netherlands War.

The Duke of Alva had reached Brussels in August 1567. A grandee of grandees and by far the most experienced soldier in Spanish service, he had been with the Emperor at Tunis, Mühlberg and the siege of Metz, before crowning his career in his brilliant campaign in Italy against the Pope and the Duke of Guise. Now nearing sixty, his silver-bearded patriarchal appearance belied a very decided nature. He had long been an advocate of stern measures against the Netherlands seigniors, whose letters of protest and side-tracking in matters of faith and obedience had filled him, he told the King, with such rage as almost to deprive him of the power of rational thought – and indeed the most charitable way of looking at his bloodstained regime in the Netherlands to come, with its executions and extortions and the pitiless sack of rebel towns, is to regard it as the work of a man who had temporarily lost his judgment if not his reason.

He was now to have his way, for under his hand as he entered Brabant was a splendidly equipped army some 20,000 strong (just under 9,000 of them Spaniards) attended by 'a marvellous number of whores', as one impressionable native reported. Their tally reached as high as two thousand on some reckonings, which even for a mercenary army seems unduly high.

The arrival of Alva at the vice-regal palace in Brussels was not however as smooth as might have been expected. The archers of the Regent's bodyguard refused to admit his halberdiers, and the first meeting between the high personages of Duke and Duchess was chilly in the extreme. At a second interview Margaret wanted to know what was the object of this mysterious mission. The Duke replied that it was to ensure that justice was respected and the edicts obeyed so that the King would find a peaceful country awaiting him

An anonymous etching of the Council of Blood in 1567 presided over by the Duke of Alva.

Courtesy Atlas van Stolk, Rotterdam.

when he arrived – an intolerable insult to a woman who with her own resources had just suppressed an armed rebellion.

The Regent was almost frantic with rage. On 29th August she wrote to Philip asking leave to lay down her office and retire from the Netherlands, being grieved, as she put it, to the depths of her soul by the treatment she had received from him. Before the year was out she had left the provinces, whose main strategic centres had meanwhile been occupied by the Captain-General's troops. Soon he was to be elevated to the Governorship. The Prince of Orange had already fled to Germany, having read the signs more correctly than the victor of St. Quentin, Count Egmont, and Montigny's brother, the Count of Horn, who listened to the blandishments held out to them by the King and the Duke, only to find themselves arrested in September, as was Montigny himself in Spain. By the end of that month a new tribunal had been established to try all those who had taken part in the disturbances – the Netherlanders were soon to dub it 'The Council of Blood'.

On 24th October the Duke was reporting to the King that, God be praised, all was quiet in the Netherlands. It was the quiet of an overwhelming fear, and soon the executions began. On 4th January 1568 eighty-four notables died on the scaffold; in February, ninety-five were charged and thirty-seven condemned; March saw a wave of arrests, five hundred in a single day. Meanwhile the Prince of Orange had been summoned to appear before the Council; *in absentia* his estates had been sequestered; and for good measure his heir, the Count of Buren, had been kidnapped from his studies at the university at Louvain.

Thus began what Alva called a 'pruning' of the King's vineyard in the provinces. He had obviously expected some counter-blow by the insurgents, though not the defeat inflicted on one of his levies near the monastery of Heiligerlee in Friesland at the hand of an army led by Orange's younger brother, Count Louis of Nassau. His answer was to hurry on the public executions in Brussels of Counts Egmont and Horn, already condemned as

Opposite: The tiny gold box in the form of a book, left below, is an Agnus Dei Reliquary; above it is a jewel of a Knight of Alcantar; to the right is a gold cross of a Knight of Malta. All three were salvaged from a Spanish wreck.
Courtesy of the Ulster Museum, Belfast.

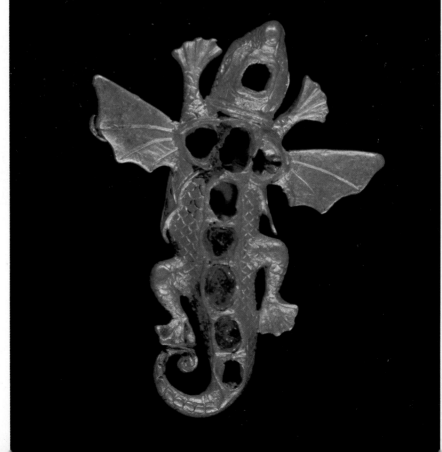

The beheading of Egmont and Horn at Brussels on 4th June 1568.
Courtesy Gemeentearchief, Delft.

rebels – a blunder, indeed a gross miscalculation, since Horn was a man of small consequence whom he thus elevated into a patriot and martyr, while Egmont was at heart a moderate whose real loyalties were less to the Netherlands than to the King. In a letter to Philip the Duke hoped that their example would be 'fruitful'. To underline the point, the first two weeks in June saw a flurry of other executions and the promise of much wider punishment as he gathered his forces and marched northwards into Friesland. There, near the small town of Jemmingen in a loop of the river Ems, he caught and destroyed Nassau's rebel force which had triumphed at Heiligerlee. Returning south, he then outmanoeuvred the main rebel army led by the Prince of Orange, shepherding it out of Brabant with hardly the loss of a man.

Victorious, secure, omnipotent, the Duke went on to introduce next year a whole new fiscal system for the provinces which had previously been very grudging in their support for the royal treasury and the royal army that was protecting them. The taxation system had been feudal and hopelessly out of date. Now it would be modernized; and in the spring of 1569 the States General, summoned to Brussels, found themselves faced with demands for three new taxes: the Hundredth Penny, a 1% capital levy, the Twentieth Penny, a 5% charge on transfers of land, and the soon-to-be-notorious Tenth Penny, a 10% purchase tax on sales. No doubt in principle these charges were not wholly unreasonable or unjust, and the Tenth Penny itself was no worse than the *Alcabala* which the Spanish people had been enduring for years. However the Duke had overlooked two vital factors. The first was the sullen resentment of the country which aligned many moderates with the extremist 'Beggars'. The second was the attitude of England.

For Philip, as for his father the Emperor, England was a constant preoccupation. Her position as a sea power on the flank of Spain's communications with the Low Countries, her trading links with Antwerp and value as a counterweight to France, all made her friendship a matter of the utmost importance, and even

Opposite: From a Spanish wreck, the Girona, *came these two jewels, a golden salamander set with rubies and a gilt bronze dolphin.* Courtesy of the Ulster Museum, Belfast.

*An anonymous engraving describing the situation in the Netherlands in the late 1560s.
The differences between the Spanish régime and the Prince of Orange are highlighted.
Alva is crowned by Anger and Discord; at his side the naked woman symbolizes the
Dutch people. Orange is crowned with Honour; next to him sits a woman representing
Freedom of Conscience and at his feet is Prosperity.*
Courtesy Atlas van Stolk, Rotterdam.

after his failure to marry her new Queen, Philip had never ceased to protest his
friendship and offer his protection. Nor were these mere words, for during the
reign of Mary Tudor he *had* very effectively protected the princess and had
been one of the main agents of her peaceful accession. The fact that ruler and
government had slipped from orthodoxy into heresy on Mary's death made no
difference to the policy of a man who did not always carry religious bigotry into
affairs of state.

He got precious little return for his brotherly tolerance; and a succession of
Spanish ambassadors in London continued to be perplexed, bamboozled and at
times enraged by the subtle manoeuvrings of the Queen and her Council.
'Things are in such a muddle that they can only be written about confusedly',
wrote the Bishop of Quadra in 1560. Some years later the unfortunate ecclesi-
astic was as hopelessly at sea as ever and confessed: 'I do not know what to think
of it all, except that these people are in such confusion that they confound me
as well.'

Most of the trouble arose over whom or whether Elizabeth would marry.
Would it be the Austrian archduke Charles or her own favourite, Robert
Dudley? Around all her dealings she threw up a smoke-screen of deception
through which shone occasional glimpses of the truth. Where marriage was

concerned Philip was perceptive enough to guess her mind. Having failed to marry her himself, he was naturally inclined to believe that she would marry no one, and that all her talk, as he put it, was nothing but a trick and a pastime from beginning to end. Yet even he never really understood how devious she was. She had a genius for effrontery, to the point of telling one Spanish ambassador that she had to dissemble but was a Papist at heart, and on another occasion, that the piratical acts in the Caribbean of which the poor man was complaining had really been committed by Scotsmen speaking English in order to mislead. Don Guzman de Silva, easily the best of Philip's envoys in the 1560s, paid a grudging tribute to this nimbleness of hers in threading a way through the maze of problems surrounding her, so that even her English favourites were as often as not bewildered and deceived.

Philip himself, with his early experience of Elizabeth, was less in the toils than most and instinctively understood both her bias against marriage and her sturdy independence of mind, however deeply it might pain him. 'Since she has been Queen,' he wrote to Quadra in 1561, 'she has never done anything according to our advice and for our satisfaction. . . .' The suffering Quadra went further in psychological insight when he wrote to Granvelle in Brussels even before the Duke of Alva's arrival on the scene: 'I am certain that this Queen has thought and studied nothing else since the King sailed for Spain but how to oust him from the Netherlands.' Her natural inclination, he added, was inimical to the King and always had been.

The potential for active hostility between Spain and England had therefore always been present from the moment these two strangely contrasted rivals had ascended their thrones. It might never have deteriorated into war but for the outbreak of rebellion in the Netherlands.

During the iconoclastic riots in the Duchess Margaret's time Elizabeth had remained neutral in action, and in thought had probably inclined towards the Spanish and legitimist point of view. Such rebels against their king deserved heavy punishment, she told Don Guzman de Silva, a man she personally respected, and this contained a large element of truth. At no time was she ever a Protestant zealot, for as a monarch and a sceptic she was politically and temperamentally opposed to rebels and extremists of any kind. However she happened also to be the ruler of a country traditionally friendly to its Netherlands trading partner across the Channel, and she was surrounded by Councillors far more hostile to Rome than she was. The arrival of Alva in Brussels had 'disturbed' her, Don Guzman reported to his King: the arrests of Horn and Egmont had provoked great 'surprise', which was a fine diplomatic understatement for the shock and outrage felt in London at this event.

From that moment chill and distrust can be sensed in the exchanges between the two governments. And there were other manifestations that would have been unthinkable a few years earlier. In the same month as the Counts' arrest (September 1567) Philip's Flemish admiral, de Walchen, put into the supposedly friendly haven of Plymouth, only to be fired on by English ships and peremptorily ordered to haul down his flag – the first such incident he had suffered in eighteen years at sea. In his instructions to a new ambassador to succeed Don Guzman – Don Guerau de Spes – Philip might continue to protest his good neighbourly intentions, and answering noises came sometimes from the Queen, but the damage had been done, and in December 1568 the English government suddenly pounced on a convoy of Spanish ships which in fear of pirates had taken shelter in Plymouth and other Channel ports, and seized all the treasure aboard.

It was daylight robbery, but as usual Elizabeth was fertile of excuses. True, the money was destined for the Duke of Alva, and true, it was money on loan to the King of Spain, but it was still technically the property of Genoese bankers and the English had not actually purloined it but were colourably engaged in 'protecting' it. The ships, so ran the argument, had been impounded for fear that they might otherwise be boarded by the French. And having regard to the heavy expense of defending a friend's money, the treasure had been unloaded on to English soil as security.

This time the Queen had nearly overreached herself. As a counterblow, Alva seized all her shipping and goods in Netherlands ports. Unfortunately for him, these amounted to only a fraction of the worth of the bullion now in English hands; and the Queen's government, noting the lack of decision among its opponents, remained unmoved by the diplomatic furore its seamen had unleashed. It was the Spanish who were left to make the overtures towards compromise. Ambassadors and special envoys scurried here and there, and one of the more clear-eyed of them put the matter in a nutshell in the course of a fruitless session with the English Privy Council: 'Well, gentlemen, then the Queen means to say, in short, that she will not return his Majesty's money': and that was exactly it.

What then was to be done? The King in Madrid and the Duke in Brussels began to toss the ball to and fro between them, the King pleading that he was a long way from the scene, the Duke, his subservience to his master. Alva was basically for compromise: he wanted his money back and a return to normal trading. As Governor of the Netherlands he was the inheritor of a long tradition of alliance with England. On 10th March 1569 he wrote to Philip that he doubted whether an open rupture at the present time would be advantageous, considering the state of the treasury, the general exhaustion in the Netherlands and the lack of ships. He recommended peaceful means.

The King on this issue was much more bellicose and inclined to enquire into the possibility of stirring up a Catholic rebellion in England with Spanish money. 'No time is more opportune', he remarked in a burst of quite unusual decisiveness. But he was still asking Alva's advice and leaving Alva to do the spadework. What inhibited him was the fact that the successor to the throne of England in the event of Elizabeth's deposition or death was the imprisoned Mary Queen of Scots, who might be a good Catholic but was politically pro-French. This was a spectre that was to haunt Spanish diplomacy down to the day of Mary's execution in Fotheringay Castle, but it was a risk that had sometimes to be faced, and about this time Philip began to toy with certain notions suggested to him by the Pope and other ultra-Catholic zealots for a more radical solution of the English problem.

Between the poles of militancy and compromise the King tended to swing from day to day. In July 1569 he wrote to Alva that the best policy was to get

Elizabeth 'to come to the point' over the stolen treasure and avoid circum-locution, which was easier said than done. More forthrightly he was writing to the Duke in November that should the Queen be shameless enough to force him to break with her, it would be well to seize Ireland, which could easily be done with troops from Spain.

And so it probably could have been done in that year or in 1570/71, when the new ambassador in London, Don Guerau de Spes, was pressing this 'Irish' solution, with urgent exhortations to his master to bestir himself and show the energy so great a business required. Far more clearly than Alva or any other of the King's advisers, Spes had seen the realities behind English policies in relation to Spain. If England did not change its religion or at least its govern-ment, he wrote in one despatch, the King could in future count on 'nothing but evil and trouble, insolence and robbery'. And on the commercial front he spelled it out in even greater detail. It was useless, he declared, to treat for a settlement with the English, because however just one's demands might be, they would always overmatch them and ask too much: freedom to trade with the Spanish Indies; freedom for English seamen from the jurisdiction of the Inquisition when on Spanish soil. These demands could be made, he added, because the English were convinced that Philip would never move to depose the Queen for fear of driving her into the arms of France.

If this was so, the English had misjudged their man for by the summer of 1571 Philip had decided on the Pope's urging to support a plan suggested to him by one Rudolfo Ridolfi, which involved a rising of English Catholics under the Duke of Norfolk supported by an invasion force of Spaniards from the Nether-lands, the assassination of Queen Elizabeth during one of her progresses through the country, the rescue of the Queen of Scots and her elevation to the English throne, together with her marriage either to Norfolk or – one final touch of fantasy – to that last of the Crusaders, Don John of Austria.

Seldom had the normally cautious King been hotter for action. Nothing, he wrote in his own hand to the Duke of Alva, nothing was closer to his heart than this single service to God. There was a great need for secrecy and no overt move should be made till the conspirators in England had shown their hand, but once that was done Alva must not lose a moment in launching the support force across the Straits of Dover. How the Duke was to assemble such a force and at the same time keep its existence a secret from English spies was not dwelt on, but everything else was, even down to the name of the expedition's commander, another Italian named Chiapin Vitelli.

The Duke had met Ridolfi, and unlike the King he distrusted him immensely as a person totally lacking in discretion. He remembered Norfolk as a weak, irresolute man. He knew all about ambassador de Spes and thought even less of him than of the plot. He did not care a *real* for Elizabeth one way or the other, but he was a man of good sense who saw the dangers of affronting Protestant opinion throughout Europe in support of such creatures, whose boastful talk filled him with scorn. What Ridolfi was proposing in the way of raising armies to kill one Queen, rescue another, capture the Tower of London and burn all the shipping in the Thames, he wrote, could not be done if the Queen of England herself joined actively in the plot. And in solemn terms he begged the

The Duke of Alva, painted in oils on wood by Moro.
Courtesy of the Hispanic Society of America, New York.

King not to allow his 'great zeal' for religion to betray him into courses which could actually destroy it by bringing all Europe about their ears.

A strange reversal of roles indeed, with the Man of Blood in Brussels preaching peace, and the 'Prudent' King the assassination of his own sister-in-law! In terms of the political morality of the times, held even by a Pope, Philip had some good arguments on his side, for as he pointed out, the English Catholics would certainly be eliminated if no help was sent them, and the Queen, whether provoked or not, would always be an irreconcilable enemy of Spain. He felt assured that God would favour His own cause and direct matters in the proper way. Yet at the very end of a letter filled with so much faith and credulity, his own basic uncertainty of mind reappeared, and he left the final decision whether to act or not to act to the Duke.

And there the matter ended, for as Alva had long foreseen, the whole ramshackle plot foundered in a welter of weakness and incompetence. It had been penetrated by English agents, and in its collapse brought down Norfolk and the Catholic cause. The Spanish were lucky that the Queen contented herself with expelling de Spes and asking for his replacement by a less headstrong successor.

The campaign in fact had been one of almost unalloyed disaster. Elizabeth sat more firmly than ever on her throne. The Duke of Alva was left hankering for his 800,000 ducats' worth of cash and merchandise. The commercial dispute dragged on till it was settled in 1573 by the Convention of Nijmegen on terms very favourable to England, which for years anyway had been profitably dumping its woollen goods in Flanders to the ruin of the local trade. More serious still in the long run for Spain was the distrust which the King had come to feel for any independently-minded Governor in the Low Countries. The results of the imbroglio and of the humiliations he had suffered were reminders of the Emperor's injunctions to trust in no one but himself. It was a lesson he did not forget; and it led in turn to the concentration of Spanish policy in the hands of a ruler who, in the words of one of his most knowing servants, was by nature incapable of deciding anything.

Chapter 9

Cross against Crescent

Don Carlos had died in July, the Queen in October; the English seizure of the treasure ships took place in December; and from August onwards the Emperor Maximilian had been formally protesting to Philip at Alva's severities in the Low Countries, thus opening up a dangerous rift in the Catholic front against heresy. Fifteen hundred and sixty-eight in fact had been a year of almost un-relieved misfortune and the fates still did not relent, for while the King knelt at his Christmas prayers in the cold of his unfinished palace of the Escorial the fires of the Morisco rebellion were springing up throughout the towns and villages of the Alpujarras mountains between Granada and the sea – Granada itself could well have fallen in the first surprise assault.

The Moriscos were the descendants of the Moors who early in the eighth century had invaded and occupied most of Spain, but had been slowly driven back in the long struggle of the *Reconquista* till the last of their Emirs had surrendered the kingdom of Granada to Ferdinand and Isabella in 1492.

The surrender terms had been generous, guaranteeing to the Moriscos the right to worship and dress as they pleased and to keep the bath-houses around which much of their cultural life revolved. There had been wisdom in the generosity, for the defeated numbered over half-a-million hard-working and productive people spread out along the Mediterranean coasts of Spain between Malaga and Valencia whom the victors could hardly massacre or enslave. They hoped to assimilate them by degrees, by the force of example and some pressure from the Church. When however it became evident that the first rush of converts – the *Conversos* or 'New Christians' – was drying up and that the Moriscos were becoming a state within a state, alien and divorced from the rest of Spain, a series of edicts of increasing severity was issued, culminating during Charles V's time in decrees proscribing the use of bath-houses, the wearing of turbans and Moorish robes, and the use of Arabic as a language and of Arab customs and feasts.

However Islam is a very durable religion, almost impossible to suppress, and forty years after the Emperor's edicts, in the reign of his son, the Moriscos of the Alpujarras (where most of the zealots were concentrated) were in fact if not in form as irreconcilably Moslem as their ancestors had been in the time of the Cid.

A map of the central Mediterranean, the scene of the Spanish/Moorish confrontation. This chart drawn by Diogo Homem and engraved and published by Paolo Forlani in 1569 was among the first to be produced on a scale large enough to be of use at sea.
Courtesy the National Maritime Museum, London.

To the Church and to the 'Old Christian' population which thought it had won the campaign of the *Reconquista* this was an intolerable affront, worse even than Protestant heresy, and in 1566 Philip reacted to the national mood by re-issuing his father's edicts in an attempt to put an end to the backsliding and pretence and force the Moriscos to conform. He had acted, he wrote, on the advice of wise and conscientious men who had told him it was his duty. The need for such a policy seemed all the greater because in the previous year the Turkish fleets had made a major sally into the western Mediterranean by attacking Malta, and though they had been driven off by the Knights of St. John, the threat of their return in alliance with the pirates of the Barbary Coast made the presence of what we should call today a Fifth Column on the soil of Spain itself a danger even more pressing than rebellion in the Netherlands. For the Valencian coastal strip was one of the richest agricultural areas in the country, and the Alpujarras lay on the flank of the Andalusian plain, less than 150 miles from Seville and the Guadalquivir, the centre of the Indies trade where the treasure fleets came to port from the Isthmus.

As in the Netherlands, so among the Moriscos. The Emperor's draconic edicts had been largely winked at on both sides. Their re-enactment by a new zealous king with a zealous Inquisition behind him brought the Moriscos face to face with the choice whether to submit or to rebel. All the old time-honoured devices for delaying things were tried, but when these failed and the King rejected even the advice of his own officials in Granada, the long-prepared rising suddenly erupted throughout the Alpujarras.

The atrocities that followed struck even contemporaries with horror. A kind of madness seized the protagonists. The Christian minorities in the mountains were wiped out with every refinement of cruelty. Priests were hurled from the tops of towers; men, women and children were disembowelled; victims had their mouths stuffed with gunpowder, to be blown to pieces; and there were reports – certainly not the first atrocity stories of their kind in history – of hearts being torn from living bodies and then devoured.

Opposite, above: An astrolabe, the primitive forerunner of the sextant, was used in Philip's time to measure the altitude of the sun, and so establish a ship's position.

Below: These two pairs of navigational dividers are lying on a 16th century map by John Baptiste Agnese. Both Courtesy of the Ulster Museum, Belfast.

Overleaf: The Battle of Lepanto, 7th October 1571, by an unknown artist.
Courtesy of the National Maritime Museum, London.

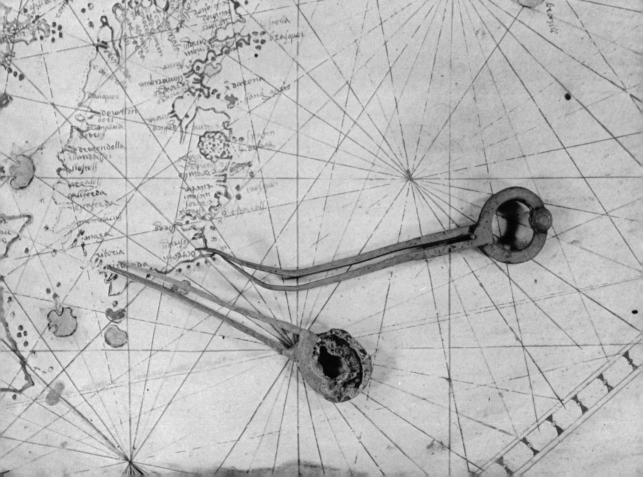

This rebellion, which threatened from day to day to spread from the Alpujarras to other Moorish communities in Murcia and Valencia, was undoubtedly the most serious threat Christian Spain had faced for centuries. It was not only a matter of what the Moriscos could do on their own, for they were known to be in touch with Constantinople and Algiers and there were plenty of havens even along that rocky coast where Turkish squadrons or pirate brigantines from North Africa could anchor.

Yet the King remained astonishingly cool, lulled perhaps by early and short-lived successes won by his troops against the rebels. Even when he was driven – partly by the importunities of the young man himself – to appoint his half-brother Don John to overall command in Granada, he took care to keep him in check by means of a powerful council of advisers and never ceased to remind him that his main duty was to guard the provincial capital, not to go campaigning in person in the mountains. 'You must keep yourself, and I must keep you, for greater things', he wrote; and one must judge for oneself how much of this was calculation of the odds and how much was jealousy of a too brilliant personality in the bud. Not till the autumn of 1569 did Philip declare a war of 'fire and blood' against the enemy; and that was partly a technicality to attract recruits by offer of a better pay scale for combatants who were now deemed on active service.

By Christmas 1569, a year after the rising, he had at last come to a full realization of the dangers, for the Moriscos had reorganized, and under a new leader were more formidable than ever. If at this stage the Turks or their Viceroy in Algiers had responded to the appeals reaching them from their co-religionists and had bestirred themselves to raise even a fraction of the fleet that had appeared off Malta four years earlier, the whole eastern seaboard of Spain could have been wrenched back from the Christians and the verdict of the *Reconquista* challenged in blood.

In Constantinople the Grand Vizier was in favour of intervention, but the Sultan, Selim II, thought only of an attack on Cyprus, a Venetian possession on his own doorstep. The opportunity was missed, and no more than a handful of Moslem irregulars came ashore from Africa to swell the Morisco ranks. The aloofness of those on either side who might have been expected to throw themselves into the struggle almost passes belief – Philip, for instance, never even visited the scene of the fighting, though he did condescend to stretch the itinerary of the 'Great Voyages' by venturing as far south as the old Moorish capital of Cordoba, where he had a meeting of the Cortes to attend to.

Such a cold, calculating reaction would have been unthinkable in Charles V. But Philip had always had a very different conception of leadership. On hearing that Don John had so far forgotten himself as to get mixed up in the fighting and had been hit on the head in consequence, he sent him a sharp reproof: 'I therefore distinctly order you . . . to remain in the place which befits one who has the charge of this business . . . for every one ought to do his own duty, and not the general the soldier's nor the soldier the general's.' It was admirable advice which he was rather to forget when he came to plan the Armada of 1588 over the heads of his expert military advisers.

Opposite: Two views of the Escorial, built between 1563 and 1584 to commemorate the Spanish victory over the French at St. Quentin, and dedicated to St. Lawrence.
Photograph Scala, Florence.

In any case in the Alpujarras, Don John, a true son of his imperial father, took little notice, and once he had slipped his leash and galvanized his armies the war moved on to its inevitable and bloody end. At the siege of the rebel stronghold of Galera, high in the mountains, he vowed not to leave a soul alive, and all but kept his promise when the town eventually fell. Some of the women and children were spared. The men were butchered, the place was fired, and the ruins sown with salt. Every Morisco atrocity was repaid with interest as the surviving rebels were hunted like beasts from crag to crag and cave to cave through the desolate uplands, till the day came when the body of the last Morisco 'king', murdered by a faction of his own countrymen, was handed over to the Spaniards and paraded into Granada, propped up by wooden boards on the back of a mule, and his severed head nailed to a gateway where for years it hung bleaching in the sun.

The King had not approved the massacre at Galera, which he refused to celebrate with the paeans of triumph that the badly frightened Church and Christian communities in Granada would have thought appropriate to the occasion. Just as he had taken no part in the fighting, so he hardly deigned to notice the fragmented, squalid, and pitiful surrenders of the Moriscos that went on through the winter and spring of 1571. But he took care to see that the fruits of victory were reaped in the most practical way. Even before the final collapse, the Moriscos of the Albaicin quarter of the city of Granada had been expelled inland, far from the coast, and this was the solution that was adopted for the whole Granadan province once the rebels had laid down their arms.

No one was exempted – not even the *Moriscos de la paz* who had stayed loyal through the troubles. Men, women and children – all were gathered together into camps and then moved under strong military guard to remote provinces of Spain, some to La Mancha, others as far afield as Galicia in the north-west. If this was an inhuman act, there have been many worse in our own time for far less cause. And at the King's command great care was taken to ensure that in their enforced Odyssey the victims' families should not be broken up or separated from one another. It was probably a just, certainly a necessary solution in the context of the political and military situation of the time, with a large Turkish fleet once more at sea. The Moriscos suffered only a small diaspora. In the next reign, under Philip's weak and ultra-pious successor, the whole race was to be expelled from the peninsula.

The Morisco rebellion had had a number of things in common with the Netherlands rising but there was one great difference: it was a Mediterranean problem, part of the confrontation between Cross and Crescent that had taken Charles V to Tunis and Algiers, and the Turks to the conquest of Budapest.

This resulted in a very different emphasis, in very different attitudes. Where the Netherlands was concerned, Philip and his Viceroy in Brussels found themselves objects of widespread hatred and suspicion even in Catholic Hapsburg Vienna. Their sole ally outside the Spanish dependencies in Italy and the Franche Comté was the Pope, and even he was more concerned with Catholic dogma than with the well-being of the King of Spain. But where the Mediterranean was concerned it was far otherwise, for on this front everyone, from the Papacy to the villagers of Sicily and Calabria and that most ingrown and selfish of powers, the Venetian Republic, had come to recognize the danger of any further advance by the Ottomans and their Barbary Coast allies. Of the major European states, only the Emperor (insured by his payment of Danegelt to the Sultan) and the French (who had a tradition of alliance with him) remained unaffected by Turkish moves in the inland sea.

At exactly what point in time the danger had been realized is hard to say, for the Turkish assault in 1565 on the gateway to the Western Mediterranean – Malta – had been turned back largely through the heroism of the Maltese themselves, and the aid promised by Philip would have come too late if he had not had an energetic Viceroy in Sicily prepared to act on his own. It was probably a case of delayed shock, for four years later, as the ashes of the Morisco rising in the Alpujarras were being stamped out, not only the King of Spain but even the Venetians were prepared to listen to the call of Pius V, the last of the crusading Popes, who had been using every power of persuasion to create an alliance of the threatened against the infidel.

On 25th May 1571 the 'Holy League' was solemnized at the Vatican to provide a force of 300 ships, 50,000 infantry, 4,500 horse, with the requisite artillery in support, to be armed and ready each spring to proceed to the Levant.

The three allies had very different aims. The Pope, a real zealot, dreamed of expelling the Turks not only from the Mediterranean but from Constantinople! The King of Spain's mind was not directed to the Aegean but towards Algiers, Tunis and Tripoli, the pirate lairs opposite the Spanish coast, and had throughout insisted that the 'perpetual' alliance against the Turks should be widened to include action against these satellites of Turkish power. The Venetians merely wanted to save their island possession of Cyprus which the Ottomans had attacked. For years the *Serenissima* had had excellent relations with Constantinople and had watched Turkish inroads into Europe with detachment, but they were now so alarmed that they were prepared to put up one third of the expenses of the League and even to allow a Spaniard to be Captain General with a papal nominee as his deputy. The Pope, besides supplying the spirituality, shouldered one sixth of the cost. The rest was to be paid for by Philip – the Morisco rising had at last alarmed him too. He was duly gratified by the League's choice of his young half-brother, Don John, to be leader of the Christian host.

Three years earlier in May 1568, on creating Don John 'General of the Sea', which meant the command of the Spanish fleets, Philip had given detailed instructions as to the rules by which his brother must be guided. Since in the King's words 'the foundation and beginning of all things and all good counsel' came from God, Don John must make His service the be-all and end-all of life. He must be pious, devout, God-fearing, a model Christian. Truth in every word spoken and the exact fulfilment of promises were the basis of credit and esteem among men and upon them the 'confidence of society' was supported and founded. 'Administer justice equally and rightly, and when necessary, with the rigour and example which the case may require', the King went on; but Don John must also be 'merciful and benignant' wherever possible. Flattery and even words 'having that tendency' were ungracious in those who spoke

A Venetian galleass at the Battle of Lepanto.
Mary Evans Picture Library, London.

them and degrading and offensive to those to whom they were addressed. Special stress was laid on the need for pure living – a truly delicious side-thwack at the Emperor's bastard from a man who himself had enjoyed his share of mistresses. Don John must walk 'with great circumspection' here, since impurity was not only offensive to God but brought endless troubles and embarrassments in its train – surely another piece of black humour on Philip's part, seeing that the problem of what to do with Don John's scandalous mother, Barbara Blomberg, now the widow Kegell and eager to marry again, was one of the many insoluble questions presently exercising his and the Duke of Alva's mind. To proceed: Don John must if possible avoid gaming, especially at dice and cards. He must reject all kinds of ostentation in dress and manners; must not eat or drink too much, since moderation was good for the health; and must always be calm and modest, affable and courteous, avoiding the giving of insults and displays of bad temper which lowered a man's dignity.

In every word and nuance of this extraordinary document, surely the oddest orders ever given to a sea-going admiral, we can hear Philip busily paying back the Emperor his father for all the lectures that had rained down on him in his own youth. What was sauce for the goose was sauce for gander. What Charles had said to Philip, Philip would say to John. 'Be more like me.' It is a document full of irony, of echoes dating back to a time before Don John was even born. And since Don John was *never* to become like Philip, we can read in it some of the clues to the strange and tragic relationship that was to develop between these two brothers. What never divided them was their trust in God, and it was altogether in the spirit of these exhortations to Christian living that the younger man set out from Madrid for Italy in July 1571 and in August, in the church of Santa Chiara in Naples, received from the hands of Cardinal Granvelle his commander's baton and the gorgeous blue damask standard of the Holy League.

By the end of that month the allied squadrons were concentrating off Messina – 208 galleys, 32 larger vessels including galleasses with artillery aboard, 75 frigates and brigantines, over 300 sail, manned by 50,000 sailors and galley slaves and 30,000 troops. Of these, 90 galleys, 24 large ships and 50 frigates were Spanish, and two-thirds of the infantry were either Spanish (8,000 of them) or Italians and Germans in Spanish pay – a generous contribution when one remembers that Philip had also to maintain an army in the Netherlands and ocean-going fleets to guard the English Channel and the Atlantic treasure routes. He had shown quite unusual energy and promptness in the arming and despatch of his galleys to Naples.

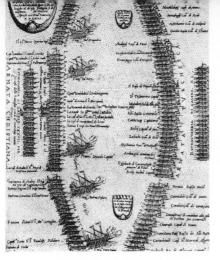

Left: The Christian and Turkish formations at the Battle of Lepanto, at the moment when the Venetian galleasses opened fire against the Turks.

Right: A later stage in the battle. Courtesy the National Maritime Museum, London.

Exactly what to do with this enormous armada now that it had assembled was however still a matter of dispute. For some unexplained reason the Venetians did not press for a hell-for-leather dash at Cyprus to save their threatened island, the final loss of which they were not to learn about till some weeks after the ceremonies in Santa Chiara. Probably it was thought that if the main Turkish fleet could be located and driven off, Cyprus would fall back of its own accord into allegiance. As for Philip's commanders, the most experienced among them, the Genoese Prince Giovanni Andrea Doria, was all for caution, and even Don John was uneasily aware of his responsibility to Philip for so huge an investment of blood and treasure. Many thought the Turks invincible at sea, and if this had been the feeling among the majority of the commanders the joint fleets could well have dallied in Italian waters as cravenly as in the previous year, when a Christian squadron had wasted a whole campaigning season with nothing to show for it. But the ardent spirit of Pius V had at last inspired the majority of the War Council which the cautious Philip had hung like an albatross round his brother's neck, and in mid-September, after days of fasting and shore visits by the ships' companies (including even the galley slaves) to confess and receive absolution in the churches and Jesuit College at Messina, the whole armament put to sea under the eye of the scarlet-clad papal nuncio, standing, arm raised in blessing, at the end of the harbour mole, while Don John knelt in golden armour among his kneeling men at arms on the prow of his flagship, the *Real*.

No one at this stage knew the whereabouts of the main enemy body as distinct from the force off Cyprus. Not till they had gingerly felt their way down the Ionian coast to Corfu and had come upon traces of Turkish raids ashore on the villages of Epirus did the Christians learn that a fleet at least as large as their own lay ahead of them in the Gulf of Lepanto. Off Cephalonia news reached them that the last Venetian fortress on Cyprus – Famagusta – had surrendered early in August, and that its commander had been flayed alive, his body stuffed with straw and hoisted to the yardarm of his captor's ship. It was a powerful incentive to the Christians to press on.

During the night of 6th October their squadrons were approaching the

An engraving of the Battle of Lepanto by Philippe Galle.
Bibliothèque National, Paris. Photograph, Roger Viollet, Paris.

entrance to the Lepanto gulf that cuts like a sword blade between the Greek 'mainland' and the Peloponnese, with the isthmus of Corinth at its tip. In these waters Odysseus had sailed home to Ithaca from Troy, and Octavian had defeated Anthony and Cleopatra at Actium to settle the mastery of the Roman world. Soon after dawn on the 7th Turkish ships were sighted ahead.

The League's line of battle was already formed – the six Venetian galleasses in the lead, to hurl their heavy shot into the advancing Turks; then the three divisions of the line, deployed as an army would have been on land; the Venetians on the left, a mixed force under the Genoese Andrea Doria on the vulnerable right or seaward flank, the main *batalla* under Don John and his deputy, Colonna, at the centre; supported by a reserve of 35 galleys under command of the Spanish marquis of Santa Cruz.

In the jaws of the Gulf the Turks had formed the usual crescent line, their commander Ali Pasha at the centre and their most experienced seaman, the renegade Christian Aluch Ali, to seaward facing Doria; but as more and more allied ships were seen rounding the headland the wings were drawn back defensively, and it was in long parallel lines that the rival navies began to close on one another in the clear light of the autumn morning.

The wind which during the night had sent the League's fleet scudding south-wards had dropped soon after dawn, and in the final hours before the battle the faithful on both sides were busy. Don John had rejected the appeals of the faint-hearted to retreat in ringing words: 'Gentlemen, the time for counsel is past, the time for fighting has come', and boarding a frigate he went down the line of ships calling on his men to do their duty by God and the Church. It was a spirit that ran through most of the fleet, even among the worldly Venetians. In Andrea Doria's squadron the young Cervantes, who was suffering from fever, rose from his sick bed to fight, to lose the use of an arm, and to remember the day as the greatest of his life. As a slight breeze stirred in the north behind the allied fleet a deep silence fell; the friars aboard each ship held up their crucifixes and men knelt to receive their blessing. Aboard the Turkish flagship Ali Pasha, a compassionate man who had not been responsible for the massacre of the captives at Famagusta, went down from his command post to speak to his Christian galley slaves. If the battle went against him, then Allah would have declared for them and they would have found freedom; if his was the victory, he promised them their liberty. He begged them meanwhile to remember his past efforts to make their lot more bearable and in gratitude to do their best for him in the coming battle. Then to the sound of Christian bugles and Turkish kettledrums the fleets came together like rival armies of ants grappling with one another.

Except on the allied right, where Andrea Doria and Aluch Ali fought a war of movement, Lepanto was not a sea battle in Atlantic terms but a series of ship to ship engagements between boarding parties of infantry using tactics not very different from those of Roman times in the Carthaginian Wars. In number of galleys engaged the Turks had an advantage of almost three to two, but not all of them were of good quality or well manned, and they were outmatched in fire power by the Christians, who on Doria's advice had cut away their *espalones* or ramming prows to give a clearer and lower field of fire for the forward-mounted guns; nor did the Turks have any counter to the heavy artillery in the Venetian galleasses.

To seaward the wily Aluch Ali outmanoeuvred Doria and slipped between his extended line and the rest of the Christian fleet, causing havoc among the Maltese galleys in the rear, but like Prince Rupert's cavalry at Marston Moor many years later he was more intent on cutting out prizes than in winning a battle, and played no part in the hard pounding at the centre where the issue was being decided.

Here the carnage was even greater than it would have been on land, for there was nowhere for the combatants to go but into the bloodstained shambles of the decks or overboard into the sea. Locked together in a death grapple, the two flagships were the stage on which companies of Turkish janissaries and Castilian infantry decimated one another and were constantly replaced by reinforcements from other ships, till observers saw the water around them running red with blood. In one of these surges Ali Pasha was killed by an arquebus shot, his head was cut off, and according to the most likely story hoisted on a pike as a trophy for all to see. It was the turning point, and by sunset the Ottoman fleet was in utter rout.

The Christians had won their greatest victory over the Crescent since the capture of Granada; greater even than the Emperor Charles's capture of Tunis; and they had won it against odds and probably their own expectations. In the course of it they had lost over four thousand dead, but the Turkish losses were much greater, and if a blustery night of thunderstorms had not put an end to any thought of pursuit hardly a squadron of the Ottoman centre and right would have made its way back to Constantinople.

Tradition has it that on the afternoon of the battle Pope Pius V, far off in Rome, suddenly broke off a conversation with his treasurer to say that the Christian fleets had won a mighty victory. The King of Spain was given no such

Titian here links the victory at Lepanto with the birth of a prince, Don Fernando, on 14th December, 1571. But the painter's divinations came to nothing, as Fernando died in 1578. Courtesy the Prado Madrid.

divine revelation: if it had not been for the high-class earthly service provided by the Venetians, he would have had to wait till late in November before Don John's official courier, Don Lope de Figuerosa, finally limped into Madrid, sorely troubled by the wounds he had suffered in the battle.

The King greeted the victory with a display of benign, impressive calm: he had been at Vespers in his chapel when the first despatch from the Venetians came in, and he did not allow the news of it to interrupt the service. A month later he greeted poor Don Lope 'as well as your Highness would be the Pope', the delighted messenger reported to his master in Sicily. Graciously the King wrote also to his victorious Captain-General: 'Brother, by a courier despatched by the Republic of Venice to their ambassador, who arrived at Madrid on the eve of All Saints, I heard of the great victory which our Lord has been pleased to give you.' Further news confirming this – and that meant Don Lope – he went on, had given him inexpressible joy, not least because of what he had heard of Don John's great courage and skilful direction of the battle. To Don John, after God, he gave the honour and thanks for the victory.

Then having praised, the King turned to administer a sharp rap over the knuckles of this now-too-illustrious youth. Don John had asked for leave to come to Madrid. That could not be thought of. He must winter with the fleet in Messina. The King must therefore regretfully postpone the pleasure of exchanging congratulations.

And that was that. On balance Don John probably earned more displeasure from his king for winning Lepanto than Medina Sidonia six years later for losing the Invincible Armada.

Chapter 10

Mutiny

The stories of The Emperor's New Clothes and of the Duke of Alva's New Taxes have much in common.

At first the illusion was complete. In April 1569 the Duke reported to Philip that he had put his proposals for the Hundredth, Twentieth and Tenth Pennies to the Netherlands States General, which had taken it well. By midsummer he was rejoicing that a majority had consented to these taxes, the largest grants ever made in one swoop by the States to their sovereign, and he even went on to prophesy that there would in future be no need of subsidies from Spain. In August Philip sent him his personal thanks and congratulations for these 'eminent services'. So much were the future financial benefits taken for granted by both King and Duke that for the rest of 1569 and most of 1570 the subject of taxation filled only a minor role in their correspondence, which became chiefly concerned with two other matters: the granting of a General Pardon to the rebels and also another item which went rather oddly with it, since it amounted to a plan for the judicial murder of that same Count of Montigny whom the Duchess Margaret had sent on an abortive mission to Madrid.

Shuttled backwards and forwards in draft after draft between the two secretariats, polished and re-polished, the General Pardon when it finally came to be published in Antwerp in July 1570 fell flat – it had come too late in the day and was too full of reservations and ifs and buts to satisfy the Netherlanders. The Montigny affair was however far more efficiently and expeditiously conducted. After a species of trial *in absentia* before Alva's Council of Troubles, the Count was duly condemned to death and the condemnation forwarded for action to Madrid. There the King and his advisers debated how best to carry out the sentence – the final plan was for a secret execution in the castle of Simancas, which would then be presented to the public both in Spain and the Netherlands as death from natural causes.

If Spanish sources are to be believed, the unfortunate Montigny, awakened from sleep at midnight and told of his fate, declared himself to be a good Catholic, admitted that the sentence passed on him was just, and thanked the King for sparing him the indignity of a public execution. Having made his confession, he was then strangled and his body was dressed in Franciscan habit, which hid the marks around his neck. His death marked the end of the round of punishments which the Duke had been sent to Brussels to inflict, and obviously no one from Philip and his Viceroy down to the executioner, the priest who gave absolution and the doctor who had been brought to the castle to lend some credibility to the tale of fatal illness, ever paused to consider that what was being done was a cruel, unjust and atrocious crime. After all, everything had been carried out with due legality.

In Brussels, now that the country was officially pacified and pardoned for its misdeeds and the fiscal revolution had been carried through the States General, the Duke was impatiently awaiting his recall. He found the ambience of the Low Countries and particularly the climate distressing. Also he was suffering from the gout. However this was only the beginning of his troubles, for it soon began to dawn on him that the matter of the taxes had not arranged itself quite as harmoniously as he in his innocence had imagined, and that many of the King's normally loyal supporters were unwaveringly opposed to anything that hurt their pockets. At the end of September 1571 the Bishop of Ypres wrote to Philip complaining of the hardship the Tenth Penny would cause to the poor now that winter was coming on, and another devoted servant of the régime warned the King that its collection would provoke widespread disturbances. Even Alva himself was soon confessing his puzzlement that the heads he had cut off on a hundred scaffolds had caused nothing like the outcry raised by this simple purchase tax. With the new year came reports of massive emigration and trade was nearly at a standstill. It was becoming clear, as three of his own Netherlands bishops wrote to the King, that whatever the States General might or might not have promised in the people's name, the people themselves had utterly rejected it.

By February 1572 the King had become alarmed by the number of reports and petitions he was receiving. Certainly, he wrote to Alva, certainly if the Tenth Penny could be collected peacefully it would be a great thing for the finances, but since the imposition of new taxes was always 'dangerous and displeasing to subjects' and trade was the very lifeblood of the provinces, he begged him to weigh the consequences very carefully before going on. Might it

In this engraving the Babylonian Whore makes merry with Alva while the Dutch ships come to ruin, the merchants cannot obtain goods and the pedlar cannot earn his bread.
Courtesy Atlas van Stolk, Rotterdam.

Left: The invasion of Brille by the 'Sea Beggars' in April 1572.
Courtesy the Gemeentearchief, Delft.

*Right: The Spanish soldiers under the command of Don Fadrique, Alva's son, murder
the inhabitants of the rebel town of Zutphen.*
Courtesy Atlas van Stolk, Rotterdam.

not be better to work out some kind of compromise? It is to Philip's credit that
he had sensed the dangers much more clearly than his Viceroy on the spot and
was reaching out for some kind of general settlement of differences with the
Netherlanders. However very typically – as in the matter of the treasure ships
at Plymouth – he was not prepared to assert his own judgment but left the
final decision to the Duke.

And there, in a long wrangle with the tax-payers, the matter might have
rested if a number of ruffianly pirate captains and their crews sailing under
letters of marque issued by the Prince of Orange (and soon to be immortalized
as the 'Sea Beggars') had not chosen to anchor – purely by chance – off the port
of Brille in Zeeland on a day when the Spanish garrison was absent on duty
elsewhere.

To their own astonishment they discovered that not only Brille but most of
the villages and towns along the seaways and canals of Zeeland were at their
mercy. It was more of an orgy than an invasion, as boatloads of men in vestments looted from the churches ran wild among the islands and mudflats of that
sombre coast. The Duke himself, as he explained in a singularly cool letter to
the King announcing this disaster, was unable to move against them with his
usual speed because of unrest and fear of 'insolences' among his shock troops,
the *tercios* – the first whisper of the mutinies that were to spell the end of Spanish
rule in the northern provinces. The correspondence between him and the King
during that spring, summer and autumn of 1572 shows small understanding of
the fact that something of decisive importance had occured. This was because
another invasion by rebel land armies under the Prince of Orange and his
brother, Count Louis of Nassau, had diverted everyone's attention from the
coast to the interior. By the time the important town of Mons in the Walloon
south had been recaptured from Count Louis and Orange's main force had been
driven out of Brabant across the Rhine, the Sea Beggars' hold on Zeeland had
spread to the neighbouring provinces of Holland, Overyssel and Gelderland,
and a sizeable slice of the country north of the river Waal with a number of
strong-walled towns had passed into rebel hands.

Into this pickle there now stepped another grandee from Spain, Don Juan de Cerda, Duke of Medina Celi, whom Philip had sent to the Netherlands in answer to Alva's constant requests for a replacement. However the man's commission had been post-dated to take effect only on Alva's actual departure from Netherlands soil, and since it happened that the newcomer's arrival coincided with the military crisis caused by the rebel invasions, he had to wait in the wings and was never destined to take office.

His mere presence in Brussels with his commission in his pocket was how-ever a fine apple of discord, and the relationship between the two dukes was to provide the only comedy in the rapidly darkening scene. They loathed one another from the start. Medina Celi, deprived of active command, accused Alva of culpable aloofness from the war, even of cowardice, a truly astonishing charge. With Christian humility Alva lamented Medina Celi's faults – never, he wrote, had there lived a more irascible or unreasonable man or one to cause him more pains and persecutions. Both bombarded the King with their shrill complaints, which formed a kind of comic counterpoint to the continuing saga of the Tenth Penny and the growing thunder of the guns.

For in the late autumn of 1572 Alva loosed his armies under his son Don Fadrique in a punitive strike at the town of Mechlin, which had unwisely opened its gates to the Orangists, and then northwards towards the rebel strongholds beyond the Waal, where Zutphen was selected as a suitable case for treatment. Here the orders received by Don Fadrique were not to leave a soul alive after its occupation, and he proved so obedient a son that the Duke was soon writing to Philip to offer his official congratulations on this 'success' which had brought matters – at least in Zutphen – to a 'satisfactory conclusion'. At the neighbouring small town of Naarden matters were more satisfactory still; for here the citizens docilely allowed themselves to be rounded up in the church where they could be slaughtered conveniently *en masse* – truly 'men of butter', as the Duke had contemptuously called the Netherlanders.

Early in the new year – 1573 – Don Fadrique's army cast its net round Haarlem, the largest and most important of the rebel-held towns in the horn of Holland. As the weeks went by the suffering inside the town was fearful, but it was little better for the besiegers in the depths of a Dutch winter, and every assault was beaten off. 'This is the bloodiest war . . . seen for a long time,' the Duke lamented to the King in his perplexity. That burghers from behind a line of walls as thin as those of Haarlem should dare defy the *tercios*, and continue to defy them month after month, was to his mind a denial of nature, and as the year wore on his testy complaints to Madrid began to verge on the paranoiac. 'I have noticed for some time', he wrote to the King that March, 'that the advice I send your Majesty does not receive your approval. . . . The tone of your Majesty's replies is very different from what it used to be.' Almost as burden-some as the war was the Tenth Penny, which both he and Philip had agreed to give up in return for an annual lump sum of two million ducats, but annual for how long? The Duke thought one thing and the Netherlanders thought the other, but it was as clear as daylight that no money whatsoever was coming in and that he had hardly a *real* to his name. Kept seven years from the clear air and sunshine of Spain, a martyr to gout, chair-bound, beset by troubles and complaints on every side, risking his life and reputation in a cause for which he

Left: Haarlem surrendered in July 1573; here the Spanish troops are shown massacring the inhabitants. The killings were less than at Zutphen.
Courtesy Atlas van Stolk, Rotterdam.

Right: A painting of the Siege of Alkmaar in 1573 by Pieter Aeriaensz Cluyt.
Courtesy Stedelijk Museum, Alkmaar. Photograph, A. Dinjan.

received never a word of thanks from anyone – his self-pity had become a disease.

In July, as some slight alleviation, Haarlem surrendered at last. It had held off fifteen thousand crack troops well supplied with siege artillery for six months, and in a final gesture of defiance and derision its starving garrison had thrown their last loaves of bread into the besiegers' camp, where conditions were not much better. A whole fleet of ships had had to be hauled overland with immense pains by Don Fadrique's engineers to cut the town's last communications with the outside world. If there were to be many more such victories Spain could hardly hope to survive them. And no sooner was the siege over than Don Fadrique's victorious troops mutinied, demanding food, loot having been denied them by the lenient surrender terms imposed on the town. In his letter to the King, Alva remarked that this indiscipline had pained him more than anything he had encountered in forty years of soldiering, yet it could hardly have surprised him, since as he well knew it was more than a year since the Spanish infantry had received their pay. Even when the mutinies had been quelled for the time being, there was still no end in sight to the Duke's troubles, for as fast as one dragon's tooth was wrenched out of the ground, another fully-armed warrior sprang up, and at the northern tip of Holland, Alkmaar closed its gates against him.

A remote market town, Alkmaar stood in the low-lying country between the Zuiderzee and the ocean behind the defensive barrier of its dykes. By cutting them the burghers marooned themselves inside a ring of water more impassable than any walls, and as the autumn high tides and gales along the coast whipped up the floods in the canals and polders, the Duke's besieging army was driven off in rout. Enraged by the failure of his 'clemency' at Haarlem to pacify the provinces, he had sworn to treat Alkmaar as he had treated Zutphen, but thanks to the elements and the ruthless energy of its citizens it survived to become the place long remembered in Dutch history 'where Victory began'.

Its relief and the simultaneous loss of a Spanish fleet off Enkhuisen heralded the end of Alva's reign in Brussels. Begun in overwhelming pride, it had ended in ignominy, with a bankrupt treasury, a rebellious people and a mutinous army. Nothing that had happened had however changed the Duke's mind one jot. Clemency had failed and would fail. Force was the only answer. Such was his final uncompromising message to Madrid. But in the interim the King had begun to tire of this advice and of a policy which brought him nothing but reproaches from his subjects and a spreading stain of war for which he could not pay. It was time for a change, perhaps over-late. The Duke's constant pleas for relief had at last been answered and a new Lieutenant Governor to replace both him and Medina Celi was on his way.

The new appointee (who had tried his best to avoid being chosen for this office) was Don Luis de Requesens y Cuniga, Grand Commander of Castile, a very different kind of man from his predecessor, a simple gentleman 'of cape and sword' who had risen by his own abilities to hold important diplomatic posts and had served also as Don John's mentor in the war against the Moriscos in the Alpujarras and at Lepanto, where his vigorous support of the flagship at the crisis of the battle had played a big part in the victory.

This time there was none of the posturing or the comic relief that had accompanied Medina Celi's ghost appointment. The Grand Commander arrived on the scene and like any sensible man of business asked for a statement of the accounts. The Duke replied that it was impossible to supply one. Requesens set to work with his officials to make his own reckoning. He found that he had just under sixty thousand Spanish, German, Italian and Walloon troops whose back pay amounted to more than one year's revenue from all Spanish sources, including the Indies. He found also the battle for the Tenth Penny in its usual state of flux.

Right at the year's end, after a series of conferences with his predecessor and Don Fadrique, Requesens sent his assessment of the situation to his master in Madrid. The Duke and his fiery son had rejected any talk of a pardon. The Grand Commander on the other hand felt that one must be published without delay. It could hardly make things worse than they were. In his view the religious question which had once divided the Netherlands was now of secondary importance, and the things that really mattered, because they out-raged the people, were the Tenth Penny, the detested Council of Troubles, and the indiscipline of the occupying troops against which many of Philip's own bishops had protested. The special courts should be abolished. And the Tenth Penny should be done away with also for good and all, in return for the best annual contribution that could be negotiated with the States General – for twelve years if possible, failing that for six, but to be got out of the way at all costs.

This was a diplomat's survey which if it had been implemented five years earlier might have saved all the Netherlands provinces for the King. However there was now an armed insurrection which Requesens had inherited along with the Tenth Penny, and the result was to turn the peacemaker into a cam-paigner busier than Alva had ever been and to mark the short period of his rule with two of the greatest feats of arms of the century: the rebel raising of the siege of Leyden by an armada of flat-bottomed boats and the still more fabulous Spanish victory at Zeirickzee, where a small force of infantry fought its way through a night of storm across the mudflats of an estuary, chest-deep in water and under fire from enemy ships and batteries.

Zeirickzee was an incident of no lasting consequence, as was the battle at Mookerheide on the borders of Germany where a Spanish army put an end to

The relief of Leyden by the 'Sea Beggars' under the command of Boisot in October 1573.
Courtesy the Gemeentearchief, Delft.

the adventures of Orange's younger brother, Count Louis of Nassau. But Leyden, like Brille, was a more decisive affair altogether. If it had fallen to the Spaniards the rebellion in the north would almost certainly have been snuffed out. Books have been written about the prodigies that saved it: the long-endured famine, the cutting of the dykes, the fleet of barges which the Orangist relieving force collected at Rotterdam and sent mudlarking through the meadows and orchards in two feet of water released from the rivers and the distant sea. A stained-glass window in the cathedral at Gouda and a fair in Leyden itself still commemorate this event of 1574, exactly four hundred years ago, which heralded the end of Spanish power in seven northern provinces of the seventeen which Philip had inherited.

Yet Leyden alone did not bring about the collapse of morale which followed among the Spanish regiments: it was just the culminating event that brought the King and his advisers face to face with the appalling fact that what in today's terms we would call a 'colonial' war was costing annually more than the total revenues of Spain. It was a realization which led in turn to a chain reaction of disaster – first, a 'Suspension of Payments' in Madrid (a nice euphemism for a mass defaulting on government loans); the closure of the great trade fair at Medina del Campo and a gradual drying up of the arteries of trade; growing alarm among foreign bankers; a freeze on credits; and the virtual cessation of the flow of ready cash between the King in Spain, his representative in Brussels, and the unpaid army of occupation in its Netherlands cantonments.

Already in the aftermath of the victory over Count Louis at Mookerheide a section of the Spanish army had given notice of its profound displeasure by seizing control of Antwerp in defiance of its own officers. 'Bread, not speeches!' the troopers shouted at the Grand Commander when he appeared on horseback to harangue them. The citizens of Antwerp, appalled by the presence of three thousand potential brigands and rapists on their streets, hastily paid up enough cash to rid themselves of their unwelcome guests – a somewhat short-sighted policy as the future was to show. But though the *tercios* had been happy to insult the Grand Commander, they had some hopes of him; he was after all their traditional paymaster and a famous leader by land and sea. His lamentably early death (from natural causes) in the spring of 1576 left them with no single person to appeal to or intimidate but only a Council of State, composed largely

'The Spanish Fury' at Antwerp during which eight thousand people are reported to have died. Courtesy Atlas van Stolk, Rotterdam.

of Netherlanders and men of straw, who clearly had neither the will nor the means to pay anyone anything and whose members were in any event soon to be arrested in an Orangist *coup* which sought to take over not only Holland and Zeeland but the entire country. The machinery of Spanish rule had simply disintegrated in front of their eyes under the enormous military, political and financial strains that had been imposed on it. *Io Saturnalia*! The Netherlands had become a free-for-all, where the loyalist-minded (still in the vast majority in every province) had no visible rallying point. And this applied particularly to the army of occupation which, apart from its Walloon members, was an alien force on alien soil, equally conscious of its unpopularity, its hunger, and its latent power.

So it mutinied. If it wanted to be fed it had probably little choice. It did so, as in all its mutinies, in a very disciplined way, each unit democratically appointing an *Eletto* from within its own ranks who would represent it, lead it to the nearest lootable town, and could be made a convenient scapegoat if the thing went wrong.

Late in October in the year of Requesens' death a body of mutineers seized Maastricht on the Meuse and sacked it with savage fury. In Alva's citadel of Antwerp far stronger forces lay waiting their opportunity. On 4th November, in an operation long remembered by the survivors among the victims as 'The Spanish Fury', they launched themselves in a concerted swoop of cavalry and infantry with artillery support on the fabulously and provocatively rich city which lay within their grasp. According to one Spanish witness who reported to the King, eight thousand died – for Antwerp had made some token efforts to defend itself. No one has ever attempted to estimate how many were robbed, pillaged, raped or burnt in the final holocaust which destroyed much of the commercial centre of the city. The cathedral escaped. The historian Motley has one ironic passage where he describes its bells chiming the hours, high above the inferno that was going on below. Centuries were to pass before Antwerp regained its old pre-eminence.

The Spanish Fury completed the work begun by the Beggars at Brille. A week later the Protestant Orangists of Holland and Zeeland and the Catholic moderates of the States General, the best of enemies at most times and deeply divided from one another, came together in the common crisis and signed the so-called 'Pacification of Ghent', which amounted to a formal alliance of the Netherlands provinces in pursuit of revolutionary social and political aims. What Alva had sown the Spanish army had reaped, and the unfortunate harvester was the King.

Chapter 11

The Fourth Marriage

Philip had found these troubles and discouragements more bearable because in the autumn of 1570, at the age of forty-three, he had married for the fourth time. The bride had been the Habsburg princess originally intended for Don Carlos: his niece Anne of Austria, daughter of the Emperor Maximilian and his sister Maria, over whose cradle he had leaned on his way to make his first journey abroad.

The princess was less than half his age: a peach-blonde Viennese, though born in Castile and entirely Castilian in spirit. And in this, as in almost everything, she matched her husband to perfection. Contemporary observers of the Spanish scene and later historians who took their tone from them have eulogized the King's happiness with his third (French) wife: there is a great deal of evidence to suggest that he was at least as contented with his fourth, this young, charming, docile member of his own family, devoted to religion and the contemplative life, who was to present him with the male heir for which his heart had longed.

The marriage took place at Segovia, always one of the King's favourite towns. A certain placid air of middle age can be sensed even through the splendours of the pageants and celebrations that marked these last nuptials of the reign. The new Queen had been born for her task. No one could look more modest or decorous, reported an anonymous Venetian who saw her at court a year later. She was slightly built, had fair hair and a very white skin – yet another proof of the dominance of the Habsburg genes in the colouring of the Spanish princes of that blood, from the Emperor Charles to Philip II and Don John. Her conduct was exemplary, noted the Venetian, who in all conscience could hardly have expected anything else. When he saw her she was dressed very elegantly in black velvet, her coiffure was adorned with jewels and she wore a chain necklace of 'inestimable value'. Close to her were six young ladies of noble birth, of whom three served at table while the others, grouped around the walls, chatted with their lovers. An idyllic scene, not at all in keeping with the usual tales of the stiff protocol of the Spanish court. And this keen observer noted one other felicitous fact – that the king dearly loved his wife.

Anne of Austria, Philip II's fourth wife, painted by Sani.
Courtesy the Prado, Madrid.

A quarter of a century had elapsed since Don Carlos had been born to Maria of Portugal. Now at last in Madrid on 4th December 1571 Anne of Austria gave birth to a prince, Don Fernando. The King had spent six hours at the bedside, and his joy at the event was reflected even in the unusual gaiety of his clothes. On the 8th, when the Venetian ambassadors came to present their official congratulations, they found him seated at a small table, wearing silver-coloured velvet breeches, silk stockings, a satin doublet, an elegant black silk jacket and a damask cloak trimmed with sable and surmounted by the collar of the Golden Fleece. His black velvet hat was edged with gold. An impressive, even awesome, spectacle. Yet the ambassadors found themselves greeted with the most urbane courtesy – gone altogether was the arrogant air which had earned the disapproval of the Netherlanders and the Germans in other days.

In a companion sketch an anonymous scribe from the *Serenissima* added a more generalized portrait of Philip in his forties.

El Alcazar, Segovia.
Courtesy the Spanish National Tourist Office, London.

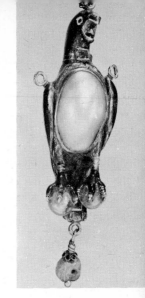

Left: Philip II with his young family.
Courtesy the Hispanic Society of America, New York.

Right: A parrot pendant in enamelled gold set with pearls. These pendants were popular in the 16th century and both Philip's daughters are wearing similar ornaments in the painting on the left.
Courtesy Sotheby Parke-Bernet, New York.

He was of medium height, well proportioned and 'more robust than delicate', no doubt the result of middle-age spread affecting even this most ascetic of monarchs. His fair hair and thick beard had become streaked with grey. His lower lip protruded, but this hereditary trait, which in the Emperor had been marked to the point of deformity, gave Philip, in this observer's view at least, an added dignity. The total effect of this word picture, as in the portraits, is one of Roman, even Stoic, equilibrium. The King's eating and drinking habits were regular; so were his attendances at set times of the day at chapel and on the Queen and her growing family: he was a man of method even in his leisure hours. Afternoons out hunting and driving in the country and *fêtes champêtres* in the gardens at Aranjuez were the rare exceptions in a régime which, in the words of this foreign observer, was otherwise devoted to 'business without respite'.

For when at his desk, where he spent more and more of his day, the King's one desire was 'to know and oversee everything'. Death was depriving him of many of his old intimates. Ruy Gomez, Prince of Eboli, died in 1575; and he had become estranged from Alva, who in the historian Cabrera's words had tired him with his too-great self-sufficiency and constant harpings on the great services he had performed for the State. The air of melancholy that had always accompanied the King had deepened as he grew older and the routine of religious devotions increasingly absorbed him. His wife was of the same mind. Her court was like a nunnery, wrote the disgusted French ambassador Fourquevaulx, who could recall the livelier days of her predecessor, Elizabeth of Valois. A very biased witness, no doubt, for relations between Spain and her powerful neighbour beyond the Pyrenees were deteriorating, yet in his contemptuous phrase Fourquevaulx had correctly sketched a style, a way of life that was to persist till the end of the reign a quarter of a century later.

It was a tone of devout piety. The King who had presided over Lepanto and the siege of Haarlem, the lord of the Indies and of the treasure fleets, was as often as not at work of choice on other vastly different matters; preferments to bishoprics and obscure curacies; the endowments of a monastery; the proper vestments to be worn by a parish priest; the transfer of the remains of his ancestors and family from their scattered graves to the solemn splendour of the Escorial; the collections of bones from far and wide. 'I believe your Majesty should consider the matter of relics', wrote the King's principal secretary, that joker in the pack, Antonio Perez, who was to cause his master untold agonies of conscience in the years ahead. 'This man has one most rare one, the Winding-Sheet from the Sepulchre, which would be very well suited to the Escorial.' This may or may not have been the famous 'Shroud' from Jerusalem which turned up in Turin in 1578 and is still preserved in its cathedral, one of the most remarkable and mysterious of all alleged relics of the Crucifixion. It certainly never reached the Escorial, but an inventory of the bones and skulls of saintly and sometimes quite fictitious persons that eventually found a home there testifies to the widespread nature of the search and to the King's bent for believing.

He was in many respects a credulous man, open to the suggestions and influence of the narrow circle of those in whom he trusted. For all his good intelligence and experience in ruling he was always temperamentally on the look-out to be instructed, to be *told*. It had started with his father's long catalogues of the rules and regulations by which he should be guided, and he never really outgrew them. He might adjudicate on this, and dictate vast memoranda on that, but at heart, as one of the Venetians wrote, he distrusted his own judgment. His own knowledge of this fact was to place him even more completely in the hands of those immediately around him, his secretaries, who, if they were wise (as Antonio Perez in the long run was not) dexterously returned the ball of indecision into their master's court and sat down patiently to await the result.

From this devil's circle of delay sprang many of the ills that beset the Spanish service across the world. Antonio Perez's own father (a much more honest and weighty man) had early come to the conclusion that Philip's natural condition was 'never to decide anything'. Some years later another sufferer was to complain: 'Although dilatoriness is usually bad in all things, it is sometimes incurable, as his Majesty's is beginning to be.' He was so tardy in deciding things that in the end he came to them 'quite out of season', wrote the Grand Commander, Requesens; and Pope Pius V in a personal letter to the King was still more direct: 'Your Majesty spends so long considering your undertakings that when the moment to perform them comes, the occasion has passed. . . .' This was natural in a man who tried to perform too much and could never distinguish between what was vital and what was peripheral. 'He filled his life with occupations', wrote Gregorio Maranon in a phrase which perhaps comes closest to an understanding of a deeply solitary and troubled life. It was easier and more pleasurable to busy oneself in filling the Escorial with the coffins of ancestors and the bones of wonder-working saints than to decide what should be done with the seventeen provinces of the Netherlands in the appalling interregnum that had followed the death of Requesens.

Chapter 12

Don John in Brussels: Escovedo in Madrid

Traditionally the government of the Netherlands had been entrusted to cadet members of the Habsburg ruling house, and after the experiments with Alva and the Grand Commander the King reverted to custom by appointing his half-brother as his Governor and Captain General.

He had done it with some misgivings, not unaware that Don John could be a difficult subordinate – in fact after Lepanto the important gain of the pirate nest of Tunis had been squandered because the headstrong young man had disobeyed orders sent to him from Madrid. Philip also knew that his brother had ambitions, natural enough in an imperial bastard, to sit some day on a throne; indeed *two* thrones, by carrying an army across the English Channel to the rescue of the imprisoned Mary Queen of Scots and the deposition of Elizabeth.

These visionary schemes, in which Philip himself never for one moment believed and which from the viewpoint of Spanish diplomacy were dangerous in the extreme, could have been scotched at source by firm instructions to Don John on no account to go adventuring. But that was never Philip's way. If he placed such an embargo on his brother the man might not consent to go to Brussels where he was urgently needed. Philip therefore made a parade of sympathizing with these ambitions, while ensuring at the first opportunity that the Spanish troops should as a peace gesture to the Netherlanders be sent out of the country, but southwards, *overland*, and not by sea, where Don John might have used them for some descent on London.

At this stage in his relations with his rebellious subjects Philip was genuinely anxious to come to terms. He had tried terror and military repression and now he was looking for a formula which would make people forget the past and restore things to where they had been in the early days of the Duchess Margaret. To a man of ingrained legalistic mind unaware of the depths of hatred that had been stirred up by Alva and the mutinous troops, such an agreement seemed well within grasp, and in his instructions to his brother he set out the new aims of his diplomacy. By 'good, just and reasonable means' and exercising 'love, gentleness and benevolence', Don John must give 'just and reasonable contentment to all' and ensure 'a true, stable and durable pacification' in conformity with the edicts of Charles V (by which all heretics could be burnt at the stake). Nor was this the end of the contradictory absurdities implicit in the instructions. A General Pardon was to be proclaimed, excepting only the Prince of Orange, who at the time was the single most powerful person in the Netherlands. Don John was given wide powers to negotiate, provided that the rights of the Catholic Church and the Crown were retained intact – a position which in two of the provinces was already lost beyond redemption. The King had brought himself to a negotiating position at the moment when all the winning cards were in his opponents' hands, and his chosen agent of appeasement was a man who dreamed chiefly of war.

The new Governor's arrival on the Netherlands scene was typical of what was to come, for in his hurry to reach the base from which he hoped to win the crown of England Don John had scorned the usual route from Genoa along the Rhine and crossed France on horseback in the disguise of a Morisco servant. His closest intimate was a scheming secretary, Juan de Escovedo, who with some assistance from Madrid was to figure in the greatest political scandal of the century by getting himself murdered with the complicity of the King. What Philip and his knight errant of a brother were doing in such company passes belief, but it happened, and it made a fine tragedy.

In the Netherlands the chain of Spanish mutinies culminating in the rape of Antwerp had created a situation in which the King's writ no longer ran in the vast majority of provinces, which had banded themselves together in uneasy alliance between the Protestant followers of Orange and the Catholics of the centre and south to form a confederation which had as its charter the treaty called 'The Pacification of Ghent', later enlarged by the 'Union of Brussels'. It was a settlement broadly recognizing the balance of power between the religious forces. Catholicism should prevail as before in fifteen provinces, the Reformed Religion in two, and everywhere the savage edicts of Charles V were suspended – all until such time as the States General should agree a final solution to the problem.

Don John, coming naked and forlorn into a situation not of his own making, found himself faced with this *Diktat* and with a country which (Luxemburg apart) seemed almost completely estranged from Spain.

He had advantages. He was young and handsome: a slight, dapper man with long blond hair and moustaches, a fine horseman, and very graceful in his bearing. He was the son of a Netherlands-born Emperor and a German mother, a born charmer and the victor of Lepanto. Even so, the task facing him would have daunted anyone; and besides, he had failings which had not escaped the notice of the Venetian diplomats, who judged him hot-headed, hasty, designing, obstinately mule headed, and (at games) a bad loser. In proof of this, he had hardly arrived in Luxemburg before his complaints to the King began. He did not like the people he had been sent to negotiate with. They were rude, insolent, had lost all sense of duty to God and the crown, and, most offensively of all in view of his designs on England, they were insisting that as the price of recognition he must send away the Spanish troops. Also he must accept their precious religious settlement. Within a matter of days of his arrival he was asking for money and talking of force as the only alternative to 'shamefully abandoning

This portrait of Don John of Austria hangs in the Escorial monastery.
The Escorial. Photograph, MAS, Barcelona.

the country'. To negotiate with such people, he told the King in one of the endless stream of letters he despatched to Madrid, one needed 'the patience of an angel'. They were men inspired by Satan – 'and may he carry them off!' he added in a typical explosion of wrath. Finding himself 'alone, without troops, without credit, without money', he begged the King to review his whole policy of détente and, if he wanted a just and durable peace, to prepare for a 'cruel and bloody war'.

It took time for these intemperate outbursts to alarm the King. Perhaps the moment when he first began to repent his choice of agent came when Don John's secretary, Escovedo, joined in the chorus with his own contributions on the theme: 'It must come to a rupture; it must come to war.' Patiently at first, and then with increasing desperation, Philip sent back his answer. There must be no rupture, no breaking off of negotiations with the States General, no matter how difficult they might be. 'The time has come to try gentleness and forgiveness' – this was the tenor of all he wrote. Don John must endure and if necessary suffer in the cause; there could be no recourse to a war which Spain could not afford. Not wholly in irony – for he depended on the man and had not as yet received very many of his complaints – he praised his brother's 'patience and fortitude' and encouraged him to keep on. This situation continued throughout the late autumn, till with the coming of the new year of 1577 Philip at last became aware of how far Don John was straying in spirit from his instructions and sent him a sharp reminder: 'I charge you again, brother, to avoid a breakdown in the negotiations and to accommodate yourself to time and necessity, the best counsellors you can have in a matter so pressing and delicate.' This was a version of the King's own favourite maxim, 'Time and I against any two others', and he added for his brother's benefit a second, often used by statesmen since: 'Policy must conform to the possible.'

Many historians have amused themselves with this quaint dialogue, and some of them have concluded that Don John's warlike and impatient nature (which he himself admitted) made him not only a poor negotiator but a disobedient and utterly unsuitable one. The correspondence does not bear this out. Don John never ceased (and nor did Escovedo) to bewail the collapse of their dreams of using Spanish *tercios* from the Netherlands to invade England: '... we are in despair and almost out of our minds; nothing else means anything to us but disgust and mortification' (this was the voice of Escovedo, but whether puppet-master or puppet was a matter of doubt). They never ceased,

147

either, to cry out against the perfidy and general wickedness of those with whom they were negotiating. Nevertheless the fact remains that dreaming always of wars and conquests – and sometimes even of a marriage with the Queen of England (at which that wily monarch had hinted to turn his thoughts from aggression) – Don John renounced his ambitions, bowed his head to the King's instructions, agreed to send away the *tercios* overland, and much against his own judgment signed a treaty with his tormentors which accepted the Pacification of Ghent and bought peace at the only price obtainable at the time. A conclave of bishops and jurists had assured him that the religious settlement contained in the Pacification was contrary neither to the Catholic religion nor to the King's authority, the two essential points on which he stood. He took leave to doubt it himself; but obedient to urgings from Madrid he turned a blind eye and signed.

He wanted however nothing more to do with people who had imposed such humiliations upon him, and even as he prepared to set out northwards for his formal installation as Governor in Brussels he began to bombard his royal master with requests to be relieved from so hateful an office and to be replaced by a more suitable successor in the person of the recently bereaved Empress, Philip's sister, or by the Duchess Margaret of Parma who had run the course before. Splendid arguments were advanced for this change. The Netherlanders, he wrote to Philip in one of his inimitable asides, had come to detest him almost as much as he detested *them*. The insults and pains he had suffered at their hands filled him with a desire to make war on them, pillage them, destroy them and bathe in their blood. And meanwhile, not to be outdone in any folly, Secretary Escovedo was sending off letter after letter to his opposite number in the royal secretariat in Madrid, the nimble Antonio Perez, urging the immediate withdrawal of Don John before his physical and mental health gave way. The proper place for his paladin of a master, he wrote, was not in any Governor-Generalship but at court, at the King's right hand, as an acknowledged Infante of Spain and head of a party which would include Antonio Perez and naturally Escovedo himself. In that position Don John would act as a staff for the King's old age – a suggestion not without humour when one remembers that Philip was not yet sixty and had just sired a son.

These letters and Perez's replies inviting further confidences were shown to Philip. The picture that was slowly building up in his mind was of an ambitious, dangerous aspirant to thrones and power, perhaps even to the throne of Spain, egged on by Escovedo, a confidant of monumental indiscretion and stupidity. At the very least there were evident objections to a Governor who had confessed in writing (to Perez) that if he were not soon withdrawn from the Netherlands he would lose his life and reputation and was in danger of losing his soul through the sin of despair. Escovedo in a parallel letter had admitted that his master was 'confused'. But the King still needed Don John, who by his treaty with the States General ('The Perpetual Edict'), signed on 12th and 17th February, had at least put an end to the war. He therefore wrote soothingly to him, congratulating him on these achievements. As for Don John's talk of replacements, he begged him not to mention it again. Don John, with his practical experience of negotiating with the Netherlanders, was indispensable. The situation demanded

Opposite: This portrait of Philip by an unknown artist in 1580 is close to Titian's view of the Prince painted some years earlier. The Golden Fleece hangs on a crimson ribbon entwined with a gold chain round his neck.
Courtesy of the National Portrait Gallery, London.

a man who could mix benevolence with discretion and courage, and all these qualities were happily blended and united in Don John! Could Philip have been serious in writing in this way after a diet of his deputy's and Escovedo's letters? He was certainly serious (or devious) enough to repeat this praise of his brother's diplomacy in a letter to Cardinal Granvelle in Italy.

For a while the settlement he had achieved seems to have steadied Don John also. The absurdities dropped out of his (if not Escovedo's) correspondence with Madrid. Not perhaps altogether, for he still found his Protestant opponents 'worse than the demons in hell'. But he had political sense of a kind, and he saw the key to the Netherlands problem in the Prince of Orange, 'the pilot', he wrote, 'who steers and sails this ship and the one who can either save or wreck it.' Therefore he opened negotiations with him through intermediaries. He could do little else, for to his own 'great affliction' he had had to witness the evacuation by the Spanish troops of the citadel of Antwerp and other strong-points and their southwards march out of the country. Now he was all but totally disarmed. As some compensation he was officially received amid popular demonstrations of joy into Namur, Louvain, and finally Brussels, where at the beginning of May he made his entry into his Governorship, to be greeted with tableaux depicting the Battle of Lepanto.

Considering the depths to which the royal prestige had sunk after the Spanish Fury, Don John had not done badly. He had reached the centre of power, the seat of patronage. If he could have possessed his soul in patience and waited for the inevitable quarrel to break out between the Protestants of Holland and Zeeland and the Catholics who remained in the vast majority in every other province, he could have played off the Fifteen against the Two and might even have thrown Orange into diplomatic isolation. He wrote to the King that he was continuing the royal policy of 'clemency', and if this had really been the case he might have justified his earlier boast to Philip that his services in the cause of peace were worth more than the conquest of several kingdoms. In fact however his activities had been more militant than he pretended. He had found even among many of the Catholics with whom he dealt a yearning for liberty of conscience in matters of religion, a thing so revolting to his mind that he prayed God that the King would never make him the means of granting it. He would much rather die than permit so great an evil, he declared – and this after himself having accepted the Pacification of Ghent which had doomed the Catholics of Holland and Zeeland to the Calvinist yoke! Perhaps this knowledge of betrayal was one of the motives behind the pressure he had been putting on the bishops to stamp down on heresy and on his appeals to the States General to break with Orange and bring the lost provinces back into obedience to Rome.

The States General which had few troops at its disposal recoiled from a solution which had defeated Alva and Requesens. Its members would probably have been happy if Don John had been able to bribe the Prince of Orange to remove himself from the Netherlands and accept the countship of Charolais as a vassal of the French king; but nothing came of that project either. The Prince was too solid and powerful an object to be wished away. Secure in his northern bastion, he was demanding that the important towns of Amsterdam and Utrecht

Opposite: Always in the background to Philip's troubles in the Netherlands was Elizabeth of England, shown here in the 'Armada Portrait'.
From the Woburn Abbey Collection by kind permission of His Grace the Duke of Bedford.

This portrait of William of Orange was painted by an unknown master after the first attempt to assassinate him.

and his own estates at Breda should be handed over to him forthwith.

These were demands hard to resist, for as Don John truly remarked, people had been 'bewitched' by Orange's propaganda and the States General constantly urged compliance. It was no pleasant discovery for the victor of Lepanto to find himself a cypher, obeyed by no one, respected by few, and surrounded, as he put it, by 'all the heresies, treasons and vices in the world'. Under the strain the last of his pacific resolutions died away and he reverted to the tone of his earlier letters to Madrid. Let the King realize the futility of 'clemency', raise a fleet (ostensibly to attack Algiers), and use it for a sudden thrust at England and the Zeeland coast. Don John himself would be very pleased to take part in this manoeuvre and to return to the Netherlands sword in hand. Let the King – for the second time of asking – prepare for a very savage and very bloody war by deciding to act as the Emperor Charles V of glorious memory would have acted! It would be hard to conceive of more tactless words.

Along with these plans went phobias, for Don John no longer felt himself safe in Brussels. Using the excuse of negotiating with some of the mutinous (and unpaid) German mercenaries left over from Alva's wars, he took himself off to the ecclesiastical capital at Mechlin (Malines). There rumours reached him that the Prince of Orange was sending forces southwards towards Namur and Luxemburg at the northern end of the 'Spanish Road' by which the *tercios* might one day return. Much of this, including talk of plots to murder him, may have been planted by enemies to goad him into hasty and ill-advised action. At all events, on the pretext of meeting the French King's sister, who was due to take the water at Spa, Don John hastened southwards, and on 24th July pounced on Namur citadel with the triumphant cry that at long last he had entered into his governorship.

By the strict tablets of the law, as the King's Governor and Captain General, Don John had of course a perfect right to possess himself of any citadel in the Netherlands he happened to want, but the practical results of his *coup* and of a similar attempt (which failed) at Antwerp were wholly disastrous to the cause of peace which he had been sent to implement. A tremendous outcry arose, not only among the Orangists of Holland and Zeeland who were committed to destroy him, but even among the moderates of the States General who in normal times would have wished him well. The effect of what seemed to everyone a reversion to the tyranny of Alva's time was to bring into being a union of Protestant and Catholic sentiment and the appearance of Orange at Antwerp and Brussels as the accepted saviour of the people. *That* position could not last either, for suspicion of the Prince's motives was too deeply imbued in too many Catholics to make him their acceptable leader for long. But the revulsion caused by Don John's aggressive acts was quite sufficient to make some of the magnates of the States General look around for a compromise candidate and to find him in the person of the new Emperor's brother, the Archduke Matthias, a biddable nonentity who duly presented himself in the Netherlands in the autumn of 1577.

After some hesitation the Prince of Orange also decided to back the newcomer. In December the States General formally invited Matthias to become Governor, with Orange as Lieutenant General in the real seat of power, and Don John was declared a public enemy. There was as yet no final break with the King, in whose name all these revolutionary steps were taken. And meanwhile, in his fortress at Namur, Don John was welcoming back the advance guard of his 'blackbeards', the Spanish veterans returning from Italy.

In Spain the King had watched the developing situation with dismay. His policy was peace. Not till the end of August did he learn how Don John had been interpreting this by the seizure of Namur. But he had been receiving almost daily proof of his brother's frantic state of mind, and in July came Secretary Escovedo to Madrid. Only Don John himself could have been a more unwelcome visitor; and on learning from Perez of his arrival the King minuted: 'The blow is about to be struck at us. We must be ready for anything. We must get rid of him (*despachar*) before he gets the better of us.' On one reading of these ambiguous words it would appear that Philip was saying that they must kill the man before he killed them.

What could this have meant? Escovedo had come to Madrid to urge the need for warlike measures in the Netherlands, to ask for money, and as a sideline to look into the possibility that his confidences in his secret letters had been betrayed. He certainly formed no kind of threat to the King. Unfortunately in the past he had said many tactless things, some of them to Philip, whom he had accused of being 'changeable' in his policies. It was also true – and the King could see it in writing in the correspondence Perez was showing him – that Escovedo had talked of political assassination, if only of the Prince of Orange. Evidently a man of action and ideas, and dangerous.

As such at least he could be presented to the King by the man who really had cause to fear him. Perez had not at the outset been hostile to Don John or Escovedo – indeed for a long time he had given them the best possible advice, to shelve their ambitions for the moment and to obey the King in everything. However the moment came when he began to show their letters to his master – probably as insurance against being accused of complicity in their schemes. And clearly he found Escovedo's arrival in person in Madrid (which he had done his utmost to prevent) a new and threatening factor. Why? Was he afraid that Escovedo would discover his affair with the Princess of Eboli, the widow of the dead favourite, with whom Philip was also supposed to be in love? And did Escovedo duly discover it and threaten to tell the King?

At one time this was widely believed to have been the cause of what followed. The Princess had charms of a kind, though she was already the mother of several children and wore a large black patch over a damaged eye. She was certainly Perez's mistress. That she was also the King's is supported by no evidence whatsoever, unless we accept in a very specialized sense her alleged remark that she preferred Perez's arse to the King's whole person. Perez's biographer, Gregorio Marañón, is satisfied that if Escovedo discovered anything compromising in the relationship between the all-powerful secretary and the lady, it had nothing to do with sex, but rather with the political alliance between them and the use they had been making of Perez's confidential position close to the King to leak information to rebel sources in the Netherlands in return for money. Treason, once proved, might account for the extreme malignity with which the King was later to pursue both Perez and the Princess. However his rage accords equally well if not better with the motive of sexual jealousy, and the observer, four hundred years after the event, may still wonder if the last word on this mysterious business has yet been said.

That is to look too far ahead into the future, for it was not until much later that Philip learnt that in one way or another he had been betrayed. At the time, he had only the information that was fed him by Perez. He proved a ready listener, the perfect dupe. Already deeply displeased by the warlike tone of Don John's letters and by news of unauthorized approaches that had been made to the Pope to enlist support for adventures against England, his latent resentment and jealousy of his brother needed little arousing and made it natural for him to see plots and disobedience everywhere. Why, for instance, had Escovedo come to Madrid without permission? Was he not Don John's *eminence grise*? What subversive aims, even of assassination, might he not be nurturing? These were ludicrous notions, yet perhaps not much more ludicrous than the letters Don John and Escovedo had been sending. Only genuine fear could have aroused the normally prudent Philip to react as he did to the fantasies that were the creation of Perez's ingenious mind – 'The blow is about to be struck at us. We must be ready for anything.' Yet these fantasies were to be translated into action which brought about the death of a man.

One of the minor mysteries in the affair is the length of time that it took the normally quick-witted Perez to act. Perhaps the answer is that like everything else in Spain even political assassination moved slowly. After all, it had taken months of labour and meticulous planning before Count Montigny had been strangled in Simancas. And of course the whole question had to be debated in the highest quarters, where the Marquis of Los Velez – incidentally a man whom Don John and Escovedo had fondly seen as their ally in a new grouping at court – helpfully suggested that the dangerous Escovedo should be given a 'tit-bit': the kind of dish a guest might have expected when dining at the Borgias.

Hilariously enough, massive doses of poison were duly served up to Escovedo on two occasions at Perez's house. A man of iron constitution, he easily survived them. It therefore became necessary to have recourse to other methods, and on Easter Monday 1578, eight months after he had come to Spain, Don John's unfortunate ambassador was waylaid in the streets of Madrid and done to death by a gang of bravoes, one of whom rejoiced in the nickname of 'The Guardian Angel'.

Perez had delicately taken himself out of Madrid some days before the event in order to notch up an alibi. No one believed in it. From the outset everyone assumed as a matter of course that he had arranged the murder. No one as yet imagined that the King was equally guilty. Yet it was so. In later statements under torture Perez was to declare that he had acted under Philip's orders, and though the probability is that the King simply agreed to a proposition put to him, his complicity is undoubted. He went further, by conniving at the escape of the assassins from his own police officers – a truly astonishing act for a man so steeped in legality. And all this in order to remove a nonentity whose only crime was a love of interference in other people's affairs.

Long before Escovedo died on that March night in 1578 the King had taken the first steps to dispose politically of his master. In the previous autumn some of Don John's secret despatches – full of expressions of venomous loathing for the States General and its pretensions – had fallen into enemy hands, and the echoes of this disaster had reached the ears of the King and his State Council. The matter was debated, and the natural conclusion was that since Don John had now lost all credibility as a peace negotiator with the Netherlanders, he had better be replaced. He had become a liability. His requests for the appointment of another Governor were therefore answered by the King's invitation to his half-sister, Duchess Margaret of Parma, to take up the burden which she had laid down in a huff on Alva's arrival in 1567, and with the same councillor as before at her side, in the person of Cardinal Granvelle.

The Duchess proved resistant to these orders without actually disobeying them. When really pressed, she pleaded an attack of gout, a heritage from her imperial father. These delays did not make the King's position any easier, for at home he was under constant pressure from the militants on his Council to return to a policy of force now that the rebels had defiantly accepted the Archduke Matthias and had rejected their legal Governor.

What should the King do? He was determined to stand by the Catholic religion and not tolerate heresy anywhere. He was determined to insist on his own sovereignty. He would have no truck with Matthias. He was being pressed by his own closest advisers to support Don John and recall the Spanish *tercios*. And yet at the same time, as his letters to Granvelle clearly show, he still yearned for peace.

The solution was a compromise – in fact a series of compromises. The *tercios* were recalled: and with them Don John won a signal but barren victory at the end of January 1578 over the forces of the States General at Gembloux. Yet even while rearming his brother, Philip was cutting the ground from under him. His aim now was, in his own words, a mixture of 'force and diplomacy', a formula which Don John himself had recently recommended. Over his Governor's head the King opened direct negotiations with the States General through a special envoy, the Baron de Selles. And he began increasingly to listen to suggestions coming to him from Vienna from his nephew, the new Emperor, Rudolf II, for a conference of all the disputing parties on German soil under the umbrella of imperial mediation. Meanwhile hostilities would continue, with Don John as Captain General, and there was talk of an army of 25,000 infantry and 5,000 horse at a cost of a quarter-of-a-million ducats a month.

In the autumn of 1578 the King issued his instructions to his delegate to the conference, the Duke of Terra Nova, an Aragonese who had served on the Council of Sicily. He would accept imperial mediation and negotiation with the rebels, subject to three points of principle – the Catholic religion and his own sovereignty must be maintained and the Archduke Matthias must go. He would accept the Pacification of Ghent apart from certain objectionable terms. For instance, Orange must not remain in the provinces, and Charles V's edicts against heresy must be enforced. In secret instructions to Terra Nova, however, the King indicated that these points were negotiable and were not to be insisted on at the cost of a breach. He was prepared, as the price of agreement, to recall Don John and replace him with a Governor of royal blood acceptable to the States – perhaps the Dowager Empress or one of the Archdukes: anyone in fact except Matthias.

It is not quite true to say that thereafter, having made his decision to go to imperial arbitration, Philip never wrote to his brother. He did – occasionally. He even sent him money, if not subsidies of a quarter-of-a-million ducats a month. But he depended no more on the man, whose appointment to the Governorship he now saw as a mistake and whose activities he judged through Perez's eyes as a lurking danger to the country and to his régime.

In fact Don John's victory at Gembloux was to prove the last of his triumphs, as illusory as his old dreams of thrones. He had some of his Spanish veterans back from Italy, but they were too few and there was still too little money to pay them. He had one consolation in the arrival at his urgent request of his friend and cousin, Alexander Farnese, the real victor of Gembloux. Otherwise it was a bleak prospect. As the spring and summer of 1578 wore on, new reinforcements reached the rebels from France and Germany. Surrounded by a ring of enemies he fell back to an entrenched camp at Bouges at the confluence of the rivers Sambre and Meuse, but there was an outbreak of spotted fever, probably typhus in the army, and in September Don John himself fell ill and was carried to a disused pigeon loft hastily furnished for his reception.

Almost from the first he seems to have known that he was dying, and perhaps in his despair it came as a relief. He still wrote to Madrid, protesting his devotion to the King. Never had he been disloyal. He had fought against impossible odds. 'I assure your Majesty that the work here is enough to destroy any constitution and any life.' This was on 20th September in the last of his letters to the King. 'Thus I remain perplexed and confused, desiring more than life some decision on your Majesty's part, for which I have begged so many times.'

When this letter reached him, the King noted in the margin that he was not going to answer it. Don John had become an irrelevance in Netherlands affairs, an obstacle to peace, an embarrassment, just as deep down he had perhaps always been an object of dislike. Indeed there was no occasion to answer. For on 1st October, the eve of the anniversary of Lepanto, in his converted pigeon loft in the camp at Bouges, Don John died.

Chapter 13

The Escorial: Portugal

At fifty, Philip was much the same man as the one the Venetian envoys had described in 1572. Now, five years later, another anonymous diplomat from the Republic took up the tale.

The King rose early and worked till noon; then dined, always punctually at the same hour, drinking two or two-and-a-half glasses of wine from a crystal glass 'of no particular value'. His health was generally good, though he sometimes suffered from stomach cramps and the first symptoms of gout had appeared. He was devoted to his wife, on whom he attended at least three times a day and with whom he slept at night – in single beds rather low-set to the floor. He was 'a very Catholic prince', a friend to the Faith, remarkable for his prudence and sense of justice and full of 'gentleness and affability'. Perhaps envoys to the court of Spain had to say such complimentary things, but the Venetians were usually men of independent mind and the reports of their ambassadors deserve respect.

By this time Madrid, which twenty years earlier had been little more than an overgrown village, had become a town of 55,000 people, infested with an urban riff-raff soon to figure in the plays and novels of the new age. Philip had deliberatley chosen it as his capital, rejecting Toledo and his birthplace of Valladolid. But since Don Carlos's death he never seems to have liked it and spent nearly three-quarters of every year in his retreats at Aranjuez, the Pardo, and increasingly at the Escorial, where his passion for country life could be combined with piety and the joys of artistic creation.

The Escorial is central to any understanding of Philip's character: half monastery, half palace: his personal handiwork and reflection. Many years earlier he had appointed a commission to look for a site not too far from Madrid in a countryside (wrote one of the fathers who knew him best) that would 'elevate his soul and sustain his pious meditations'. The commission had settled on a spot near a village, in a plain overlooked by mountains that gave some protection from the north wind and where there was a good supply of water, timber and building stone. On 23rd April 1563 the foundation stone had been laid – St. George's Day, dedicated to England's patron saint, a thought not

Above: In this painting by Jordan, Philip and his architects inspect the building of the Escorial.
Courtesy the Prado, Madrid.

Below: An anonymous painting of the Escorial in the 17th century. The painting gives a bird's-eye view of the vast building and illustrates the rigid ground-plan, a symbolic reference to the gridiron on which St. Lawrence was martyred.
The Louvre, Paris. Photograph, Giraudon, Paris.

without irony as it was largely at the Escorial that the Armada was to be planned. The architect was Juan Bautista de Toledo, who had worked in Rome under Michelangelo and modelled his central chapel on the master's original plan for St. Peter's. Twenty years later the fabric was completed – under another architect, Juan de Herrera, but in the presence of the same chief surveyor, Brother Antonio de Villacostin, who had seen its beginning.

Year by year the King had watched his palace rise out of the rock of the sierra. In the early days he had lodged in the curé's house in the village, but as soon as there was enough accommodation to house the reluctant colony of Hieronymite monks whom he had chosen to inhabit San Lorenzo el Real, the royal monastery of the Escorial, he moved them in, and moved in himself into adjoining apartments where he could keep an eye on them and urge on the builders.

By March 1575 the masons were ready to lay the foundation blocks for the pillars of the cupola, and a grand fête was held, with tournaments and bull-fights and a procession in which even the oxen that led the stone from the quarries had their honoured part, garlanded for the occasion. Imperious commands went out for everyone to work at full pressure; and as fresh teams of workmen were brought in, it seemed to those who marvelled at this eighth wonder of the world, while privately condemning its ruinous expense, as though the whole of Spain and her tributary states in Europe and the Indies were toiling at the project, as Egypt had laboured under the Pharaohs to build the Pyramids.

Conceptually a remembrance in stone of the gridiron on which St. Lawrence was martyred, the Escorial has always struck most observers as a massive quadrilateral with a church embedded in its centre. If its walls reflected those of the Alcazar in Toledo and other grim castles in Spain, its rich interior was surely derived (however unconsciously) from that Moorish tradition that hid its treasures, like its women, from the prying eyes of the world. Only the treasures of San Lorenzo were not dedicated to Mammon but to God. The King had not yet moved into the small bare workroom with its window overlooking the high altar where he was to be most at home in the last years of his life; but already the tone had been set and the apartments he shared with the Queen and his growing family had a modest and makeshift air compared with the gold and glitter of the great church, adorned with masterpieces by Titian, Cellini and Roger van der Weyden.

Modest too were the entertainments offered the royal inmates who shared San Lorenzo with the monks. Three or four times a week when in residence they would go out driving in the carriages, shooting deer or rabbits with arquebus and cross-bow, at which the two eldest girls excelled; and there were picnics by the fountains in the arbours and gardens that Philip loved. It was a great event when the villagers came up to dance in front of the palace on a feast day, or when by special request of the Queen the shepherds drove their flocks under the windows so that the children and her ladies could watch the sheep-shearing. The arrival of the jawbone of a whale that had gone ashore off the coast or of exotic visitors from the East, including an elephant and its mahout, were enough to convulse the court; and great was the joy at the occasional banquet given by the monks, as in the autumn of 1575, when the menu included a mixed salad with melon, capons, fried ham and liver omelettes, roast game, a goose-liver pâté, smoked leg of mutton, cheeses, quinces, apples, pears and preserves.

Even such simple pleasures were perhaps too demanding for the Queen. She was still very young, but already inclined to shut herself away indoors. The King had noticed it, and many years later warned his daughters against such an unhealthy way of life. But what did he expect? In the space of six years Anne of Austria brought five children into the world and was pregnant of a sixth when she died. What time had she between *accouchements* to enjoy herself like other women? Though Philip undoubtedly loved her and did his best according to his lights to care for her, she was in a very real sense a sacrifice made on the altar of his dynastic ambitions. It was typical of their relationship that she was to die giving birth to a premature stillborn child in strange surroundings, far from home, accompanying her husband on a campaign of aggrandizement and conquest, the fruits of which within eighty years were also to crumble into dust.

Apart from the fighting at the beginning of the reign against the French in Italy and Picardy, which had been forced on him, and his war of containment against the Turks, Philip's foreign policy had been almost wholly pacific. Suddenly in 1579, when he had been on the throne for nearly a quarter of a century, the mood altered and the last two decades of his life were to be marked by almost continuous aggressions.

Had the King's character undergone a change? Certainly a new note of decisiveness appears in his correspondence from the beginning of the 1580s onwards, a new trust in the correctness of his own judgment which makes his relations with his later servants very different from his tentative treatment of Alva in the days of the Blood Council and the Tenth Penny. But this is only half the story. If some of the causes of this growing self-confidence lay deep in the King's nature, a release of energies which his fourth marriage had brought out, they lay also, to a far greater degree, in the changing international situation around him. He became aggressive because circumstances – opportunities – favoured aggression. The cycle began with Portugal.

To most Castilians the very existence of such a kingdom in the west of their peninsula was a reproach dating back five hundred years to the time when the peoples of Oporto had set up an independent state which was to grow into a vast trading empire stretching around the globe. The connexion had never been renounced, even after the attempt to reassert it had been bloodily repulsed in the thirteenth century on the field of Aljubarrota, and Spanish monarchs had spent a great deal of their time and energies in marrying themselves and their children to Portuguese princes and princesses in the hopes of producing a Spanish heir to the splendid property when the Portuguese male line at last ran out.

In 1578 after many disappointments these hopes seemed on the verge of fulfilment. The Portuguese king, Sebastian, an unbalanced and excitable enthusiast much in the Don John mould, allowed himself to be drawn into a web of Arab intrigue and lost his life and his entire invading army in Morocco at the battle of Alcazar el Kebir. Since his successor was his great-uncle Henry, a blameless but aged cardinal who seemed unlikely to father children, the European rulers began furiously to concern themselves with the problem of succession that would arise when the old man died. There was a respectable claimant to the throne, the Duchess of Braganza, a thoroughly frivolous one in the French Queen Mother, Catherine de Medici, and a certain Don Antonio, Prior of Crato, descended on the wrong side of the blanket from a younger brother of the Cardinal, the people's choice without a doubt; but by strict hereditary right the new heir to Portugal could hardly be other than the king of Spain, impeccably descended in the female line from King Manoel the Fortunate.

Armed with the best credentials, Philip naturally wished to act in strict accordance with the law – it was the kind of claim he could argue better than his own jurists. Son of a Portuguese mother, the Empress Isabella, widower of a Portuguese wife, nephew of one queen of Portugal, brother of another, and uncle of the last Portuguese king but one, he could hardly doubt his unique fitness for the role that centuries of history had prepared and reserved for him. He had every hope that these claims would be accepted by the Cardinal/King and the 'Estates' which had assembled to decide on the succession. To help them come to the right conclusion he sent them his Portuguese favourite, Don Cristobal de Moura, with pockets weighed down with enough ducats to convince any waverers where justice lay. But the stakes were high: little short of total domination of the sea routes to Asia and the Americas and a monopoly of their trade. No chances must be taken with such an inheritance in sight; it was time to turn to advisers on whom he could absolutely rely. He therefore brought Cardinal Granvelle out of semi-retirement in Italy to Madrid as his chief adviser: a subtle statesman well versed in diplomatic niceties. And to make doubly sure, he recalled the Duke of Alva to command the army that was being raised to invade Portugal if peaceful methods failed.

When in 1580 the old Cardinal/King died the chances still were that the Regency Council would deliver the kingdom without a fight. The Portuguese people, in their hatred of things Spanish, preferred the bastard Don Antonio. So it had to be war. In June, Philip, accompanied by the Queen, reviewed the army near the frontier at Badajoz. It was a bad year for sickness among the troops, and soon Philip himself fell dangerously ill. He recovered, but the Queen, six months pregnant, was not so fortunate in her doctors, who applied the sovereign remedies of the times and effectively bled and purged her to death.

Philip made his retreat to a monastery, as customary after such disasters. He had lost a wife and a companion whom he loved and who suited him very well, but never for a moment did he allow himself to be diverted from his plans. His invasion forces by land and sea converged on Lisbon, which fell at the cost of only a token struggle at the bridge of Alcantara, and in the spring of the following year the Portuguese Estates at Thomar accepted the inevitable and recognized Philip as their king. There were only minor inconveniences. 'You will have heard', he wrote to his elder daughters on the eve of the ceremonies, 'that they want to dress me in brocade, much against my will: but they tell me it's the custom here.' A few weeks later he made his formal entry into Lisbon.

It was the apogee of the reign. After five hundred years the whole of the Iberian peninsula had been united under one hand. Ruler of half the New World, as defined in the famous papal demarcation in his great-grandparents' time, Philip had now acquired the huge unexplored territory of Brazil, together with a chain of islands and trading posts stretching around the world, from the Cape of Good Hope, the Red Sea and the Persian Gulf to the shores of India, the East Indies, Indo-China and Macao on the borders of China itself. Also he now controlled the enormously lucrative spice trade and the Portuguese fleets.

That this overwhelming triumph should have been reflected in the King's personal life in a relaxed tenderness of mood has often surprised historians who turn from the brutal events of the campaign to the charming letters from Portugal to his two elder daughters which centuries later came to light in the archives at Turin. There should be nothing surprising about it. The King was a man like any other and loved his children – at least those of them who did not, like Don Carlos, seem to set themselves up against him and threaten his regime. Exiled in a foreign land and with no wife to console him, he naturally turned to the two people he trusted most and through whom he could in imagination embrace the much younger children of his fourth marriage : his heir, Don Diego, his other son, Don Philip, and the baby of the family, Maria, who had been born only a few weeks before the royal cavalcade had set out for Badajoz. The letters, covering two years from the spring of 1581, when the King was awaiting his recognition by the Portuguese Cortes at Thomar, to March 1583 when he returned home to the Escorial, are exactly what the unprejudiced observer might have deduced from the known facts of Philip's life and from a reading of his interminable state despatches, remembering always that they are the products of his leisure hours : they are prolix, fussy, fumbling, repetitive, prosaic, and for all these reasons they are deeply touching.

The King wanted above all things to communicate. But he was not very good at it. There were no secretaries to interpret or dress up his words. In one letter to his second daughter, the Infanta Catalina, then convalescent from smallpox, he anxiously discusses the lasting effects of the disease : 'Your sister and the Count write me to the effect that you won't have any marks, I mean scars, the others don't matter ; they were only afraid there might be one near your nose . . . but if there are only a few, as I pray, then that's nothing. You can't know yet, since you don't tell me about it.' Under the casual phrases the troubled thoughts for the future appear, almost as though the writer were aware of the doom hanging over his family, which three generations later was to bring his line to an end. He had after all already lost four wives and two heirs to his kingdom – Don Carlos, followed by the eldest of his children by Anne of Austria, Don Fernando – and he had learnt not to expect too much from life. On hearing that his eldest surviving son is ill, perhaps of smallpox, he writes resignedly to the Infantas : '. . . if this were so I wouldn't be too grieved, since it would be better for him to have it now rather than later on. All the same, I can't help feeling anxious until I hear the nature and character of the illness. . . . The care that both of you take of your brother encourages me to hope that he will be all right.'

This note of concern is always present. Are the two small boys warm enough

The Infantas Isabella Clara Eugenia (left) and Catalina Michaela (right), painted by Sanchez Coello.
Courtesy the Prado, Madrid.

in the winter at the Pardo and the Escorial? Are the girls taking enough exercise? Is Don Diego working at his reading and writing and the necessary new study of Portuguese?

> I think he will have managed to fill in the coloured letters: this is why I am sending you others . . . and I've got some more. Make sure that he occupies himself in filling them in, but little by little, so as not to tire himself, and let him sometimes copy them. He will learn more that way and I hope by this means acquire a good hand.

To encourage the boy, there is the promise of a writing desk made of wood from the Indies, and later news of a gift of an elephant from the Portuguese viceroy in the East. Attempts at painting are assessed and progress charted. The King had not only to be a father to his children: he had to be a mother too. Therefore he discusses with his eldest daughter the intimate matter of 'the secret', the delay in the appearance of menstruation which troubled her. Nose bleedings, he wrote, were in the circumstances to be expected and were actually favourable signs. At the same time he praised his second daughter's spartan devotion to boiled roots and medicinal syrups. Teething problems in the younger children are discussed, with many a reminder of past troubles with Catalina, a backward child in this regard. 'They've written to me to say that your little brother (Philip) has cut a tooth; it seems to me that it's taken its time, since it's three years ago today that he was baptized. . . .' But was it three years or two? The King puzzled over the matter. He was troubled about his memory and what his poor head could carry – he was not, he confessed, quite sure what age even Diego would be on his next birthday. Happily not all the family were laggards in this matter of teething, for the youngest girl, Maria, was a stalwart exception: 'It seems to me that your little sister's canine teeth are coming very early: they must be replacements for the two which I'm on the verge of losing: I don't think I'll still have them when I return.'

This sense of time passing, depriving him of the day to day enjoyment of his children, is reflected very often in the letters. He is impatient to see them all again, but since this can't be, he hopes for the next best thing:

> If you've taken measurements, let me know how much you have grown since I last saw you, and send them to me taken very exactly with ribbons. Add your brother's to them. I will be delighted to see them, though I would be happier still to see you all. I trust in God it will be soon; beg it of Him, you others. . . .

And he rejoices in any evidence of their prowess: in Diego's dancing lessons; the fine impression Philip makes in his new white suit; and his elder daughters' skill with the cross-bow, though not without a paternal rebuke for certain inaccuracies in their reports:

> . . . you must both of you be great shots judging by your success with the deer and so many rabbits. You, my eldest, tell me that your brother distinguished himself at the sport. I think you mean that your sister did, to judge by what you write further on – but you've put an *o* instead of an *a* and have also left out a word. I think you must have written the letter in a hurry.

In return he faithfully reports his own experiences at a boar hunt, at the preliminaries of an *auto-de-fé* (one of the few repellent passages in the letters), at a grand naval review of his fleet, soon to be off for Terceira in the Azores to defeat the last surviving supporters of Don Antonio, and on a trip up the river to the castle of Belem on a day of boisterous weather. He provides a rueful picture of himself at a great ceremony, dressed in his black mourning, the only dignitary in the whole assembly not wearing the new fashionable bootees; and there are glimpses of a mass sung at the monastery of Descalcas by choristers of the chapel royal (who sang very badly) and perhaps more rewarding performances on various instruments by a group of galley slaves. Naturally the children are given a grandstand view of the *Corpus Christi* processions and of the dancers dressed as devils – just like those painted by Hieronymus Bosch – which might however, he fears on reflection, have frightened Don Diego, though they were really 'good devils'.

Many passages in the letters reveal one of the chief solaces of Philip's life: his love of nature. He is moved by the majesty of the Tagus and its shipping; by the sight of gardens and fountains at Cintra; the smell of roses and orange blossom and early violets in the spring. Shut up in his palace, its walls so thin that he can hardly sleep at nights for the clocks of the town striking the hours, he is seized with nostalgia as he remembers the peace of the gardens at Aranjuez and the song of the nightingales. Strangely enough it is not his great passion, the Escorial, that moves him, but always Aranjuez. Are the new fountains working? Does the clock keep good time? Any gifts from that favoured spot are enough to awaken memories:

> The peaches have arrived in such a state that I wouldn't have known what they were if you hadn't written to tell me. I haven't therefore been able to try them, which I regretted very much, because, coming as they do from

Left: Isabella Clara Eugenia, by Sanchez Coello. Courtesy the Prado, Madrid.

Centre: This onyx cameo of Philip II by Pompeo Leoni is very like the one carried by his daughter (left). Crown copyright, the Victoria and Albert Museum, London.

Right: Catalina Michaela, subsequently the Duchess of Savoy, by Sanchez Coello. Courtesy the Prado, Madrid.

the little garden under your window, they would have given me so much pleasure.

In this love of nature the King was an earnest seeker after truth. He sends his daughters a box containing what he has been told is a sweet lime, but he takes leave to doubt it. Surely it is too large for a sweet lime and he fears that it may be just a common or garden sour one. What do the Infantas think? He has a great desire to be instructed. But also to instruct. The bird which his daughters declare must be a heron is *not* a heron but a much smaller creature altogether. Also the jonquils they say have been sent from the gardens at Aranjuez must actually have come from the fields. He pontificates on what the Infantas may wear at a wedding – yes, gold ornaments can properly go with black, provided they are not too ostentatious. This theme of humility constantly crops up. Catalina must not be too proud at being taller than her slightly older cousin, the Archduchess Margaret of Austria (then visiting Spain with her mother, the Dowager Empress Maria), nor must Isabella be too puffed up at being taller than her aunt, even without her shoes, since this comes 'more because she is very small than because you are very tall'.

The Dowager, who was the King's sister and also his mother-in-law, came on from Spain to Portugal, and Philip hurried to meet her at Almeirin. They had not met for twenty-six years, and how much had passed in the world during that time! Defying protocol, the King got down from his coach to greet her and they spent some minutes in each other's arms. 'You can imagine the pleasure she and I had in seeing each other again', he wrote to the Infantas, and from that moment the Empress's name comes up time and again in the letters and always with affection.

Royal personages in such a correspondence are only to be expected, and the King had taken care to bring a tame one with him to Lisbon in the person of his nephew, the Cardinal Archduke Albert, whom he was to make his viceroy in

Portugal and much later to marry to his eldest daughter Isabella. The Archduke figures on and off in the letters: a somewhat remote figure endlessly watching ceremonies out of windows. Much more dramatic are the appearances of far humbler persons: servants and hangers-on of the court; in particular Madalena Ruiz, an elderly dwarf of uncertain temper whose tantrums and peccadilloes charmed and at times alarmed the King. A titanic quarrel between her and one Luis Tristan is reported in depth for the Infantas, who were in regular correspondence with them both – the unfortunate King himself had been drawn into the imbroglio by failing to rebuke Luis, as for some unrecorded reason he ought to have done:

> I did not hear the quarrel but I think it was she who began it by treating Tristan with scorn in front of my nephew. She's gone off in a very bad temper with me, saying that she wants to leave and that she will kill him, but I think that by tomorrow she will have forgotten all about it.

Madalena in fact was a problem, and the King did not attempt to hide the grisly truth from his daughters:

> I think now that Madalena is not so cross with me as she was, but she's been ill for some time, she's been purged, and is still in a bad temper. Yesterday she came here; she is in a sad state, feeble, old, deaf and semi-infirm. I think all this comes of her drinking. . . .

Things were rather worse however when Madalena was *not* drinking, for then she became really ill. So ill that she told the King she had lost all taste for wine; 'which for her is a very bad sign', he added understandingly.

Sometimes abusive, usually cantankerous, forgetful, a glutton for strawberries, sea-sick when taken on a boat, and devoted to music in the form of a soprano so fat as to be unable to get through a door, Madalena was a therapy all in herself, a constant refreshment for the King's spirit which at times fell very low. He was not in fact fated to leave Portugal without suffering yet another crushing blow, perhaps the worst of all. A week after the Portuguese Estates at Thomar had acclaimed Philip as their king, they had recognized Don Diego as heir to the throne. That had been in the spring of 1581. Eighteen months later, as Philip was preparing to return home, Diego died in the royal palace at Madrid. The attack of smallpox which had spread through the whole family of children had not spared the boy.

To Granvelle, Philip wrote one of the saddest and most resigned of all his letters:

> It is a dreadful blow, coming so soon after all the others, but I praise God for all it has pleased Him to perform, submitting myself to His divine will and praying Him that He will be content with this sacrifice.

Summoning the Estates to Lisbon, he got them to accept Don Philip in the dead boy's place. No reference to the tragedy appears in the letters to the Infantas. Probably he could not find the words.

Opposite: A detail of one of the tapestries of the 'Honours Series' made in Brussels in the 16th century. The Series came into Philip's possession when it formed part of the wedding dowry of his first wife, Maria of Portugal.
Courtesy of the Tapestry Museum, La Granja de San Ildefonso, Segovia. Photograph Scala, Florence.

Chapter 14

Parma

The death of Don John was followed by six of the most perplexing years in the history of Spanish involvement with the Netherlands. The cast was large; the play, with its plots and sub-plots, impenetrable; and the King's own commitment is shown in the avalanche of letters and instructions that continued to flow from him even at a time of tragic personal bereavement and during his seizure of an entire new empire in Portugal.

His correspondence makes compulsive reading and proves the astonishing work load he carried through months and years of triumph and disaster. No topic was too great or too small for his attention: the rape of a kingdom and the appointment of a new abbess at Maubeuge; a treaty with rebellious provinces and a pension to be paid a Scottish refugee; negotiations with kings and remuneration for a local councillor; the elevation of a lord's land into a marquisate, the conservation of game in the forests of Brabant and the choice of a Chief Ranger. Through it all shines a constant care for the Church in all its manifestations: concern over the theft of reliquaries by heretics; an order for the payment of 9,000 ducats to Christopher Plantin for the printing of a Bible; the appointment of an archdeacon at Arras, a bishop at Tournai; the transfer to the seminary at Douai of certain choristers of the Chapel Royal whose voices had broken, and replacements for them, to be selected by a retired organist at Mons. Concern for justice was just as marked. What other king, one wonders, would have bothered in the midst of all his other troubles to bend his mind to the matter of a claim presented by a widowed countess for 20,000 ducats allegedly promised to her husband before the King himself had even been born? The relic collector shows up too; for at the Escorial a great number of bones, bodies and skulls were being assembled, and in the very year of the Armada Philip was concerning himself most deeply over the availability and authenticity or otherwise of the head of St. Lawrence, said to be in the abbey of Gladbach and in some danger of being snatched by the Archbishop of Cologne. It was a quarter of a century since Philip had last seen the Netherlands, but he still prided himself on intimate knowledge of the administration of its councils, abbeys, bishoprics, even parishes, and of most of its leading figures, a remarkable

Opposite: Silver candlesticks and the remains of a decorated silver dish give a glimpse of daily life. Courtesy of the Ulster Museum, Belfast.

Alexander Farnese, the Duke of Parma.
Mansell Collection, London.

number of whom had survived the wars and executions of the times.

That one man can have carried in his head such a vast array of facts and on the whole should have judged the many interests involved so wisely is a remarkable tribute to his memory and expertise. Widowed for the fourth time, a martyr to gout and stomach cramps, nearly dead of a fever that had carried off his wife and plagued with problems from all round the known world, the King continued to apply himself unremittingly to his self-imposed task of overseeing everything. His paternal care for his subjects was never more deeply impressive. But, where the Netherlands was concerned, he never counted for less – a fortunate thing for any biographer of Philip who would otherwise have to follow every crazy convolution of Netherlands history during these chaotic years. The King might concern himself with *minutiae*, and expect with certainty to be obeyed. But for the first time since Alva had ceased to dominate the stage, the great issues of policy that decided the fate of the Netherlands were only formally settled in Madrid, and were in reality the work of a Governor General on the spot. On the one occasion between 1579 and 1585 when Philip and his agent differed on an important point of principle, it was the King who in the end gave way. Only later, when the first triumphs were over and the Armada against England was being planned, did the King's part in the story become once more crucial to Spain and to an understanding of his nature.

On his death bed Don John had handed over the insignia of office to his lifelong friend Alexander Farnese, Prince (later Duke) of Parma. It was an unauthorized act whose justification was the need to avoid another such disastrous inter-regnum as had followed the death of Requesens.

Parma was thirty-three years old, the grandson of an emperor, great-grandson of a pope, and already a man of mark who had fought with distinction at Lepanto and Gembloux. Only in the surface glitter of a late Renaissance prince did he resemble his unhappy predecessor. He was a much warier person, far more calculating and adroit: all things to all men. The foremost soldier of his age and reckless of his own personal safety, he was the most methodical of commanders, who rarely took a foolish or unnecessary risk where his army was concerned. When it was prudent to be merciful he avoided massacres and even the sacking of towns; but he could be as ruthless as Alva if he felt the need. A diplomat by instinct, like most Italians, he had learnt from Don John's mistakes how to treat the Netherlanders and his morbidly suspicious master in Madrid.

Not too many complaints, no intemperate abuse, no parade of ambitions, no hint of rivalry, but instead a steady, dutiful submission to the King – these, during the early days, were his methods and the basis of his power.

His situation at first was extremely delicate. He was accepted in Madrid as temporary Governor and Captain General in the crisis caused by Don John's death, but royal policy was really directed towards getting a settlement with the 'generality' of the provinces at the conference under imperial mediation due to assemble in Cologne, and he was to have no part in these negotiations, of which he was merely kept 'informed'. He was seen simply as a stakeholder defending what was left of the Spanish Netherlands. Even here his freedom of action was restricted, for the King was fearful of the bad diplomatic consequences that would follow a defeat in the field and had warned him on no account to risk one. Clearly Philip looked for very little from this stop-gap appointee who would as a matter of course be replaced by a Viceroy of royal blood the moment the Cologne negotiations succeeded.

However it happened that Parma had glimpsed an important shift in the power balance in the Netherlands which had escaped less perceptive mortals and saw an opportunity waiting to be seized. The Ultras among the rebels had grossly overreached themselves. The Prince of Orange had prevailed on the States General to accept a new 'Religious Peace' which in fact revoked the Pacification of Ghent by allowing the worship of either religion *in all seventeen provinces* until such time as a national council should decide otherwise. Orange himself was a moderate who believed in liberty of conscience for everyone; however his henchmen both in Holland and Zeeland and among the radical demagogues of the big towns had been interpreting this policy as a licence for themselves to worship as they pleased, and to require everyone else to worship as they – the demagogues – pleased also. In Ghent, always the most radical of Netherlands towns, Calvinist zealots had set up a religious reign of terror, and news of this had naturally distressed the moderates of the States General and enraged the staunchly Catholic Walloons of the French-speaking south. The nobility had also taken alarm at the levelling trends in the new Protestantism which seemed an attack on their privileges far more damaging than anything attempted by the King of Spain.

What Parma was witnessing, and alone had the wit to recognize, was the gradual break-up of the unnatural coalition which had faced Don John. He had recognized it very early, within a matter of weeks of Don John's death, and had sent his appraisal of the situation to the King. If the Walloons could be wooed away from the militants, many of the Catholic centre and almost the whole of the nobility might follow them. Therefore unlike the King, who saw the solution of the problem in a settlement with the 'generality' at the Cologne conference, Parma knew that the only way to the restoration of Spanish power lay through negotiation with the individual states – a policy of step by step, of 'creeping diplomacy', to win over first the Walloons, then the central provinces of Brabant and Flanders, before turning to confront the Orangist states lying beyond the line of the great rivers Maas and Waal.

Early in 1579 this division into power blocks came into the open with the formation of the Protestant 'Union of Utrecht' in the north and the Catholic

'Union of Arras' in the south, leaving between them a mass of uncommitted states and towns whose allegiance to either party was there to be won. All that was needed from the Spanish side was diplomacy and patience: things could not be rushed. And the approaches must first be aimed at the Walloon provinces of Artois and Hainault, which were the most approachable (because of their fervent Catholicism) if also the most dangerous (because of their proximity to France and the attraction that might be exercised over them by the freelance Francis of Alençon, Duke of Anjou, the French king's brother and the most potent foreign meddler in Netherlands affairs). Right from the first, therefore, Parma began to bait his line and cast in the Walloon direction.

Sure enough the fish began to rise and he was able to report these stirrings to the King. Encouraged in his turn by moves which contrasted with the stalemate in the negotiations at Cologne, Philip began to see the situation through Parma's eyes and recognized the virtue of working (as he put it in a letter to his servant) to weaken and divide the enemy. The full diplomatic weight of Spain was shifted back from Cologne to the Walloons.

And step by hesitant step the provinces of Artois and Hainault responded to these advances and returned to their old obedience – at a price. Parma's appointment as Governor must be limited to six months, after which he was to be replaced by someone of royal blood. The Pacification of Ghent (that hardy annual which elsewhere had been uprooted by the new religious peace) must be ratified, which meant an end to the edicts of Charles V. And the Spanish troops, which had been sent away to Italy by Don John and had returned to win Gembloux, must be sent away again, to be replaced by a national army of Walloons.

It was a settlement on terms hardly favourable either to the King of Spain or his agent; but if Philip had qualms, Parma had none. He was signing away his only reliable troops and his governor-generalship, but he saw further and sensed that he and they would become indispensable once the ink was dry on the treaty and the two Walloon provinces had passed back into the Spanish camp.

So it proved. The *tercios* were dismissed – not however before they had captured and sacked the important stronghold of Maastricht, one of the keys to Brabant. Before long, under the threat of French invasion and Protestant sectarian outrages, the Walloons were clamouring to have them back. And the matter of the governorship made even better comedy: a burlesque triangular tug of war between the King, his chosen vicereine of royal blood (the Duchess Margaret of Parma), and the Prince of Parma, her dutiful yet determined son.

The King wanted the Duchess as Head of State and the Prince as Captain General of the armies. The Duchess would have liked her viceroyalty, but saw she could only get it at her son's expense. Her letters to Madrid in answer to her royal brother's demands to be obeyed without further delays or arguments are small masterpieces of evasion and strongly suggestive of a put-up job within the Farnese family. As for Parma, he never ceased to profess his total submission to Philip's orders. Had he not personally begged his mother to assume the reins of government, only to be rebuffed by her refusal? He begged to be allowed to lay down his office to make way for her and for leave to come to Spain in person to

An allegorical representation of the political situation in the Netherlands in 1580. The Low Countries are represented as a cow fed by Elizabeth, ridden by Philip and milked by William of Orange.
Courtesy the Rijksmuseum, Amsterdam.

explain things. The King easily dodged this suggestion, all too reminiscent of the importunities of Don John and Escovedo. By no means must Parma think of coming to Madrid: he was indispensable in the Netherlands, where the reconciled Walloons were demanding him as their Captain General – the only man who could command their armies; under the Duchess Margaret of course.

It was a game that three could play, and it happened this time that the King was in a minority of one. Circumstances were against him, for with Anjou in arms and knocking at the gates of Flanders it was hard to refute Parma's repeated argument that a division of powers between Governor and Captain General would prove fatal to the country. It must be all or nothing. Either Parma must have the governor-generalship, or he would resign and withdraw from the provinces – and here, in this sharp (though tactfully phrased) alternative presented to the King, we have the measure of Parma's greatness and the courage he could show in tight situations. Without the support of his all-powerful uncle in Madrid he was nothing: a mere Italian princeling. He was putting his whole career in jeopardy: and indeed in the end this show of independence was neither forgiven nor forgotten. But in the short-term his argument was irresistible, and after a decent delay of several months he was finally appointed by the King as Don John's successor to what was still a shadow viceroyalty of the southern fringes of the Netherlands.

The taking of Maastricht had been the first proof of Parma's genius as commander in chief of a Spanish army. Many of the garrison were massacred: the siege had lasted an unacceptably long time and an example was needed to persuade other towns on the road back to Brussels. The lesson did not go unobserved; nor did the diplomatic initiatives the victor had been taking with the Walloons, the nobility, the States General, and indeed with anyone who would listen. Being a fortunate diplomat, Parma was actually helped by events which at the time must have seemed highly prejudicial and dangerous to his cause: in particular by the reappearance in the provinces of the Duke of Anjou, now suitor for the hand of the Queen of England and candidate for the sovereignty of the rebellious Netherlands – no less.

For in 1581 the Orangists of Holland and Zeeland and the States General had at last tired of the fiction of carrying through a revolution in the name of a sovereign whom in reality they had deposed. They had dismissed one royal governor (Don John), ignored another (Parma), and had appointed a third (Matthias), while still pretending obedience and insisting that the constitutional position had not changed. This farcical situation failed to survive the shock of Philip's own action in publishing a 'Ban' of outlawry against the Prince of Orange, inviting adventurers to assassinate the man, and of Orange's riposte in his 'Apologia', a document which accused the King, among other crimes, of murdering Don Carlos, Elizabeth of Valois and the lately deceased Emperor Maximilian. The fiction of loyalty had collapsed, and the States General followed the Orangist provinces into a formal abjuration. Having rid themselves of one king, it became necessary to appoint another, and the names of several candidates were hawked around. Holland and Zeeland would have no one but Orange, but the rest were eventually persuaded to offer the sovereignty to Anjou, who of all the self-seeking and untrustworthy persons who had intervened in Netherlands affairs was decidedly the worst.

No one had really wanted him, except the Prince of Orange, who saw the need for enlisting French and English support and believed that a candidate who was a 'Son of France' and also a suitor for the Queen of England's hand would attract both. But the support was not forthcoming; for in the delicate diplomatic game of alliances that was being played between Paris and London it was not found to be prudent or convenient for Elizabeth to marry Anjou or for the French king to support him too openly. Fairly substantial forces were given him – enough to have won a crown if Anjou had had a grain of Parma's patience or intelligence – but the vain and ambitious man overplayed his hand. Finding himself, like Don John and Matthias before him, no more than a figurehead or Orange's lackey, he attempted to seize Antwerp from his own allies by a military coup, failed miserably to take it, and eventually withdrew in disgrace to France, where a few months later he died.

The whole adventure had benefited no one except Parma, who had continued his diplomatic and conciliatory overtures to the rebels and in the meantime had been picking up towns here and there, as he worked his way northwards into Flanders and Brabant. In November 1581 he had taken Tournai; in the autumn of the next year he collected Diest, Dunkirk, Nieuport and Zutphen; by April 1584 he had Ypres; in May, Bruges surrendered; in September, Ghent; in March 1585 he entered Brussels. Of the important centres south of the great rivers only Antwerp stood out against him, and that was closely besieged, with its land and sea communications cut.

Down they had all gone, those bastions of rebellion, and along with them the leaders he had faced – Anjou, dead of phthisis at Château Thierry; Orange, wounded by one assassin and despatched by a second a few months later in his own house at Delft in July 1584. In retrospect we can see that every year about this time was for Parma an *annus mirabilis*. Fame and prestige were his and the aura of uninterrupted success. Yet as one reads his correspondence one sees deeper. He was constantly plagued by troop mutinies, treasons, delays, intrigues, in the service of a dilatory master on whom he depended for all the sinews of war. The period had arrived when treasure receipts from the Indies were rapidly increasing and the King tried not to be niggardly, but there was never enough money for the huge task involved in reconquering a country and

The assassination of the Prince of Orange at Delft in 1584.
Courtesy the Gemeentearchief, Delft.

mending its broken economy. The earlier tone of optimism was soon to give way to a darker mood, very reminiscent of Don John, and in January 1583 came the first of Parma's complaints in a *cri de coeur* that the King must have forgotten him and the Netherlands. This was very bad language to use, noted the King when he received this letter – an element of distrust had come into their relationship and was never to leave it.

That winter for Parma was a time of deep distress, when he feared that the whole country might be lost through discontent and mutinies. At the darkest moment the tide turned with Anjou's brutal attempt on Antwerp which lost him sympathy throughout the rebel-held territories – a 'near miracle', Parma called it. When the triumphant march into Brabant was resumed with the captures of more towns, the King rejoiced with him: 'Send me always such good news. . . . After God, it is on Farnese that victory depends!' But in the camp before Antwerp in the harsh winter of 1584/5 the flame of victory again burned low, and in February the Governor General was complaining that he had not a single *real* to his name.

For eleven months Parma had to sit down to the hard grind of the siege of this largest of Netherlands towns, then one of the greatest in Western Europe. His engineers had to throw a huge fortified bridge across an estuary, more a sea than a river, as he rightly described it. The enemy breached it with a ship filled with gunpowder, but it was repaired and it strangled the communications of the city. The whole operation was regarded in Europe as a masterpiece of military art. On 27th August 1585 the long campaign came to its climax, and a few weeks later in Spain the King came running in the night to the door of his elder daughter's room, crying exultantly: 'Antwerp is ours!'

Chapter 15

The Armada

The good father and family man who penned the letters from Lisbon to his daughters had just raped one neighbour's property in Portugal and was meditating something of the kind against another.

The germ of the idea which in the fullness of time grew into the 'Invincible' or 'Most Fortunate' Armada lay far back in Philip's life, perhaps in the humiliations he and his courtiers suffered at English hands during their probationary months in England. He had borne them with patience, and patience was certainly needed. In the years after Mary Tudor's death he had had to watch the heretic Elizabeth refuse his hand and his advice, see his ambassadors ill-treated and expelled, his ships and money seized, his towns and treasure routes in the Indies attacked by English pirates, and his rebel subjects in the Netherlands sustained by English gold. Perhaps the strangest thing about the Armada of 1588 is that it was delayed so long and that England was not treated twenty years earlier in the way that the Count of Feria had recommended, sword in hand.

The King had long shrunk from such confrontation. Meekly, over the affair of the treasure ships at Plymouth, he had accepted Alva's advice to work for a negotiated settlement, and in the same spirit he had discouraged Don John's dreams of invasion. He had even accepted Elizabeth's covert support of Orange and her dangerous flirtation with Anjou. True, there had been moments when he had toyed with plans to have her assassinated or deposed, but he had never been whole-hearted about it, because the heir to the English throne was Mary Queen of Scots, a French-orientated princess who might prove even more troublesome. Since Elizabeth for her part was careful to limit the piracies of her sea captains in the Caribbean and her involvement in Netherlands affairs, and since the King of Spain did not possess an ocean-going fleet large enough to

Opposite: Philip II's daughter, the Infanta Isabella Clara Eugenia painted by Sanchez Coello. Courtesy of the Prado, Madrid. Photograph Scala, Florence.

Overleaf: A detail of a panel painting entitled The Defeat of the Spanish Armada *by an unknown artist. The galleys of Mediterranean warfare have been replaced by galleons more suitable for the rough Atlantic weather.*
Courtesy of the National Maritime Museum, London.

A page from Breve compendio de la sphera y de la arte de navegar *by Martin Cortes which was used as a manual of navigation for pilots sailing to the Spanish Indies.* Courtesy the National Maritime Museum, London.

protect the treasure routes while mounting a full-scale invasion of England, or even of Ireland, the fragile peace had survived.

Progressively during the 1580s these deterrents to war ceased to apply.

One of the most sensitive areas affecting the two nations was the Indies.

In 1492 Columbus had stumbled on their outriders in the Caribbean while looking for a sea route westward to the Spice Islands of the China Sea. In later voyages in 1498 and 1502 he discovered the existence of the mainland of South America and sailed along the shores of Mexico, but it was still some years before more than a glimmer of the real wealth and size of the new continents began to penetrate the official mind. However there was a restless, rootless element among the new settlers in the islands more willing to take risks, more open to the rumours that reached them from the natives and from ships' crews driven off course in those waters, of lands far away where there was gold in abundance for the taking.

The response was simple and unquestioning. Small expeditions were fitted out to travel into the unknown: admirably adapted for the conquest of a few villages or islands. In fact they encountered powerful empires numbering millions of souls, which without more ado they attacked and conquered.

Between 1518 and 1522, when he was appointed Governor and Captain General of 'New Spain', the Conquistador Hernando Cortes destroyed the Aztec empire and took Mexico. Its capital city was a town of at least 300,000 inhabitants, larger than Seville. He had sailed off to this assignment with 550 Spaniards, 250 native allies, 15 horses and 10 small guns. No one has ever calculated the odds. In 1511 Vasco Nuñez de Balboa sighted the Pacific from a treetop on a ridge in Darien. Spanish flotillas were soon launched on it. The exploration spilled over into Honduras, Guatemala and the Colombian coast east of the Isthmus of Panama, the famous Spanish Main. Still more fantastic exploits were reserved for the Pizarro brothers and their partner Diego de Almagro, minor gentry from impoverished Estremadura. After a reconnaissance of the Peruvian coast in 1526, Francisco Pizarro set sail from Panama in December 1531 with 182 men and 47 horses. Within five years he had destroyed the huge empire of the Incas, founded the city of Lima and annexed Peru and parts of Bolivia. Meanwhile Almagro had subdued the northern half of Chile. In 1541 Francisco de Orellana discovered the headwaters of the Amazon and followed the river to its mouth.

Opposite: A detail of the triptych The Garden of Earthly Delights *by Bosch, among Philip's favourite painters.* Courtesy of the Prado, Madrid.

Pizarro enters Cuzco, Peru, in 1533.
Mary Evans Picture Library, London.

Nothing in the Chivalry Books, the popular reading of the day, with their tales of giants and sorcerers, could have exceeded the reality of these extraordinary feats carried out across unknown seas and deserts and jungle and some of the highest mountains in the world. And not even the fabled gold of El Dorado could have matched the mineral wealth that lay buried in the soil, soon to be discovered by Spanish prospectors and mined by Indian labour. Almost as remarkably, these conquests of the wild men were in a matter of a few decades brought under control by Spanish administrators, to be tidily organized into viceroyalties, provinces, municipalities and councils, while at the same time the Church and its militant wing of missionary friars moved in to convert the Indians and protect them from the worst extortions and cruelties of the conquerors. Churches and monasteries were going up in every populous centre; and soon there was an establishment of archbishops and bishops to match anything in Spain itself. Needless to say, the Holy Office was soon very much in evidence.

By the time of Philip's accession the groundwork had been done and the Spanish empire in the New World was a working reality in the whole enormous territory from California to Chile. Such heady and almost uninterrupted triumphs had their natural effect on the Spanish people who had provided the dynamic behind this unparalleled explosion of energy. The Conquistadores themselves had been practical men who had not troubled themselves unduly about divine aid and had simply gone in with the sword, but in the aftermath of their victory it was hard for others not to see something miraculous and God-given in the results. Had not Christ's vicar on Earth, the Pope, assigned this part of the (then undiscovered) world to Spain in the bull *Inter Caetera* of 1473? The wealth that came out of its mines was Spanish; and as new discoveries were made in the field and new techniques in the processing of metals introduced, it could be seen that Providence had not failed to underwrite the Spanish economy with enormous gifts in cash – two million ducats in the year of Philip's accession; four millions annually by 1580; in the 1590s, eight millions; a fifth of which went to the King and played a significant part in financing the Netherlands war. Armed convoys brought the specie from the Main and Mexico to Sanlucar on the Guadalquivir (in the later years of the reign to Cadiz).

That the new wealth brought with it a rise in prices and a galloping inflation was a fact not wholly appreciated in Spain. People saw only growth and affluence arising from this treasure house beyond the seas. The Indies became for them not only a livelihood and a practical investment, but also a kind of

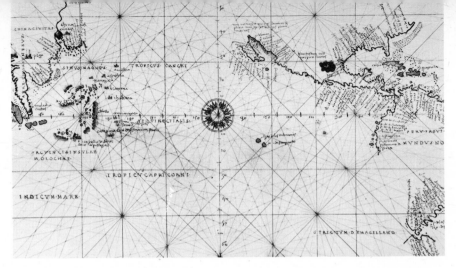

This map of the Pacific Ocean drawn by Baptiste Agnese in 1555 is from an illuminated atlas of twenty-five folios. The coast of Peru explored by Pizarro's Conquistadores can be seen on the right.
Courtesy the National Maritime Museum, London.

tribal totem touched with magic which they felt they must protect from the impious hands of trespassers.

For a while these trespasses were hardly noticeable. The incursions of French corsairs into the Caribbean were spasmodic, and the first Englishmen who went there were moved only by the profits to be won by bringing slaves from West Africa to work the great estates. But even this commerce, so welcomed by the settlers, came to be frowned on by the royal officials, and in 1567 a slaving fleet commanded by John Hawkins was caught in harbour at San Juan de Ulua and severely mauled. To mark the lesson, the Inquisition got hold of some of the captured Protestant seamen and treated them appropriately – it was a barbarity never forgiven in England.

One of the survivors of the disaster at San Juan was the young Francis Drake, who had not played a very heroic part in the battle. He was however to return. In 1571 he carried out a reconnaissance of Darien. It was across this narrow neck of land formed by the Isthmus of Panama that the treasure convoys of silver from the Peruvian mines crossed the continental divide to load at the Atlantic ports. It was a very tempting target, and vulnerable, for the sea approaches were not well policed, and the jungle that flanked the land-route was inhabited by tribes of escaped African slaves, the Cimaroons, very hostile to Spain. All this Drake had noted. In 1572 he stormed the Caribbean terminus of the trade, the town of Nombre de Dios; waylaid one of the mule trains on the road; and following in Balboa's footsteps, climbed a tree on the central ridge of the isthmus, from where he saw the waters of the Pacific.

The way and the means had been charted, and from now on the aggression was almost continuous. In 1576 one of Drake's colleagues of the Darien expedition, John Oxenham, launched some light-craft in Pacific waters; in 1577 Drake himself, on his circumnavigation of the world, sailed northwards from the Straits of Magellan past Valparaiso and created havoc among Spanish shipping off the coasts of Peru; in 1585, a larger expedition under his command swept down on the Caribbean, taking the port of Cartagena and Santo Domingo, capital of Hispaniola, the symbol of Spanish rule.

This was unacceptable. From being irritations, English raids had begun to threaten the safety of the treasure routes and the very existence of the Spanish empire in the Indies. At the same time, the English commitment to the rebel cause in the Netherlands was growing from the provision of money and diplomatic support to the landing of an army commanded by no less a person than the Queen's favourite, the Earl of Leicester. Possibly the King might have swallowed these insults and provocations too, like all the others, if in the meantime he had not found the means of avenging them by building himself a fleet and winning a fine reinforcement of galleons in Portugal.

Thus the rivals had become set on a collision course. The Queen had not deliberately willed it – she remained till the very end hopeful of some peaceful outcome while doing nothing to bring it about. There were times when she remonstrated with her sea captains for their piracies and played with notions of a Netherlands truce, but she made no very serious attempt to halt the drift to war. One of nature's fatalists, she let things take their course, trusting blindly to the luck that had brought her safely through so many dangers.

The normally more tentative Philip had nerved himself at last to action. After years of self-control his bitter resentment of England and of his exasperating sister-in-law broke out into the open in a letter dated 12th September 1583 to Parma, then nearing the climax of his triumphs in Brabant: 'To round things off we must put an end to the aid the rebels are receiving from England and bring that kingdom back to Catholicism.' He added more cautiously – and more typically – that this might well have to wait till Queen Elizabeth died, but at least it was a beginning. What, he asked, did Parma think about the prospects? It was a repetition of his running to Alva for advice at the time of the crisis over the treasure ships.

At the end of November the Governor General replied, equally guardedly, that the 'Enterprise of England' was largely a logistics problem, and a more difficult one than might be supposed at first sight. Philip had placed some hopes in a Catholic rising in England which for years had been promised by refugees, but Parma took a more sceptical view of these gentry and knew they would never deliver. If talk of the project leaked out, as it probably would if allies were brought in, the French might throw in their lot with England: something which Spanish diplomacy had always striven to prevent. His advice was naturally wrapped up in a desire not to be seen to thwart the King too openly, but it was clear enough – conquer the Netherlands first and leave the English till later.

Left to himself the King would probably never have come to the point of sending out an Armada. The specific plan for one had come from the Marquis of Santa Cruz, Spain's foremost seaman, who in the Portuguese campaign had defeated off the Azores a French squadron which he believed – incorrectly – to have included some of the royal galleons of England. From this fortunate event the Marquis had conceived such a poor opinion of English seamanship and courage as to lead him to conclude that they could be beaten without much difficulty off their own coasts and an army landed. He had served with distinction at Lepanto in Don John's fleet and shared some of his vainglorious illusions.

In the planning development that followed, three intelligences were therefore at work, and never in unison. This is the key to the Armada story. The King was cautious – his letter to Parma had been only a sighting shot. But by 1585 the diplomatic and military climate had greatly improved. By the Treaty of Joinville, on the last day of the old year of 1584, the ultra-Catholic party in France headed by the Duke of Guise had allied itself with Spain to bring pressure to bear on Henry III to disinherit his heir, the Huguenot Henry of Navarre. One dangerous factor had been taken out of the argument and France converted from a threat to a client state of Spain. The Ottoman Turks, who might have made trouble in the Mediterranean, were militarily engaged elsewhere. Even the rebels in the Netherlands seemed, with the close investment of Antwerp, to be on the point of collapse; and on the 17th August, the very day on which the great city fell, the King wrote to Parma with orders to prepare a scheme for the invasion of England.

That it should have been to Parma that he had turned is proof both of the King's strategic sense and of his basic distrust of the sea, an element that had greatly distressed and all but shipwrecked him on his return from the Netherlands in 1559. Spain was far from England, separated from it by hundreds of miles of turbulent salt water, and the Marquis of Santa Cruz's indent, when it eventually arrived, called for so enormous and ruinously costly a force – 516 ships, 240 barges and pinnaces, manned by 30,600 sailors and 63,000 troops – as to put it out of court at once as a serious plan. On the other hand the all-conquering royal Netherlands army stood conveniently close to England, at least on small-scale maps, and in a moment of euphoria which he must later have regretted its commander had proposed to sneak across the Straits of Dover in a matter of ten to twelve hours – eight in good weather with a following wind – at the head of a much more modest army, 30,000 strong, carried in flat-bottomed barges under the escort of 25 warships sailing from Flemish ports. This plan did not rule out some kind of Armada from Spain, but it was seen in a supporting role; and to judge from a letter written by Parma's agent, Piatti, to the royal Secretary Idiaquez in Madrid, it is clear that Parma was suggesting it should arrive off the English coast some time *after* his own landing on enemy soil.

The King was enchanted: it was exactly what he wanted to hear. He did not for the moment give much thought as to how Parma's thirty thousand could be assembled and loaded aboard their barges in secrecy close to enemy coasts or to what would happen to them if the weather should be rough or the English fleet appeared during the crossing. The plan in its neat symmetry satisfied the pedant in his nature: its promise inflamed his mind and induced in him a most unusual recklessness. The dockyards were set to work to produce the ships for Santa Cruz's share in the enterprise, and in the autumn of 1586 things were sufficiently advanced for the King to sound the general call to battle in a letter to Parma in which he insisted that the time had come without doubt for an operation to rescue Catholicism in England from its foes – an end to which Parma was now to apply himself with energy. This was a call to the Governor General to support a projected Catholic rising in England (the Babington Plot) which, like all other such projects before it, was penetrated by English spies and collapsed ignominiously, fatally compromising the imprisoned Mary Queen of Scots, who went to the block for it early in 1587 in Fotheringay Castle.

This engraving of Sir Francis Drake is attributed to Hondius, c. 1583.
Courtesy the National Portrait Gallery, London.

Mary's death sharpened passions and combativeness on both sides and made the Armada certain. The English government was no longer restrained by fear of a popular rising of Catholics against it, for Elizabeth's apparent heir was now the Calvinist James VI of Scotland. The Spaniards were no longer held back by the thought that they might be deposing one uncongenial woman to set up another. They had some hopes of James, with whom Parma's agents were in touch. The tempo quickened, and in June 1587 the King once more discussed with Parma the planning details of the enterprise. The Spanish fleet's main duty, he wrote, was to protect the treasure convoys from the Indies, and it could not be expected to arrive in the Channel in advance of Parma's crossing. Indeed, as the King truly remarked, Parma himself *had not asked for any such thing*, either in his letters or through the mouth of his personal envoy, Piatti. Philip was therefore envisaging three phases: firstly, Parma's invasion launched from the Netherlands ports; secondly, a diversion in Scotland (Parma's concern again); and thirdly a fleet attack from Spain directed by Santa Cruz. The rest of the letter was concerned with the provision of the necessary money – 700,000 ducats over and above the normal allocation to the Netherlands for that year, and proof in itself of the King's extreme eagerness to get to grips with the enemy.

Earlier that spring, a fleet commanded by Sir Francis Drake had swept down on the almost undefended roadstead of Cádiz, causing immense damage to shipping and supplies. It was a demonstration of English sea power which was not lost on Parma. For months he had been pretending that he could put an army across the Straits without help from Spain, but now his tone altered dramatically and in July he protested that his own squadrons could be no match for the English now that the secrecy on which he had always insisted had lapsed and his concentration of barges was known to the enemy.

It was a remarkable *volte face* but the King uttered no reproaches, for he too had noted, and had remarked on, the brilliant daring of Drake's raid. From that moment he appreciated that the two wings of his assault forces could not operate apart but must complement each other. 'I have therefore been convinced', he wrote to Parma, 'that the most advantageous way will be to join your forces there with ours at the same time; and when a junction is effected the affair will be simplified and the passage assured.' The target for Santa Cruz's Armada must therefore be moved up-Channel from the Isle of Wight to what the King called 'the Cape of Margate', the North Foreland, and its approach must be signalled to Parma ahead of its arrival. 'You in the meantime', the King went on, 'will be quite ready, and when you see the passage assured by the arrival of the fleet off Margate, or at the mouth of the Thames, you will, weather permitting, immediately cross with the whole army in the boats. . . . The most important thing of all is that you should be so completely ready that, the moment the Marquis arrives at Margate, you will be able to do your share without delay.'

This was a considerable improvement on the King's previous thinking, but to anyone with the least knowledge of sail and of conditions to be expected in the Channel, even in summer, it displays great ignorance. The letter assumed that Santa Cruz's galleons could linger in the Straits while messages passed to and fro between them and the Flemish ports. To be fair to Philip, he had remarked that time might be short, because Santa Cruz had no safe anchorage off these shores. But suppose the weather were rough? The King had recognized that in such an event Parma could not put to sea. The winds could blow for days, and what then would happen to the Armada in the Straits? The letter assumed also that in good weather Parma's barges could come out on call like carriages out of a coach-house, which altogether ignored the fact that the ports might be blockaded by English or Zeeland ships. Perhaps the fictitious twenty-five 'warships' which Parma had included in his original plan had misled Madrid on this absolutely vital issue. The King's failure to appreciate the point is proved by his parallel instructions to Santa Cruz ordering him to join Parma 'as agreed' off Margate. Actually of course Parma had 'agreed' to nothing of the sort, and was soon to make his position clear in a despatch from Brussels in which he disclosed the true condition of his 'fleet'. The boats, he wrote, were not fit for anything but the shortest crossing; they could not manoeuvre or take roundabout routes; they were too small to fight, only capable of sailing in fine weather, and so low in the water that 'four English frigates' would send to the bottom as many of them as they happened to meet – a very likely chance now that the English and Zeelanders were aware of what was being planned.

After this plain speaking no one in Spain should have remained wholly ignorant of the real situation existing in the Netherlands ports from which the landing force had to be launched. Had he lived, the Marquis of Santa Cruz, for all his dislike and jealousy of Parma, would probably have read the message correctly, for he had experience of the problems involved in working with allies during the Lepanto campaign. Unfortunately for Spain he happened to die that spring, leaving everything in confusion and every lesson to be re-learnt by his successor.

Even as the Marquis lay on his death bed the King had already fixed on that unfortunate: the Duke of Medina Sidonia, an Andalusian grandee of immense

A silver coin bearing Philip's head and the date 1588 issued in Milan. Despite the wealth from the New World Philip was plagued with financial difficulties throughout his reign.

Collection Thomas. Photograph, Roger Viollet, Paris.

wealth and small experience of campaigning. If he had known as much about naval warfare as he did about marketing salted tunny fish the Armada would have been better conducted, a cynical friar was to write when all was over. Indeed no one was better acquainted with his own failings than the Duke himself, who on learning that the royal eye was fixed on him had sent a truly poignant letter to Secretary Idiaquez, stressing his own incapacity on every count, from ignorance of fleet management to a chronic tendency to sea-sickness. There must, he argued, be other men more suited to this kind of employment.

Sternly the King overrode every objection in a letter written in his own hand: 'I am quite confident that, thanks to your great zeal and care, you will succeed very well. It cannot be otherwise in a case so entirely devoted to God's service as this.' The fact was that Philip needed a commander of sufficient social weight to overawe the professional captains of the fleet and to speak up as an equal to Parma during the actual operation off the English coast. His best seaman being dead, he turned instinctively to his richest territorial magnate. There was the added advantage that Medina Sidonia was a modest and devoted soul who would carry out orders to the letter: a great improvement in this respect on the crusty old sea-dog, Santa Cruz.

The high command of the enterprise had therefore significantly changed. But nothing else had. The Pope – Sixtus V – a notorious miser and a man who hedged his bets, continued to promise millions in gold but cannily waited for the invasion to happen. And Parma's letters continued to arrive, each more pessimistic than the last, envisaging some 'heavy disaster' which God might be preparing to punish them all for their sins. Time and time again he repeated his inability to cross the Straits without the helping hand of the fleet from Spain. Would it not, he asked, be better to come to some accommodation with the English which might lead to their withdrawal from the Netherlands? The Queen seemed willing to discuss the matter – her peace envoys were shortly to land at Ostend.

Misled by reports from his recently expelled ambassador to London, Don Bernadino de Mendoza, to the effect that the English had few ships and most of them rotten, the King regarded peace talk merely as a means of lulling his sister-in-law's suspicions while he prepared the weapon to strike her down.

The terms he set were obviously wholly unacceptable and included freedom of worship for Catholics in England besides compensation for English wrong-doing in the Netherlands, which would amount, he noted grimly, to 'an exceedingly great sum'. It was surely as though he had become infected with the spirit of Don John, whose energies in his last years had been almost wholly directed to a conquest of the heretic island. Could a feeling of guilt over his treatment of his dead half-brother have been one of the elements that led Philip to the despatch of the Armada? His instructions to Medina Sidonia, now firmly saddled with the command of the enterprise, certainly have a flavour of the victor of Lepanto and Gembloux. 'As all victories are the gifts of God Almighty, and the cause we champion is so exclusively His,' he wrote, 'we may fairly look for His aid and favour, unless by our sins we render ourselves unworthy. You will therefore have to exercise special care that such cause of offence shall be avoided on the Armada, and especially that there shall be no sort of blasphemy.'

Moral welfare was therefore an integral part of the operation – more than 180 monks and friars were aboard the fleet to ensure it. If there had been a tenth as many pilots with knowledge of the Straits or if the strategic plan had been as well thought out in all its implications and at all levels as the religious services, the daily masses and *Ave Marias*, the result of the enterprise might have been very different. Actually on the face of them the King's orders to Medina Sidonia had taken due note of Parma's warnings about the condition of the Netherlands barges and seemed to promise a competent and unified operation: '. . . you will sail with the whole of the Armada and go straight to the English Channel, which you will ascend as far as Cape Margate, where you will join hands with the Duke of Parma, my nephew, and hold the passage for his crossing.' However the King then went on to add that *in any event* Medina Sidonia must keep well clear of the French and Flemish coasts because of the danger of shoals – the exact place where Parma was most going to need the presence of the helping hand to get his transports to sea. This was the require-ment which the Governor General kept repeating in despatch after despatch: 'I am sure that your Majesty will have adopted all necessary measures for the carrying out of the task of protecting my passage across. . . . Failing this, and the due co-operation of the Duke with me, *both before and during the actual landing*, as well as afterwards, I can hardly succeed as I desire in your Majesty's service.'

So much for the confusion in the grand strategy. But tactical matters were almost as disastrously adrift: for while realizing that the English would be likely to rely on their long-range guns and keep their distance, the King was instructing Medina Sidonia if it came to a battle (which if possible he should avoid by 'drawing the enemy off by a diversion or otherwise') to boldly lay himself alongside the enemy and board him. The slower and less mobile force was therefore being credited with the ability to decline a battle or to engage in close action at choice.

Meanwhile in Lisbon the fleet was being assembled – 20 galleons, 4 galleasses, 4 galleys, 44 armed merchantmen, together with frigates and storeships: 130 sail in all with a complement of 30,000 men. The galleys were worse than useless in northern waters and some of the merchantmen performed poorly in bad weather, but the Portuguese galleons and those of the Spanish 'Indian Guard' were all first-class ships. Every kind of detailed provision was being made for the personnel. Rations had been laid down on a scale that must have warmed the contractors' hearts. Every man aboard was to receive daily $1\frac{1}{2}$ lbs. of biscuits or 2 lbs. of bread. Every Sunday and Thursday the men would receive 6 oz. of bacon and 2 oz. of rice; on Mondays and Wednesdays 6 oz. of cheese and half that quantity of beans or chick peas; on Wednesdays, Fridays and Saturdays, 5 oz. of sardines or 6 of squid, cod or tunny fish (the Duke's speciality). Oil and vinegar must be served on all fish days, and the water ration was 3 pints for all purposes, including that of diluting the issues of sherry or Candia wine. No less rigorously attended to were the men's spiritual needs, as laid down by the Admiral in his sailing orders:

> From highest to lowest you are to understand that the object of our expedition is to regain countries to the Church now oppressed by enemies of the true faith. I therefore beseech you to remember your calling, so that God will be with us in what we do.
>
> I charge you one and all to abstain from profane oaths dishonouring the names of our Lord, our Lady and the Saints. . . . Each morning at sunrise the ships' boys, according to custom, will sing 'Good morrow' at the foot of the mainmast, and at sunset the *Ave Maria*. . . .
>
> Since bad weather may disrupt communications, a watchword is laid down for each day of the week: for Sunday, Jesus; and for the succeeding days, Holy Ghost, Most Holy Trinity, St. James, The Angels, All Saints, and Our Lady.

In fact the only thing that was not agreed – was never to be agreed – was the overall plan. It sounds incredible, yet it was so. The Spanish wing of the operation had till the very last no clear understanding of the limitations of its Netherlands partner or of that partner's inability to put to sea of itself. The proof of this appears succinctly in one of Parma's letters to Philip:

> He [Medina Sidonia] seems to have persuaded himself that I may be able to go out and meet him with these boats. These things cannot be. . . .

'God grant that no embarrassment may come from this,' noted the King on the margin of the letter when it finally reached him. But by that time Medina Sidonia and the Armada were beyond correction or recall.

On 20th April at a ceremony in Lisbon cathedral in the presence of the Viceroy, the Cardinal-Archduke Albert, the sacred standard of the expedition was blessed by the Archbishop and carried by the Duke of Medina Sidonia to the Dominican Convent, where it was laid on the high altar as an act of dedication and then carried through the streets to the flagship through ranks of kneeling sailors and men at arms. The ships had already been searched to make sure that no loose women were aboard, and all ranks had taken communion and been absolved. It was to be the Lepanto campaign all over again, with even greater emphasis on the religious nature of this crusade against another Christian state, whose Queen was not much more backward in commending herself and her cause to the deity.

The King was not present at the ceremony. The creator of the Armada was never to see it sail. Had he perhaps come to doubt the issue? Throughout the summer religious processions were being held in almost every Spanish town and village to invoke God's blessing, and at the Escorial the masses and prayers were continuous. Yet for a month after the dedication of the standard the Armada was held in the Tagus estuary by contrary winds, and hardly had it got to sea in the third week in June than it was scattered by a storm off the coast of Finisterre.

From the haven at Corunna, astonished and alarmed by the malevolence of the weather which attended an undertaking 'so commended and devoted to God', the Duke of Medina Sidonia sat down to write his comments for the King. His squadrons were limping into port, but in what shape?

> To undertake so great a task with forces equal to those of the enemy would be inadvisable, but to do so with an inferior force, as ours is now, with our men lacking in experience, would be still more unwise. I am bound to confess that I see very few, or hardly any, of those on the Armada with any knowledge of or ability to perform the duties entrusted to them. I have tested and watched this point very carefully, and your Majesty may believe me when I assure you that we are very weak. . . . The opportunity might be taken, and the difficulties avoided, by making some honourable terms with the enemy. Your Majesty's necessities also make it desirable that you should deeply ponder beforehand what you are undertaking, with so many envious rivals of your greatness.

The pessimism of this strange despatch was only equalled by the sense of realism it displayed. The Duke had come to know his fleet as well as he knew himself, and he was to prove a remarkably accurate prophet of disaster. The poor sailing qualities of the storeships and some of the armed merchantmen were now realized. He was not to know that the water supplies would also prove defective through the use of unseasoned wood in the storage casks. But whatever the King in his secret thoughts may have made of this plain speaking, outwardly he gave no sign. 'Great affairs involve great difficulties', he had written to Parma the previous autumn, and his philosophical acceptance of this maxim had not changed. To Medina Sidonia he replied firmly that the operation must go on. Probably he agreed with his Admiral that the storms had been sent by God 'for some good and just reason', though he interpreted the message differently. And in fact the winds that plagued his ships were also to keep at bay an English raiding and reconnaissance squadron, thus powerfully contributing to the element of surprise when at the end of July the Armada appeared off the Cornish coast.

On 22nd July it had got to sea at last out of Corunna on a day of deceptive calm. Far off in Brussels the Governor General was lamenting his lack of money. In Rome the Pope was still shilly-shallying over his subsidies, unimpressed, so the Spanish ambassador to the Holy See reported, by news of the daily intercessions to God being made throughout Spain. Who believed now in the great 'Enterprise'? Not Parma, who for months had been playing down the part he could usefully play in it. Certainly not Medina Sidonia and his captains, soon to

The engagement between the English fleet and the Spanish Armada off the Isle of Wight.
Courtesy the National Maritime Museum, London.

be struck again off Ushant at the entrance to the English Channel by another inexplicable storm, which cost them the flagship of the Biscayan squadron and all four of the galleys. The mood of resignation and self-doubt infecting its commander, even after the fleet had successfully re-formed and its lookouts on the morning of 30th July had sighted land, is shown by the very prayers he ordered in thanksgiving to God for safely 'bringing us thus far'.

Yet the armament he commanded that morning when he sent off his first operational despatch to the King, 'in sight of Cape Lizard, on board the galleon *San Martin*', was the most formidable fleet of sailing ships that had ever been assembled – 125 vessels from every quarter of the Spanish empire, ranged so tightly together, like a vast floating fortress, that in the light winds which had followed the gales the faster and more mobile English were unable to do more than pick at them. A double spearhead of Spanish and Portuguese galleons led the way up-Channel, with three of the galleasses in support. Behind them came the *San Martin* and the mass of storeships, covered by four squadrons of the rearguard spread out like a comet's tail. Watchers on the shore either saw or imagined a crescent shape – a very strange formation for the fleet of the Most Catholic King. The impression it made on everyone who saw it was one of immense power and purpose – the forest of masts, the banners, the sails blazoned with red crosses, the slow remorseless progress along the coast.

For many months the King had been at work planning his Armada down to the last detail. The only thing he could not command was the weather, but at this crucial moment even that had favoured him. His fleet had weathered the gales and was at sea. The English were in port in Plymouth. The tale of Drake's famous quip during the game of bowls on the Hoe cannot disguise the fact that he and the Lord Admiral – Howard of Effingham – had been caught at a dis-advantage from which it required their nimblest seamanship to save them. At Terceira in the Azores, Santa Cruz, finding the French squadrons supporting Don Antonio in a similar trap, had ended by destroying them. The moment in the Channel soon passed: the light breeze did not bring the Spaniards on fast enough to catch the English before they got to sea out of the Sound and took up their station in the shelter of Rame Head. But even when the enemy had got to windward of him on Sunday 31st July, Medina Sidonia still had the whole coastline of southern England lying temptingly open on his port bow; and if the defences of Plymouth were too tough a nut to crack, there were other easier havens lying ahead – Torbay, and the narrows of the Solent, which the movements of the English fleet to windward of the Armada had uncovered.

The King's original plan had been for an attack on the Isle of Wight. Aboard the Armada were nearly 19,000 seasoned troops, many of them earmarked as reinforcements for Parma after his landing in the Thames estuary. Suppose they had been used against the island and the Hampshire coast? Many of the Queen's best companies were absent in the Netherlands: her available levies were of mixed quality and the towns on the road to London were largely undefended. Of course there was a risk: and the Armada's captains, after debating the matter, declined it. Perhaps they were wise to decline it in the presence of so strong an enemy. But in any case they had little choice, for in Philip's final plan the descent on the Solent on the eastward run had been expressly forbidden. Tied to the orders given it in Spain, the Armada continued its stately advance towards a non-existent rendezvous.

The spate of messages sent out by frigate from the Spanish fleet to its Netherlands partner perfectly charts this journey to disaster. On 1st August Ensign Juan Gill was sent off to ask Parma exactly where the Armada should *wait for him*. There was also a demand for pilots with knowledge of the Flanders coast, which suggests that at last Medina Sidonia was aware that his first target lay on the south side of the Dover straits, near Dunkirk, and not off Margate. All the other illusions remained as firmly rooted as ever in his mind. On 4th August, distressed by the way the English would not let him board them but kept cannonading at a distance, he begged Parma to be ready to put to sea at once to meet him, and asked also for supplies of shot and powder. Next day he was demanding that Parma should send him 'forty fly-boats', the light craft which in fact were a speciality of the rebel Zeelanders and of which Parma was almost wholly deficient. Given 'fifty fly-boats', Medina Sidonia was saying on the 6th, he could 'continue to resist the enemy' till Parma could come out to join him with the rest of his fleet and they could go together to seize some port where the Armada could lie in safety. 'I beg you to hasten your coming out', he repeated on 7th August. That was Sunday, and the Armada lay at anchor off Calais, thirty miles from Parma's loading base at Dunkirk but determined to venture no further without firm news of the Governor General's intentions.

That same day in the Netherlands, after receiving another of Medina Sidonia's envoys, Parma sat down to reason matters out with his master in the Escorial who would probably not get his letter for another three weeks to a month. He referred to Medina Sidonia's notion that he could come out not only to meet him but now apparently to *help* him. This, he remarked, was evidently impossible, since he was blockaded in his own harbours by rebel units and in any case the ships he possessed were only 'canal barges', not fighting craft fit for the sea. How many times had he said it! The mutual imcomprehension existing between the allies was nearing its final point of absurdity, for while the Duke was urgently awaiting Parma and his fly-boats at Calais, the Governor General at Bruges was simply waiting for the Duke. He was not even on the coast, let alone embarked, though he had concentrated some barges in Nieuport and Dunkirk and an army to put aboard them. Was this not enough?

Following the fire-ship attack on the Spanish Fleet they fell back in confusion to the waters off Gravelines where the English closed in the next day.

Courtesy the National Maritime Museum, London.

Lord Howard of Effingham, the Admiral of the English fleet.

Courtesy the National Portrait Gallery, London.

Parma's enemies – and they included eye-witnesses from the Armada – said at the time and continued to say that he had misled everyone; that his invasion barges were few in number and in a deplorable state of unseaworthiness; that nothing was prepared; that no more than a little window-dressing had even been attempted. In anguished letters to the King, Parma denied these allegations. It was not true, he wrote to Philip, that his forces were not ready to play their full part in the plan. Only the malicious could say such a thing. But the plan called for the Armada's physical presence off the Flemish coast and its control of the Straits, and where was it?

There was some substance in these arguments. Parma could only have heard of the Armada's arrival at Calais on the evening of Sunday the 7th, and by nightfall on the 8th he was at Nieuport, where the loading of the men was at once begun, followed at dawn next morning by similar operations at Dunkirk. Yet through the endless protests and the explanations the dismal truth shines through: that the barges were not ready; were unsuitable to their task; that the men to be put aboard them had no confidence whatever in their mission. In any case by the evening of Monday the 8th the storms were blowing again along the Flanders coast and there was no chance of even well-found ships getting out of port. Nor was there any longer a Spanish fleet capable of escorting them. For while the black comedy of loading troops aboard the barges was being played in the harbours at Nieuport and Dunkirk, the Armada, once again at sea, was already to leeward of them and in deadly danger off the Zeeland coast.

On the evening of the 7th the Armada had lain inshore off Calais, with the English squadrons anchored to seaward and just out of cannon range. Then about midnight, according to Medina Sidonia's official report:

> Two fires were seen kindled in the English fleet, and these two gradually increased to eight; and eight ships with sails set, drifting with the current, came straight towards our flagship and the rest of the Armada, all burning fiercely. The Duke, seeing them approach and that our men had not diverted them, and fearing that they were explosion ships, gave orders to let go the cables, and also for the rest of the Armada to do the same, intending when the fires had passed to return to the same position.

So much for good intentions. But the damage had been done, and in a scene of wild confusion the Spaniards cut their cables and jostled out to sea, losing one of the galleasses and two of the big Portuguese galleons in the process.

Next morning, off Gravelines, the English closed in and pounded the Armada as it tried desperately to re-form. By nightfall all the fight had been beaten out of it and it was in flight north-eastwards out of the Straits. At dawn on the Tuesday the Armada's pilots saw a line of shoal water directly ahead on the Zeeland Banks. 'From this desperate peril in only six-and-a-half fathoms', wrote the Duke, 'we were saved by the wind shifting by God's mercy to the southwest. . . .'

The men aboard saw the divine hand extended over them to take them clear of the shoals. But it was no 'Catholic wind', for it settled the fate of most of them. With a south-wester blowing there could be no return to the coasts of Flanders and the short way home to Spain. All that could be done was done. A council of war was held aboard the flagship; some who had failed in their duty in the fight were hanged at the yard-arm; and new sailing orders were issued to every captain – they were orders only for escape. Off the Scottish coast the English turned away to re-fit. The sea and the winds and the unfamiliar coastline were now the enemies to be fought. In the 'Long Forties' south of the Norway Channel some of the battered ships went down. Water was running short. As the fleet rounded Scotland and the islands and turned south-westward on 21st August into the Atlantic it once more encountered contrary winds which held it in those latitudes for nearly a fortnight. More ships dropped out: only forty-four of the first-raters were still under the Duke's control when on 3rd September the wind at last went round into the north and they were able to set a course for Spain.

This disciplined remnant, which included most of the ships of the Indian Guard and the Portuguese royal squadron, obeyed the sailing orders to keep well out into the Atlantic and survived. Few of the ship's companies on the unweatherly or damaged vessels that were driven towards the Irish coast or who ventured ashore there for food and water ever got back to Spain. Of the muster

The Armada's route round the coasts of Britain as seen in an engraving by John Pine.
Courtesy the National Maritime Museum, London.

roll of 130 ships that had left Corunna barely more than half came back, and the ratio for personnel was even worse, for two-thirds of the 30,000 aboard never saw their homes again. Shipwreck, disease, starvation, thirst and the hangmen working for English governors accounted for those who never returned.

The sufferings of the fugitives make poignant reading. Now and again a crew led by a resolute captain fought its way out of trouble and lived to tell the tale, but most of the story is only to be read in local traditions of ships aground on that westward-sloping Irish coast from Donegal to the mouth of the Shannon and in reports of skin-divers of our own times in search of treasure trove. The saga of one such ship, the galleass *Girona*, can stand for all the rest of the lost company.

Galleasses were galleons fitted with oars – a hybrid derived from the Mediterranean galley. At Lepanto their fire-power had played a big part in deciding the battle, but they were less at home in Atlantic waters. Four of them sailed with the Armada. Their flagship, the *San Lorenzo*, lost her rudder off Calais and fell into enemy hands. But her sister ship the *Girona* sailed on another thousand miles to meet a grimmer fate.

Her captain was Fabricio Spinola, a Genoese, and she carried 121 seamen, 244 extra hands, mostly galley slaves, and 186 troops. Well handled, she survived the panic in Calais Roads, the running fight off Gravelines and the dangerous passage into the Atlantic, to come safely ashore on the north-west coast of Ireland at Killybegs in Donegal. There she jettisoned most of her guns to make room for survivors from another Armada ship, the *Duquesa Santa Ana*, which had been wrecked nearby at Loughos More; and there were 1300 men aboard her, far more than double her complement, when she sailed out of Killybegs, going not south-westwards, because Spain was too far away, but back towards the coasts of Scotland, where her commanders hoped to be able to re-provision in safety.

She never got there, for at dawn on 16th October she was wrecked on the Rock of Bumboyes near the Giant's Causeway on the Antrim coast – and of her 1300, five men struggled ashore alive.

The place where they landed is still marked on maps as Port na Spaniagh, so the last voyage of the *Girona* has never been completely forgotten. What she carried aboard her in the way of perishables we shall never know, for when her grave was found, nothing was left of her except some lead sheeting, some nails, lead ingots from the ballast, a few pieces of rope, some cannon balls and parts of the guns not off-loaded at Killybegs. But other items have come to light as a result of underwater exploration led by the world renowned marine archaeologist, Robert Sténuit, whose finds are now in the Ulster Museum in Belfast, and these relics are not from the ship but from her crew. In a recent article the museum's Keeper of Antiquities, Laurence N. W. Flanagan, describes some of them: two astrolabes; several pairs of navigational dividers; a collection of elegantly worked table forks; a silver perfume flask; a long gold chain; gold buttons, bracelets, rings and crosses; a tiny bronze figure from a crucifix and a set of exquisite cameos of Roman emperors made of lapis lazuli in gold frames set with pearls.

The jewels alone are striking proof of the wealth and confidence of the society that sent out the men and the ships. There are no memorials of the unfortunate galley slaves who must also have died in these treacherous waters. But two other items found by the Sténuit expedition touchingly recall for us the human

These are part of the engraved pack of Armada playing cards which illustrate episodes in the campaign.
Courtesy the National Maritime Museum, London.

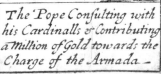

The Pope Consulting with his Cardinalls & Contributing a Million of Gold towards the Charge of the Armada

The Army of 1000 horse, and 22000 Foot, which y Earle of Leicester comanded when hee Pitched his Tents att Tilbury

Don Alphonso Duke of Medina, Cheife Comander of y Spanish Fleete, & John Martin Recalde, a great Seaman.

The English Fleet whereof the Ld Charles Howard was Ld Admirall & Sr Fran: Drake vice Admirall.

element that underlay the grandiose and doomed enterprise. One of them is a ring, probably given by a girl to her lover or husband before he sailed, inscribed *No tengo mas que dar te*, 'I have nothing more to give thee.' The other is a plum-stone – from Killybegs? Or from some orchard in Spain in that stormy summer of 1588?

It was only slowly that news of the calamity reached the outside world. The victors themselves were for a while uncertain where their enemy had got to; and in the Netherlands it was not till the end of August that Parma could use the bleak word 'disaster' in a letter to the King.

Meanwhile reports of quite another colour were being put about – many of them by the Spanish ambassador in Paris, that same Bernadino de Mendoza who had talked so slightingly of the English ships and was now purveying tales of some great Spanish success. Throughout Europe the rumours spread – to the Netherlands, to Germany, to Rome, where the Pope retained his native scepticism. Some reports had Drake a fugitive from the battle: others made him a captive aboard the *San Martin*. The slowness of communications naturally added to the normal fog of war; and Spain, on the far periphery of the continent, was the worst served of all.

The King allowed himself to hope. As late as the end of September, only ten days before the *San Martin* came limping home into Santander, he could still dream of some happy outcome. But a full month earlier the rationalist in him had accepted the fatality. His grief was greater than one could possibly describe, wrote Secretary Idiaquez to Parma on the last day of August. But it was grief kept under rigorous control, as another of Idiaquez's letters makes clear – the King was 'very much afflicted' but kept up his courage, consoling himself with the thought that he had acted throughout with 'good Christian motives'. It was this stoicism, attested to by his secretaries, combined with memories of the restraint with which his father had received the news of the victory over the French at Pavia and he himself the triumph at Lepanto, that made later admirers imagine a scene in the Escorial in which, barely pausing in his daily labours at his desk to hear the full tidings of disaster from a messenger from the Armada, he wrote on, his face as impassive as a statue's.

Yet if this was legend, it enshrined a truth: and the proof of it is in the King's letters that autumn, which maintain an admirable calm, even when he knew that all was lost, and rise to truly Christian heights of resignation in a letter that October to the Spanish bishops: 'We are bound to give praise to God for all things which He is pleased to do. Now I give thanks for the mercy He has shown. In the storms through which the Armada sailed, it might have suffered a worse fate. . . .'

What this failure meant to him, who had 'sacrificed' so much (in Idiaquez's words), appears both in the serious illness that beset him that autumn and in certain phrases in his letters to Parma, very revealing of his tormented state of mind and of his longing for some reassurance, some crumb of comfort. On 3rd September, on hearing that the English too had suffered losses in the battles, he imagined that perhaps after all the Governor General might be able to carry out his part of the plan and get his barges across the Straits. Failing that,

The Prince of Parma coming to Dunkerk with his Army but too late is received by the Spaniards with reproach

More then halfe y Spanish Fleet Taken and Sunck

Severall strange Weapons taken from the Spaniard which were provid to destroy y English

The Spaniards bewailing y misfortune of their friends

Four more cards illustrating episodes in the Armada confrontation.

he hoped that Parma would at least capture the Isle of Walcheren from the Netherlands rebels as a springboard for some future invasion. It was particularly desirable, he wrote forlornly, that the year should not pass without *some* substantial success.

Chapter 16

Death of Parma

The solace Philip yearned for was not forthcoming: the year ended on the sombre note with which it had begun. In fact another blow was to fall on him from a wholly unexpected quarter, for in December his French allies of the Catholic League, the Duke of Guise and the Cardinal of Lorraine, foolishly ventured into the royal parlour in the castle of Blois, where the French king had them both murdered.

The news, wrote Philip, caused him 'great affliction'. Yet indirectly it was to open up new fields, new prospects of aggrandizement.

Henry III was the last of the male line of the house of Valois: he had been married for several years without issue, and his tastes anyway were not for women. The murder of the Guises in Blois had been a last desperate attempt to assert his authority in a country divided by the rival factions of the Catholic League and the Huguenots under the heir presumptive and first prince of the blood, Henry of Navarre. The assassinations badly misfired. The catholics, who predominated in Paris and in most of the big towns, denounced the king as a blood-stained tyrant; and deserted by almost everyone, he had no option but to throw in his lot with Navarre and the Huguenot army.

The religious wars in France had been continuing on and off for twenty years, but now at last the country was faced with the prospect of a Protestant victory in the field and an eventual heretic succession. The League had been deprived by the murders at Blois of its two dominant personalities: its fighting and moral strength had been seriously weakened. By the Treaty of Joinville the dead men had attached Philip to their interest; and now the surviving chief of the clan, the Duke of Mayenne, renewed his appeals to Madrid to save the country for Catholicism.

After his failure with the Armada Philip had reverted to his habitual caution. Any help given to the League, he instructed Parma, must be discreet, for he could not afford an open breach with the French king. Matters however radically altered when in August 1589 Henry III was in turn struck down by a Catholic assassin.

In his dying moments, while recognizing Navarre as his successor, the king had begged him to return to the Roman church. There seemed not the least likelihood however that Navarre would do it. What course then should Philip adopt? To recognize a heretic was out of the question. The best *interim* plan seemed to be to support a Catholic candidate in the person of the Cardinal of Bourbon, even though he was a prisoner of the Huguenots in La Rochelle. 'France is the important issue now', wrote Philip to Parma, who would have to supply the army to underwrite Mayenne and the League. Even if it meant denuding the Netherlands of troops, it was a risk that Philip was prepared to take.

Parma's standpoint was entirely different. His mother had been vicereine of the Netherlands; he himself had been married there; and his personal commitment was to the reconquest of the whole country. He had disliked the project of the Armada because it had interfered with this aim; and uneasily aware of the growing wealth and power of the rebel states of the north, he disliked intervention in France even more. His enemies – and he had many since the failure of the Armada – were not wholly wrong when in their spiteful letters to Madrid they dubbed him 'the Man of Flanders'.

Throughout 1589 and 1590 a battle of wills therefore began to develop between the King and the Governor General – Philip demanding that Parma should lead a Netherlands army into France, and Parma resisting these instructions as best he could, by appeals to the poverty of the country, the mutinous state of the army, the dangerous strategic situation, and his own increasing ill-health. Meanwhile the moment of crisis drew nearer. In March 1590 the cavalry which Parma had reluctantly sent into France to help Mayenne was cut to pieces in Navarre's victory at Ivry and its leader killed. Cardinal Bourbon died uncrowned. The Huguenot army closed the ring around Paris, and by midsummer the food supplies of the capital were running out.

On 20th May Philip ordered Parma to march as soon as possible. A month later, stressing the dangers to Spain and Catholicism if Paris fell, his orders were more peremptory. On 24th June the despatch to Parma was marked by an annotation in the King's own hand: '. . . I neither ask for nor want words, but acts, and that is what I hope for from you.' The tone of exasperation is unmistakable.

Parma's replies to the orders sent him only added fuel to the fire. Towards the end of July he was writing that the impossible was being asked of him. How could it be supposed that with his limited resources in a ruined and restive country he could hold the line against the northern rebels, suppress the mutinies raging among the *tercios*, and have troops to spare for France and Mayenne? He was already a very sick man, suffering from the dropsy that was soon to kill him. Yet still protesting his desperate situation, he took the road to Paris, outmanoeuvred Navarre's Huguenot army, and relieved the starving city in one of the greatest military operations of the century – a pearl to set beside his captures of Maastricht and Antwerp.

Barely had he done so than fresh demands began to rain down on him from Madrid, for with the death of Cardinal Bourbon Philip had begun to pursue the wider dream of placing his elder daughter by Elizabeth of Valois on the throne of France. The French had a rule governing the monarchy – the so-called

An anonymous portrait of the Infanta Isabella Clara Eugenia whom Philip hoped to place on the throne of France.
Musée de Versailles. Photograph, Roger Viollet, Paris.

Salic Law, derived from the days of the Frankish tribes, which debarred women from the succession. This rule did not apply in Spain, and Philip saw no reason why it should apply in France either. Airily he dismissed such traditionalism as a 'pleasantry' unworthy of respect. However it was now vitally necessary to take physical possession of the country he hoped his daughter would inherit, and Parma was therefore instructed to stay where he was, near Paris, and on no account to return to the Netherlands while the business of the succession was still undecided.

Pleading sickness in his army and the dangerous state of Netherlands affairs, with a rebel offensive under way, the Governor General ignored these orders and returned to Brussels – then again set off for Spa to take the waters. The King had to accept the *fait accompli* and assure the truant of the confidence he felt in him. But throughout the winter of 1590/91 the Governor General found himself bombarded with orders to return to France. The Huguenots were advancing again. Chartres fell to them; Rouen was besieged. On 22nd May Philip ordered Parma to march by 1st August at the latest. He would feel himself badly served otherwise, he added in a menacing aside. On 30th June he described the intended invasion as 'the most important service' that Parma could render, and one that must on no account be delayed. To back this up, a royal envoy was sent to the Governor General to urge him into action, and on 4th August the King added the final touch: 'You know my wishes, I have opened my heart to you. To satisfy me you must leave at once, and you will see how contented I shall be.'

The King had spoken in the clearest possible terms. Yet not till 16th November did the Governor General at last set out, having spent the intervening months in trying to check the rebel offensive which had opened against Nijmegen, the key bridgehead on the Waal, and in some plain speaking with a vengeance directed to Madrid. On the last day in August, in the course of a long lamentation on the deplorable condition of the loyalist provinces under his care, he had remarked that the Netherlanders felt themselves abandoned by the King.

In just such despairing, accusing terms Don John had written to his master from Namur in the weeks before his death. Now the wheel had come full circle. Perhaps in his heart of hearts the King had never wholly approved of Parma: an Italian, a foreigner, whose European fame, like Don John's, was another reminder of how the Emperor's most glittering talents had been passed on not to the legitimate but to the illegitimate line. Only reluctantly had Philip made him Governor General of the Netherlands. The appointment had been forced on him by the Duchess Margaret's reluctance to stand up to her son and by Parma's own intransigence and ambition. Great results had flowed from it, ending in the reconquest of the southern provinces. Yet from the time of the capture of Antwerp onwards little had gone right. In his early letters, when the Armada was being planned, Parma had suggested an active role for himself, only to draw back and plead his inability to get his barges to sea. At the moment of truth in August he had done nothing. Why? Very hostile reports had been circulating in Europe as to the state of preparations in Nieuport and Dunkirk: accusations in fact of a gross failure in duty.

Even given that failure, the King still had need of Parma. But whereas in the days of triumph before Antwerp he had felt almost an exalted trust in his nephew – now it was only a union of convenience. There were too many tales abroad of the misdeeds and even of the dangerous ambitions of this man whom he had raised up and placed in command of the greatest concentration of Spanish power surviving now that the Armada had been blown away on the winds. It was said that Parma had never wanted the success of the 'Enterprise'; that he had been bought by the English, the hated enemy; and was lukewarm in the affair of France. It was said, with justification, that he surrounded himself with Italians and kept Spaniards at a distance. The desperate and demoralized state of the Netherlands provinces could be read in Parma's own letters – he never tired of stressing it. Who but he was to blame for it? Corruption was rife at every level of his administration – the Spaniards said it, and it was true. It had always been true. Certain units of the Spanish army in the provinces were in open mutiny. They had mutinied under Alva and Requesens. Never mind. As long as Parma obeyed orders and marched where he was told, the King would overlook all his offences and ignore every rumour, while storing it all up. Yet Parma was really on probation. The long delays that followed the orders of August 1591 to march into France, and the complaining, almost defiant, tone of Parma's despatches from Spa, finally settled the matter in the King's mind. Perhaps the very successes of his nephew's long reign in Brussels added to the bitterness of his mood as he reflected that after so much promise and glory his faith had been betrayed – on the coasts of Flanders in '88, and now again, three years later, when his greatest ambitions seemed on the verge of being realized. No time must be wasted. He had replaced Don John. He would replace his equally insubordinate successor.

Opposite: Philip is no longer portrayed as the man of action in this portrait by Sanchez Coello; his sombre, religious nature is stressed in the black habit relieved only by the white ruff at the neck and wrists. The Golden Fleece now hangs on a black cord.
Courtesy of the Prado, Madrid. Photograph Scala, Florence.

So in December, verbal instructions were given to a special envoy, the Marquis of Cerralvo, to go to Brussels and ensure by the most tactful possible means that the Governor General should set out at once to Spain for 'consultations'. To sweeten the pill, and to get the disgraced minister out of the Netherlands without open scandal, Philip added some blandishments of his own in a letter to the victim. He would have liked to have so indispensable a person everywhere at once, he wrote, but since this was impossible, he felt the greatest need was to have him in Madrid. Would Parma please oblige by setting out at once? Cerralvo's verbal instructions were then placed in the form of a written *aide-mémoire*.

While these machinations were going on behind his back, Parma was performing the last of his services to his master by again invading France and raising the Huguenot siege of Rouen. But this time there was a heavier price to pay. Navarre's forces were more aggressive and more skilfully handled than outside Paris two years earlier. While attacking the small town of Caudebec, and well forward as usual with his troops, Parma was wounded. Rising from his sick bed he extricated the army from a dangerous situation in face of superior forces. But there was now nothing for it but to retreat to the Netherlands, where in his absence the rebel offensive from the north had gathered strength and forced the loyalists back across the Maas and the Waal by the capture of the key bridgeheads.

From Spa, where he had retired in a last attempt to mend his broken health, he wrote to Philip on 12th July the most poignant of his letters, in which while admitting that faults had crept into his government, he protested that in everything that concerned faith, zeal, sincerity and devotion, he had never failed in his duty.

This had almost certainly been true until 1588, when the conflict between the King's ambitions in England and then in France came into conflict with Parma's more correct and realistic judgment that it was *in the Netherlands* and not elsewhere that Spanish power should be exerted. Was it true any longer? The King had come to a decidedly contrary conclusion, and on 4th July, eight days before Parma's letter was written, had issued further instructions for his removal and recall in a patent given to the Count of Fuentes, in place of the Marquis of Cerralvo, recently deceased.

Not till 23rd November did the new messenger reach Brussels, to find the bird flown. On the 11th Parma had left the city to begin his third and last incursion into France on the business of getting the Infanta elected to the throne. He got no further than Arras, where death struck him down before Fuentes could find him.

It had been an unequal duel between a monarch and a subject wholly dependent on him. No other European ruler, except perhaps Elizabeth, had such a servant to maltreat and disgrace. On 6th December the Archbishop of Cambrai reported the 'inestimable loss of a prince so valorous and zealous in the service of God and the King'. And he spoke no more than the simple truth.

Opposite, above: Philip II's apartments at the Escorial remain very largely as they were during his lifetime. This is the throne room.   Photograph MAS, Barcelona.

Below: An enamelled gold pendant in the form of a bat set with emeralds, rubies and pearls and made in Spain during the second half of the 16th century.
Crown copyright, the Victoria and Albert Museum, London.

Chapter 17

The Disgrace of Perez

In one sense Philip's life can be seen as a series of personal confrontations. The rivalry with the Valois, the Turk and with the Queen of England arose naturally out of the political situation into which he had been born, as did the duel to the death with the Prince of Orange which ended in 1584 with the Protestant leader's assassination at Delft. Yet the same pattern recurs in Philip's relationships with his own servants: time and time again we meet the same sequence of trust and dependence shading off into doubt, impatience, a growing suspiciousness, and at the end a cold, remorseless hatred, concealed till the last moment from the victim about to be struck down. It was as though, with a few rare exceptions, the King found it impossible to rely on anyone who showed independence of mind or was in a position of power that could even remotely threaten him. Outside the family circle of his daughters and sisters and his nephews, the Archdukes Albert and Ernest, those whom he trusted were very few: Ruy Gomez, Prince of Eboli, and Don Cristobal de Moura, both Portuguese, the elder Feria, the Dukes of Medina Sidonia and Savoy, Cardinal Granvelle, and on a lower level some of his secretaries and confessors. Most of the greater figures of the reign fared very badly. Alva was exiled; Don Carlos died in prison; Cardinal Espinosa fell from power for concealing an item of news, took to his bed and never got up from it; Egmont was executed; Montigny was strangled in Simancas; Don John and Parma were removed from office, their health broken by their immense services to the state.

The King was no tyrant. Even his darkest acts were motivated by reason of a kind. He ordered Egmont's execution and planned Montigny's in person because he regarded them both as traitors, and he replaced Don John and Parma because they had failed to carry out the orders he had so clearly and constantly given them. Yet behind the justifications and the excuses there lay in every case an element of the vendetta, the intrusion of an intensely personalized jealousy and suspicion of those around him which may have sprung from the insecurity of his motherless childhood, and which developed as he grew older into a kind of paranoia in which his father's warnings against too great a trust in others became translated into a morbid distrust of people's motives and a determination to punish all those who in the least degree failed him. The destruction of Don John and of Parma were casebooks in such methods, but the best clinical detail of all can be seen in the King's treatment of his secretary Antonio Perez and of Perez's mistress, the widowed Princess of Eboli.

Perez's credentials for the post he long occupied were of the highest. His natural father had been the trusted secretary and intimate of the Emperor, and being thus the bastard son of a pillar of the Establishment, Antonio enjoyed that status, half noble, half servile and wholly dependent, that particularly appealed to Philip's taste and was met with on a much higher rung of the ladder in Don John.

Allied to brains, quick-wittedness, great powers of application, boldness, a handsome figure and an aptitude to please, this made for success at the Spanish court, where the tentacles of a vast bureaucracy provided plenty of pickings for those alert enough to snatch them. It happened also that this talented and far-sighted young man had attached himself to the faction in Madrid led by the King's boyhood friend and favourite, the Prince of Eboli – and this at a time when the other leading figure in Spain, the Duke of Alva, was embarking on his disastrous governorship of the Netherlands. Not content with one protector, Antonio had two others: Doña Ana de Mendoza y de la Cerda, Eboli's wife, and the Marquis de los Velez, one of the most powerful figures on the Council of State.

Nominated Secretary by Philip in July 1567, Perez took office in November of the following year and soon made his mark. He began to be indispensable: a busy, diligent man, always attentive to his master's business but also very resourceful and fruitful of ideas. Before long he had established himself so firmly in office that we find him daring to instruct the King how to relax mentally and how to sit most restfully in a chair! Even his growing wealth and the grandeur of his establishment of town and country houses were not displeasing so long as Philip was satisfied that the man himself was wholly devoted to his interests and that this magnificence was simply a reflection of the wealth and splendour of his court. A series of events broke up this accord between the monarch and his most confidential servant: the death of Eboli; the liaison between Perez and the widow; lastly and calamitously, the crisis over Don John's governorship of the Netherlands and the murder in Madrid of Juan de Escovedo.

In his early dealings with both these men Perez had been friendly and loyal; indeed he had been personally responsible for recommending Escovedo's appointment as Don John's secretary. But for one reason or another the moment arrived when he began to play a double game, by arousing their impatience and anger with the temporizing King, while using their unguarded letters as evidence to feed Philip's jealousy and distrust of his half-brother. Perhaps the motive was fear of being supplanted at court by this ambitious pair.

All this had worked like a charm while both Perez's victims were far away in the Netherlands and he could win credit for protecting his master from non-existent plots. But it was a different matter when, suspecting some double-dealing at court, Don John's personal adviser arrived back in Spain on a mission of enquiry. Escovedo in Madrid was no longer a sitting target for the expert marksman at Philip's side: he was a standing danger to Perez and to his mistress, Eboli's widow.

Exactly what Escovedo discovered and threatened to tell the King will never be known with certainty. Sepulveda, who as the historian of the Escorial must have come upon many secrets, makes no bones about accusing Perez of betraying information to rebel elements in the Netherlands; and it could well be that these treasonable dealings also concerned Portugal, where the Princess of Eboli was ambitious to marry off a daughter to the son of the Duchess of Braganza, close in line to the succession to the throne. Much later, when denouncing his secretary's misdeeds, Philip was to declare that they were 'of so grave a nature' that no vassal had ever before been guilty of their equivalent – and these words can hardly have referred only to Perez's sexual liaison with the Princess, unless indeed the later popular tales were right in making her the object also of the royal affections.

Whatever Escovedo discovered, it was certainly grave enough (as we have seen) to cost him his life in a street assassination in Madrid on the night of Easter Monday 1578. Perez had earlier convinced the King that as Don John's evil genius Escovedo was a menace that had to be eliminated, and the royal assent had been given to this act of instant justice. For some time the King remained convinced that the brutal and cowardly crime had been a necessary act of state to protect his regime against plots emanating from Don John's entourage in the Netherlands.

However after Don John's death his papers and effects were brought to Madrid and it became clear at last that whatever his faults may have been, the victor of Lepanto and Gembloux, that seeker after thrones, had always been a devoted servant of his master. Fresh then in the King's memory must have been his brother's poignant appeal on learning of Escovedo's death: 'Be pleased, I entreat you, to let me stir your memory and kneel in supplication. I shall do this by every courier, in all matters touching the dead man, till full justice be done. . . .'

In March 1579, almost exactly a year after Escovedo's death and nearly six months after that of Don John, Philip made his first move to disencumber himself of his secretary by summoning his old confidant Cardinal Granvelle from Rome. He had the greatest need, he wrote, of his advice and presence to help him in his work, which at that time included the planning for the conquest of Portugal.

What had happened in the background was that popular rumour in Madrid, which had long identified Perez and the Princess of Eboli with Escovedo's murder, had at last emboldened Perez's rival in the secretariat, Mateo Vasquez, to lay accusations with the King against them both. Philip had shown these accusations to Perez, while at the same time assuring him of his own continued support: 'As long as I live there is nothing to fear, for though others may change, believe me, I am unchangeable.' Behind this facade of words he allowed Mateo Vasquez to incite Escovedo's family to press on with litigation against the murderer. Perez and the Princess of Eboli's arrogant response to the rumours

This stern portrait of Philip II is by an unknown artist. He is wearing a richly decorated
suit of armour and the Golden Fleece hangs on a ribbon about his neck.
Courtesy the Rijksmuseum, Amsterdam.

and their threats of vengeance against Mateo were simply grist to the King's
mill: he would use them in his good time to bring them down.

Granvelle reached Madrid on 28th July. That night the King worked with

Perez as usual, and obviously the dispute between the two secretaries was discussed. After they parted, the King sent him a written note, ending: 'Your own particular business will be despatched before I leave, at least that part of it which lies with me.' Even Antonio's quick brain does not seem to have picked up the delicate nuance of menace in the words. His arrest and that of the Princess of Eboli followed at once. The King's urbanity to the couple whose destruction he had planned over weeks, months, had never varied. 'God keep you from the King's too great kindness', the saying went, and it was true that the honeyed words and the marks of royal favour were never more evident than in the moments before the *coup de grâce* was given. So it had been with Egmont in the last letters from Madrid before he was handed over to the executioner. So it had been with Parma, in whom Philip had declared his undying trust while the messenger bearing the news of his disgrace was actually on the road to Brussels. 'He moderates every passion', wrote the Venetian, Contarini, of the King. 'He conceals his thoughts beneath an air of blandness. One never knows whether he is contemplating rewards or punishments.'

How true. Perez had walked blindfold into the trap. Since he had in his possession, though well hidden, certain papers of an extremely compromising nature concerning Philip's part in the murder of Escovedo, he probably thought that they would not *dare* arrest him and risk the scandal that would result. For by nature he was a gambler and still believed he held the winning cards.

The King remained in no kind of hurry. Concerned with the problem of Portugal, he did not unduly concern himself with the two political prisoners whose teeth he thought he had drawn. There was as yet no official charge of murder; the arrests on the face of them had merely been preventative measures to ensure Mateo Vasquez's safety in face of the threats that had been made to do him damage or dispose of him as Escovedo had been disposed of. At first Perez was only kept under house arrest, and in 1580, for a while, he was even allowed to go out and about in the town. Similarly the Princess was removed in 1581 from her fortress prison to her own palace at Pastrana, where she was given a long rope and ample opportunity to ruin herself by intrigue.

Then once more the jaws of the trap snapped shut. The Princess was confined to her room and her windows had bars put on them. Her fate was to be deprived of the guardianship of her children and finally to be cut off from the light of day till she died of her sufferings at the age of fifty-two. The King was not a forgiving man. And in June 1584, with the affairs of Portugal safely settled, he instructed his officials to lay charges for Escovedo's murder against Perez himself. The cat-and-mouse game was entering its second phase. An attempt by the victim to find sanctuary in the church of San Justo next door to his home was frustrated; and clapped in irons, the unfortunate secretary was hustled off to the fortress of Turegano near Segovia, while a special tribunal enquired into his affairs and eventually handed down a sentence of two years' imprisonment, ten years' banishment and suspension of his office as secretary. He was still allowed the company of his wife and children, and only after another unsuccessful attempt to escape was he once more manacled and his small 'court' in exile dispersed.

The remarkable tenderness and tolerance shown to the accused were not of course due to any compassion on Philip's part. Perez received special treatment because he was a very special kind of offender who possessed hidden means of injuring the King and striking back at his accusers. Some of his papers had been seized, but not all of them, and it was therefore necessary to walk warily. In March 1586 Philip carried this policy of *détente* to the point of ordering Perez out of close confinement and back to Madrid, where the secretary remained for well over a year, a most ambiguous inhabitant of the capital. Even the sentence of banishment had thus been revoked and his term of imprisonment was also cut down.

Then once again in the summer of 1587 the screws were tightened and Perez was transferred to the castle of Torrejon de Velasco. His Aragonese cousin Diego Martinez, one of the principals in the Escovedo killing, had been arrested; another, Antonio Enriquez, 'The Guardian Angel', had turned King's Evidence and was telling his gaolers many interesting things. The full weight of Castilian law was at last to be exerted against the man who had instigated a murder now nine years old.

Yet incredibly, in March 1588, Philip seemed to relent and brought Perez back to Madrid. He was still unsure of his ground. The criminal suit, however, continued to be pressed and statements were taken from both Perez and his wife. They amounted to comprehensive denials of murder. Perez was therefore given another turn of the screw, with two months' close captivity, and was then returned to Madrid for further questioning, in what no doubt his gaolers hoped would be a more receptive frame of mind. In August 1589 he was subjected to prolonged cross-examination. Still he persisted in his denials, even when the royal confessor, Father Chaves, arrived to reason with him. Perez may have been fortified in his attitude by his success in buying off the Escovedo family in return for a financial settlement, but he now had the King in person to deal with. In December 1589 Philip instructed the judge he had appointed to the case (Rodrigo Vazquez de Arce,* President of the Finance Council) to advise Perez to disclose the causes which had led him (Philip) to consent to Escovedo's death as an act of State, and on 4th January he followed this up in a remarkable letter to this same Councillor: 'You can tell Antonio Perez from me . . . that he knows very well the knowledge I have of his having Escovedo killed and the causes he said there were for it.' For Philip's conscience now imperatively demanded to know whether the reasons Perez had advanced to justify the killing were sufficient or not. 'So that I order him', the King went on, '. . . to give a particular account of them. And let him explain and tell you the truth about the causes he told me of . . . together with everything that has happened about this affair.'

Was it an olive branch or a trap? Perez seems to have thought the latter, for he simply repeated his denials of being implicated in the murder.

As a response it was singularly inept, and on 23rd February he was put to the rack and the pulleys to wring some truth out of him. All his life he had been a pliant man, born to please, and at this crisis in his fortunes he did not deny his nature or disappoint his torturers. If they would only stop, he remarked after a while, he would tell them whatever they wanted. And he was almost as good as his word. A tale was unfolded of Don John's dangerous ambitions and treasonable dealings with foreign agents and of Escovedo's part in these intrigues as prompter, culminating in the man's sudden and unexpected arrival in Madrid –

---

* Not to be confused with the King's secretary, Mateo Vasquez.

Part of the main altar in the Chapel of the Monastery in Guadalope showing the sacristy which was formerly Philip II's writing desk.
Photograph MAS, Barcelona.

for what purpose? According to what Perez was now saying, he had discussed the matter with the King, and as a result the Marquis of los Velez had been consulted about what to do with this sinister newcomer to the capital, and had suggested poison – a method that was attempted but for some reason failed. Other methods had then been used.

These vague accusations, dancing round the real point at issue and showing no reasonable grounds for Escovedo's execution, were not helpful to Perez. If he had persisted in them, without stating baldly that he held proof of the King's complicity, he would certainly have gone to the scaffold within a matter of weeks, for his agents in the killing, Enriquez and Martinez, were vying with one another to denounce him to his judges. However even in this forlorn plight, Perez could still depend on friends and on his heroic wife, eight months pregnant but devoted heart and soul to his rescue at whatever cost to herself. In Holy Week 1590, just over twelve years after the death of Escovedo, Perez slipped away from his persecutors – in woman's disguise, said the legend. His men had horses waiting. 'It would have been very good to take him, and it has been very bad to let him go free', noted the King in his own hand on hearing of the flight. 'Presumably he will go straight to Aragon.'

He was right. Perez was making for the frontier, carrying with him the fuel for the last great political crisis of the reign.

Aragon was a completely different entity from Castile. Its great cities – Saragossa, Valencia, Barcelona – looked eastward towards the Mediterranean, not westward on to the Atlantic like Seville. Its acceptance of a strong centralized monarchy had always been more grudging than in the sister kingdom; its Cortes were less easily handled and far less generous in grants in aid; and in the person of its *Justicia mayor* (Chief Justice) it had kept a reserve of legal power remarkably free of control from Madrid.

Growing unrest had begun to mark Aragon's partnership with her more populous and dynamic neighbour. It was therefore into a situation and a country ripe for mischief that Perez had projected himself in his headlong flight. He was not at this stage however bent on any revolutionary measures. Almost his first step after reaching sanctuary in the Dominican monastery at Catalayud was to write to Philip asking for forgiveness, and only when it became clear that this plea had failed did he appeal to the protection of the Chief Justice, who lodged him in the Charter gaol in the Aragonese capital of Saragossa. Meanwhile a jury in Madrid was investigating his case, and on 1st July 1590 its President, Judge Rodrigo Vazquez de Arce, signed sentence of death upon him.

It was now evident even to Perez's naturally buoyant nature that half measures would no longer do. Perhaps the relaxed atmosphere of the Charter prison and the sympathy he found everywhere for his cause emboldened him to come off the fence and accuse Philip directly of ordering Escovedo's murder. The new tactics seemed successful for a while. Fearing that the Aragonese would dismiss the accusation against the prisoner, with all the damaging effects to the royal prestige that would result, the King took the extraordinary step of withdrawing personally from the suit, while new charges were substituted of betraying State secrets, tampering with despatches, and escaping custody – charges to which there was clearly no defence, even in Aragonese law.

Perez turned to fresh plans for escape, this time into France, to find shelter with the Huguenot armies of Henry of Navarre. This was a major error on his part, for it involved a taint of irreligion, and the Spanish Inquisition now intervened in the case with charges of heresy.

On 24th May the Holy Office ordered the accused's transfer from the Charter gaol to its own dungeons in the Aljaferia Palace. It was the signal for an outbreak of mob violence in the capital, long simmering with discontent against the régime and the ecclesiastical hierarchy: a small hint of the events at the Bastille nearly two hundred years later. The tocsin was rung and enraged crowds crying out for liberty surged outside the palace of Philip's personal envoy, the Marquis of Almenara. Attempts by Chief Justice de Lanuza to calm the riot only added fuel to the flames; he himself was threatened with death, and the unfortunate Almenara, who had been arrested for his own safety and was being marched off to gaol, was attacked in the streets and sustained injuries from which he died a fortnight later. So threatening had things become that the Viceroy of Aragon, the Count of Chinchon, decided to humour the crowds by ordering Perez's immediate return from the Inquisition's dungeons to the Charter prison, and this was carried out to immense popular acclaim, the rescued hero being drawn through the streets by his enraptured public like a Roman emperor in a Triumph.

'So they have killed the Marquis!' was the King's cool response to this when the news reached him. For once he showed little hesitation: he was probably not sorry that the chance had come of teaching the Aragonese a lesson. But where others less experienced might have blundered into excesses, his strict sense of justice helped him to keep his head. 'My intention', he declared, 'is only to keep their Charter and not allow people to contravene it.' This restraint may also have been partly due to his understanding of some of the difficulties involved, for it was by no means clear whether a Castilian army could legally invade Aragon – a fact which naturally troubled so 'correct' a man.

The problem solved itself because the Aragonese nobles, after receiving a hint or two from the royal secretariat as to the latent dangers of the situation, began to look with disfavour on popular excitement in Saragossa. And these doubts as to the legality and wisdom of what was being done in the name of liberty had also affected the Chief Justice, who had been the first to be moved by Perez's plight and had been his main protector. As separatist talk began to grow among the minor gentry, and the campaign of lampoons and street ballads grew in volume along with talk of Perez's imminent escape, the Chief Justice tightened his precautions in the Charter gaol, transferring his prisoner to a safer room. Hissed in the streets for his pains, he went home to die, to be succeeded as Chief Justice by his son, also named Juan de Lanuza, an inexperienced man incapable of resisting popular pressure and indeed all too ready to invite it by open partisanship for the mob.

In this web of passion and intrigue the Holy Office alone had not relaxed its grip or altered its aim: it had a heretic to judge and reconcile to God. On 24th September plans were laid for Perez's return from the Charter gaol to the Aljaferia Palace. Two thousand troops filled the central square of Saragossa as the Inquisition's local representative claimed the prisoner from the new Chief Justice. Riots at once broke out; groups of armed men came out of the side streets to attack the soldiers, many of whom went over to the mob; the bells of the church of San Pablo were rung; and those nobles who had come to see the show were fortunate to escape with their lives. Perez was unshackled, released, and once more carried out of a prison in triumph.

But this time his will was broken. The Camille Desmoulins of a premature revolution, he was not of the metal to be its Danton or St. Just. All he had really wanted was to return to his desk in Madrid. Horses had been provided for him and with them he escaped from Saragossa, only to wander fecklessly back in the disguise of a muleteer. As the Castilian troops closed in on the rebellious city in November he fled abroad, never to return to Spain. A forlorn wanderer, now in Paris, now in London, he published in 1594 his *Relaciones*, which accused Philip of many crimes but still left the door partly open for the reconciliation of which he dreamed. Charming, able, industrious, a brilliant intriguer in the shadows, he had never had the moral weight to match himself against an opponent just as elusive but far more powerful.

The King survived the crisis with aplomb. He had Juan de Lanuza hanged for his part in the resistance to the royal troops, and a few other examples were made, but by and large he remembered the oaths he had taken to respect the laws and customs of his difficult kingdom beyond the Ebro and never pressed things too far. By a pleasant irony the insurrection even turned to his advantage, for when he assembled the Cortes at Tarragona to pronounce a general pardon, his grateful subjects voted him 600,000 ducats payable over three years, the largest grant Aragon had ever made him.

Chapter 18

The Last Years

Under his many burdens the King had begun to age rapidly, and what small appetite for wordly display he had shown in the days of his marriage to Elizabeth of Valois had long since vanished. 'He has no other pleasures, no other contentments, than to live with his monks in his house of San Lorenzo,' wrote Father Sepulveda, who saw him wandering its corridors dressed in black like a doctor of law.

This growing withdrawal from the world, almost amounting to an aversion from it, emerges clearly from the reports of the Venetian ambassadors accredited to Madrid during the last years of Philip's life. 'He loves solitude and deserted places,' noted Thomas Contarini, who retired from office in 1593. This taste for asceticism could be seen even in the furnishings of the royal apartments, whose walls were kept bare in summer and only hung with tapestries in winter as some protection against the cold. Contarini observed that the royal audiences which had been such a regular and popular feature of the reign had been severely cut down and that the King now rarely showed himself in public.

The picture of the ageing widower and recluse has a certain poignancy. The King took no pleasure in any distractions, reported Francisco Vendramino, Contarini's successor at the Spanish court, echoing Sepulveda's words. As a Venetian – a wordly race – he rather overlooked the consolations of religion and the joys of artistic patronage that existed for Philip at the Escorial and gave to his life that serenity to which the ambassador himself paid tribute. 'Such is the justness, the calm and constancy of his spirit', Vendramino wrote, 'that he never shows himself affected by the misfortunes and adversities that have befallen him. He is of remarkable gravity and listens to people attentively, even to those who bother him with trifles. He prides himself on an excellent memory. . . . He keeps his word. . . . Of the two virtues that princes should possess, that of justice distinguishes him particularly; liberality is not in his nature. . . . This parsimony causes people to say that no one in Spain uses a hundred ducats better than the King. . . . He bears up under injuries, but he does not forget them. He writes night and day, and people say that what his father won by the sword, he preserves with the pen.'

Portrait of Philip III, by Velazquez.
Courtesy the Prado, Madrid.

The truth of this portrait is proved by the delicious malice that so evidently inspires it. Clearly Vendramino did not approve of parsimonious kings or crowned bureaucrats, and one even senses between the lines the memory of some personal rebuff on the financial front suffered by the devoted ambassador. But the respect is equally evident. No tyrant or senile miser could have evoked such a tribute – not from a Venetian. The King's virtues of courage, constancy and love of justice shine out from Vendramino's words. Here was a man who had suffered greatly but had kept his inner composure and faith.

This was fortunate because the family circle around the King had contracted like much else of his life since the death of Anne of Austria. Of his children by her, only one survived: the future Philip III, an amiable youth, even less robust than the father he tried his best to imitate. Vendramino judged the Prince to be of 'peaceable disposition' and possessing 'generous sentiments'. A lukewarm judgment, and it is clear that for all the affection he felt for his son, Philip for his part remained deeply troubled by the boy's lack of vital force and will.

Far happier was the King's relationship with his two daughters by Elizabeth of Valois. The invaluable Vendramino supplies us with another of his pen portraits of the elder Infanta, Isabella Clara Eugenia, a girl, he noted tartly, 'of rare beauty but getting on in years'. 'On her birthdays', the ambassador went on, 'she has taken to saying that it would be better to conceal them than to celebrate them. A very virtuous lady, she lives as retired from the world as a nun. Her father loves her very much and often discusses important affairs with her.'

Portraits of Isabella are in the Prado gallery in Madrid, and we can judge for ourselves the accuracy of this verdict by a man of the world on a young woman whom he obviously saw as a victim of Philip's dynastic ambitions and perhaps doomed for ever to remain a spinster. The resemblance to her beautiful French mother is very striking, but there is more pride in the face, and the arrogant marmoreal calm expected of a Spanish Infanta.

Her sister Catalina was an altogether livelier person. Being only a cadet, she was not kept endlessly waiting for some grand alliance that would win her a throne, but was married off to a mere duke, the ruler of Spain's satellite, Savoy, in a love match that produced a battery of children. From an observer in Turin

In 1587 Philip commissioned Nicole Granello, Lazzaro Tavarene and Fabrizio Castello to decorate the sixty-yard-long wall of one of the galleries of the Escorial. The scene depicted here is the Battle of Higueruela where John II defeated the Moors in 1431.
Photograph MAS, Barcelona.

we have an agreeable glimpse of her in the early days of the marriage – a rather plain girl but full of fire, with a high colour and great natural dignity, lording it lovingly over her husband and his small dukedom with all the magnificence of a Queen of Spain. Her early death in November 1597, just after her thirtieth birthday, was yet another in Philip's long sequence of bereavements. Like her elder sister, she had been very dear to him – people had noted the affecting nature of the parting between them when, after the marriage at Saragossa, Philip had travelled on to Barcelona to see the bride off on her way to Italy.

Beyond the family, the King's circle of intimates had also narrowed sharply with Perez's disgrace and the deaths of Granvelle and Alva following upon that of Eboli. The King still had many able servants, of whom the Count of Fuentes was an outstanding one, but the general level of his administration at the end of the reign was noticeably less dynamic and self-reliant than it had been at its beginning. Where Alva and Don John had argued and initiated policies, Philip's later servants merely waited and obeyed. Thomas Contarini, writing in the 'nineties, singled out the two most important men at court: Juan Idiaquez, a Biscayan, and Cristobal de Moura, a Portuguese. 'They agree in never proposing anything of consequence if they can help it,' noted the ambassador; and added with delicate malice, 'They get on well together.' No doubt they did. A drab uniformity had become the mode. In the Arts of course it was a different matter, for the great era of Spanish classical culture was about to begin – had indeed begun, with Cervantes and Lope de Vega alive and active, El Greco at work on his altar-pieces, and the Escorial built. But in the sphere of the political and military struggle in Europe the tide of Spanish greatness was on the turn – an ebb tide.

In the Netherlands the ebb had begun well before Parma's death with the transfer of the main Spanish military effort from the provinces to France, and it continued to accelerate as more and more Spanish troops were drawn away in pursuit of the dream of a throne in Paris for the Infanta and as the rebel Calvinist states which had allied themselves in the Union of Utrecht tightened their unity and found a military leader in Prince Maurice of Nassau, William of Orange's second son, who was to carry Parma's mastery of siege warfare to even greater geometrical perfection.

The response from the Escorial to this dangerous challenge was sluggish. The King never wholly lost interest in the Netherlands; indeed in the end he was to hand over its loyal provinces to his favourite child; but from the moment of Henry III's assassination and the opening of other opportunities in France he no longer gave it priority in his thinking. During Parma's invasions of France a very ancient warrior, Count Peter Mansfeldt, who had been one of the Duchess Margaret's senior advisers and whom both Parma and Fuentes judged to be senile, had been left to defend the provinces from mounting enemy attacks from the north. One of his chief aides in this task was an even older veteran and survivor of Alva's wars, the nonagenarian Colonel Mondragon; and superbly did this incredible old man acquit himself against an opponent in Prince Maurice a quarter of his age. But neither of these relics from the past were given the money or the troops to do more than mount the most limited counter-offensive. 'So many officers and so few men!' lamented Mansfeldt of the once formidable army that Alva and Parma had commanded. And the royal navy in the provinces was in much the same case: it had a fine establishment of admirals and vice-admirals but hardly a ship fit to put to sea – the complaint is there in the correspondence.

The neglect of his armed forces in the Netherlands was partly due to lack of money and partly to the fact that Philip had once more turned to his old policy of trying, under Imperial mediation, to get some kind of compromise settlement with the rebels on almost any terms so long as they included a token acknowledgement of his sovereignty and guaranteed freedom of worship for the northern Catholics. Yet even these modest aims were unobtainable, because the secessionist provinces were doing commercially too well out of the war and were aware of the crippling financial burden that the struggle was imposing on Spain – the King was fortunately not to know that with one comparatively short interval the war in the Low Countries had still another half century to run.

With a policy of *détente* in view, Philip's appointment to the governor-generalship in Brussels of his Austrian nephew, the Archduke Ernest, can be seen as a tactful gesture towards the mediator, the Emperor Rudolf, and to the Netherlands people. No one could have accused the Archduke of being another Alva – he was a stately valetudinarian who in the words of one Spanish observer 'lived like an angel' but was otherwise somewhat unfitted to his task by reason of bad health and total incapacity for war or affairs. Yet another Spanish complaint was that where Parma had relied on Italians, Ernest surrounded himself with hordes of Germans. A good man for the governorship of a minor province. Yet obsessed with his ambitions in Paris, the King spent all his energies urging this fat and indolent nominee of his to act as though he were another Parma. 'Although what has happened in France has brought things to this present pass', he wrote, 'it is not the less necessary . . . to intervene there. On the contrary, we must busy ourselves all the more, since the danger to religion which has always been my chief care has increased. . . .' He was determined, he wrote, not to abandon the defence of the faith, trusting in God, whose cause it was. He did not mention his ambitions to seize a throne. So to France Ernest must go.

Fortunately perhaps for everyone the Archduke barely survived a year in office before death removed him. Affairs had run gravely downhill under his stewardship. Yet during all this time since Parma's death, there had been on the spot and available in Brussels a relative of Alva's of exactly the same stamp of fierce and energetic resolution: the Count of Fuentes, whose great talents in war were never to be used against the northern rebels and whose efforts were to be devoted towards placing the Infanta on the throne of France, a political and military dead-end which the realist in Philip should have recognized. 'Without an obvious miracle, there is no hope whatever of obtaining what is wanted', Parma had warned him of these high-flown schemes, but this advice, like much else that Parma said in his later years, had been disregarded. Perhaps it was the failure of his Armada against England that made Philip so stubborn and deaf to reason; perhaps he too ardently went on demanding 'some consolation' for that shattering defeat.

His failure to understand other people's customs and prejudices is comically displayed in instructions he drafted for the spokesmen who were to put his case to the French States General which Mayenne had assembled in Paris to decide on the succession. The glib, humourless assumptions and the mental blindness speak for themselves:

> The right to the French crown, since the last king, Henry, died without issue, belongs without any doubt to the Infanta, the lady Isabella, in the right of her mother Queen Elizabeth, eldest sister of the said Henry. . . .

This was at the very best debatable. 'The said Henry', Henry III, had been a third son. A daughter of Henry II – Marguerite of Valois – was still alive.

> To the objections which could be raised to this, on the ground that the Salic Law excludes women from the succession to the throne, it is easy to reply, as the French themselves admit, the matter of the Salic Law was sheer imagination and violence without foundation or reason.

(The French had admitted nothing of the sort.)

> Since it is thus that the crown of France belongs to the Infanta by right of blood, we must bend every effort to make the States General declare her *reine propiétaire* of France. If this truth is hard for them to swallow and they prefer . . . to proceed by election, they are obliged . . . at least to give her by election that which is due to her by succession, that is, to name her their Queen.
>
> If it should become clear that the French are intent on remaining in their present miserable state instead of recognizing the Infanta as their Queen, as they ought, we will not oppose their election of a King, provided their choice is entirely acceptable to His Majesty: . . .
>
> If this point is reached, the best course for them would be to leave the choice entirely to His Majesty. . . .

Who would imagine from this fatuous self-complacency that Philip was really a suppliant for favours whose interest depended on keeping French Catholic opinion sweet, in default of which the whole French nation might well swing away to support the real heir presumptive, Navarre? However not many of Philip's state papers were ever wholly absurd, and in later paragraphs of this *aide-mémoire* the King did go on to consider the possibility that in spite of all good sense the French might still insist on making their own choice of the person to rule them, in which case he was prepared to accept the candidature of one of his Austrian nephews or even of the young Duke of Guise. If he and his representatives had had the sense to propose Guise from the start as a husband for the Infanta, he might have managed to block Navarre's ambitions and consign him for ever to the shadows – a formidable thought for Europe and indeed for the world, for in that event there would have been no Louis XIV, no Louis XV, no Louis XVI, and conceivably no revolution of 1789.

However the approach of the Spanish plenipotentiaries to the States General when it met in 1593 was truculent, self-pitying and inept. Philip had set the tone himself in a letter to the delegates: 'There is good reason why you should recognize your own welfare in this matter and acknowledge all that I deserve from your kingdom by giving me satisfaction. . . .' There was a constant and most tactless harping on the services which he had rendered to France – and this from the ancestral enemy and victor of St. Quentin! Even when the moment came when the Spanish delegates were asked whether Philip would be prepared to give his daughter in marriage to a French prince, the chance was not snapped up, and only when it was too late was Guise's name mentioned as Philip's choice for this honour. It was tempting providence to act in this way when faced by an opponent as astute as Navarre, who saw how war-weariness and national pride were combining to lead Catholic opinion towards thoughts of compromise, an end to civil war and the ejection of foreigners from the country. He himself had problems – he was only the leader of a minority, and being a sensible hedonist as well as a man who loved his country, he did not want to spend a lifetime marching Huguenot armies all over France through blood and desolation – not if there was a better way.

In the spring of 1593, suddenly inspired, he expressed his willingness to be instructed in the Catholic religion. In July, strengthened by a declaration of the *parlement* of Paris condemning foreign interference, he abjured Calvinism. It was the master stroke. On 27th February 1594 he was crowned Henry IV at Chartres and on 22nd March he and his advance guard entered Paris without having to strike a blow. A man of infinite humour, he courteously saluted the Spanish contingent as it marched sullenly out of the Porte Saint Denis: 'Commend me to your master, but don't come back.' Eighteen months later he was received into obedience to Rome, his many cheerful sins absolved by the papal blessing, and on his formal declaration of hostilities against his neighbour beyond the Pyrenees, the Most Christian and Most Catholic kings were once more at war.

Opposite: A large part of the buildings of the Escorial are devoted to the monastery and seminary of the Order of St Jerome. The Court of the Evangelists illustrated here is at the heart of this section facing one wing of the church. Walkways are provided on the first and second floors for monastic meditations. Photograph Scala, Florence.

Stalemate in the Netherlands . . . diplomatic defeat in France. On the third front, against England, Philip was to fare even worse.

In 1589 Drake had entered the Tagus and burnt part of Lisbon, a tit-for-tat for the Armada of the previous year. English efforts to press the issue of war had then languished for a while, but in the summer of 1596 an Anglo-Dutch fleet commanded by the Lord Admiral, Howard of Effingham, surprised the still almost open harbour of Cadiz and put ashore a landing force under the Queen's new favourite, the Earl of Essex, which stormed the town and held it for a fortnight. As if this painful humiliation were not enough, the *Flota*, one of the two annual treasure fleets which should have been on its way back to the Indies, happened to be in harbour and was destroyed by the invaders, who could hardly have hoped for such a windfall.

'War with the world but peace with England' had been the Duke of Alva's prescription for a foreign policy. It was not that of the Spanish people or their King. National honour had been involved in the defeats sustained in the Caribbean, in Drake's raids on the homeland in '87 and '89 and the disastrous Armada battles. Essex's sack of Cádiz was the last straw, threatening as it did the livelihood of all those who lived by the Indies trade and indeed the whole economy of Spain. The King prayed that he might be spared long enough to avenge the insult; and he was speaking not only for the Church and the nobility but also for the vast majority of his subjects, cradled in the belief of Spanish invincibility and now faced with defeats as puzzling as Montezuma's Aztecs had experienced in the days of the Conquistadores.

The popular response in men and money was heroic. An Armada more powerful than its famous predecessor of '88 was fitted out in a hurry and launched in the late summer of 1596, with Ireland as its target – only to be blown away by gales off Finisterre. In 1597 a third fleet suffered a similar fate. The legend of 'the Protestant Wind' enshrined a century later in the English ditty *Lilliburlero* had a long ancestry behind it.

But Cadiz had not only been a blow at morale; it was also a symptom of a perhaps incurable disease, and as such had a profound effect on those who watched by the bedside of the failing Spanish economy.

Theoretically that economy should have been the marvel of Europe – as indeed it was, except to its bankers. After so many centuries of change in the value of money, actual figures can only be misleading, but Spain's resources and revenues were certainly much greater than those of any other European state of the time. Its King could draw on contributions from his Cortes of Castile and Aragon; from the immensely wealthy Spanish Church which made him a variety of grants; from the Italian dependencies and the Netherlands, the wealthiest provinces in Europe; and finally from the proceeds of the Mexican and Peruvian mines.

Yet at the moment of Philip's accession, his father's expenditure on his everlasting wars in Africa, Italy and Germany had run up a load of debts amounting to twice his income, plus a liability for state bonds (*juros*) two and a half times as large. This had led to the first Suspension of Payments in 1557, with the creation of a floating debt at interest of five per cent. As the reign wore on, the contributions from the empire began to fall away. Naples, Sicily and

Opposite: Titian's The Crucifixion *which hangs in the Sacristy at the Escorial.*
Courtesy of the Escorial. Photograph Scala, Florence.

Milan began to demand injections of cash instead of providing it. The crown of Aragon produced virtually nothing. The rebellion in the Netherlands turned these productive provinces into a drain down which went millions of ducats. By 1575 the Crown's debts to its bankers had doubled and amounted to nearly five times the revenue from all sources, while the war in the Low Countries was in itself costing annually nearly twice the Crown's *quinto* or fifth of the proceeds of the American mines. In contrast with falling revenues elsewhere the receipts from these mines continued to grow and had quadrupled in value by the 'nineties. Yet even here, paradoxically, the results were dire, for this release of a flood of gold and silver on to a primitive market had led to a skyrocketing rise in the prices of food and raw materials.

No one understood then the symptoms of an inflation, the only remedy for which would have been to curtail the supply of money. The Spanish economy had many built-in disadvantages which made it particularly vulnerable. Its potentially most productive units were the ones to be taxed: tax immunity had been bought by the upper echelons of society. The Church continued to support the Crown with grants, but an army of monks in their cloisters, grandees on their estates and the urban unemployed were hardly dynamic in any mercantile sense – the *bandoleros*, the smugglers of the sierra, were altogether more helpful in adding to the mobility of trade. Too many vested interests continued to shackle the country to outdated modes and to an outlook that was in painful contrast to the commercial drive of the English and the rebellious Netherlanders of the 'United Provinces'. The royal government and the Cortes were equally helpless in face of the problems of the times. All their remedies recoiled on them. Attempts to peg the prices of necessities only led producers to turn to the luxury trades, checked by sumptuary laws which led to a depression and a shortage of goods at home. In this topsy-turvy world in which, as one critic was to write, Spain seemed to be living 'out of the natural order of things', it was no wonder that further remedies seemed to lie in a ban on exports and the encouragement of imports, or that the specie from the Indies should have landed up, not in the hands of producers in Spain, but of money-lenders in Germany and Genoa. Meanwhile, under the constant drain of war, expenditure continued to rise till in a moment of despair the King himself declared his situation to be 'beyond remedy'.

After the Cadiz raid in 1596 even the foreign bankers who had been buoyed up through so many storms on their inflatable interest rates began to doubt whether the Spanish economy could be kept afloat much longer; and in consequence Philip found himself faced for the third time with a financial crisis.

Many of the causes lay in his maladministration and in the over-strain he had imposed on his country. But that was not how he himself saw it. In a state paper of November 1596 explaining and justifying another Suspension of Payments he put much of it down to the calls made on him as Catholicism's standard-bearer against heresy, and the rest to the stranglehold the bankers and merchants had acquired 'by grievous charges, discounts and interests' over the royal revenue, coupled with the 'unhallowed practices with bills of exchange' indulged in by those who had abandoned good husbandry and agriculture for 'gain and profit to the disservice of God and the kingdom'. It was the *cri de coeur* of a man hopelessly out of touch with events:

> And now the said merchants who hitherto have given on bills of exchange such moneys as were necessary to provide for the protection of our royal state and to carry on the war which we are waging for these righteous and special reasons, refuse to do this any longer and make difficulties in further dealings with us, seeing that they have in their own hands and power all the royal revenues by means of the said pledges, certificates and transfers.

The King's remedy for this situation was of sublime simplicity – since he could not pay his debts, he would (for the time being at least) renounce them by 'liberating' all charges on his exchequer.

> Accordingly we suspend and declare suspended all such assignments made by us in any manner whatsoever since September 1st 1575 and December 1st 1577 unto this date, to the said merchants and traders, whether of taxes, gifts, domains, rents, or any other property or revenues whatsoever, on account of such bills of exchange or other advances. And we order the moneys coming from such pledged property to be henceforth paid into our royal treasury, for the support of our own necessities, declaring from this day forth all payments otherwise made to be null and void.

The Spanish armies around the world and the bureaucracy were still responsive to the impulses and directions of the royal will: the foreign bankers and the hard-pressed economy of Spain were not. This attempt to default, when added to the physical and moral damage the English had inflicted at Cadiz, dried up the last trickle of credit. For two years no convoys sailed from Spanish ports to the Indies, and internal trade in the peninsula came almost to a standstill. It was no use threatening those who held the mouth of the sack into which the nation's wealth had been escaping for forty years. Their grip could not be wished away; and to his credit the King had at least the saving grace of being able to recognize some of the realities in the end.

The financial *diktat* he had attempted to impose was therefore soon withdrawn. And in the last two years of his life he turned back to the source of the mischief and set about winding up his commitments in the Netherlands and France.

Of these, the French problem was the easier, because under the energetic direction of Fuentes the Spanish armies in Picardy had captured a number of towns, including Calais, and Amiens, only eighty miles from Paris. Amiens was soon lost again, but the new king of France had been given another proof of the fighting power of the *tercios* and was in the mood to compromise.

By the Peace of Vervins in 1598 the two antagonists gave themselves a breathing space on much the same terms that had been agreed at Câteau-Cambrésis nearly forty years earlier. Philip had gained nothing territorially, but neither had he lost anything, and the fervent Catholic in him could take comfort from the fact that by his unflinching support of the old religion he had at least prevented a Huguenot triumph in France and had helped to make a

Papist of his free-thinking brother monarch. There could still be no peace with England. And in the Netherlands the collapse of the negotiations with the rebels under the mediation of Vienna and a victory by Prince Maurice over a Spanish force at Turnhout made any general settlement impossible. Yet something might perhaps be done, politically if not militarily. At this point Philip's own paternal feelings came also into the reckoning. If the Infanta Isabella had been cheated of a crown in Paris, she could at least be given a substitute one in Brussels, along with a husband in the person of the Cardinal Archduke Albert, the most useful and biddable of her Austrian cousins, who had proved his worth as Viceroy of Portugal.

Right at the end of his life therefore Philip reverted to that plan of separating the Netherlands politically from Spain which his father the Emperor had formed at the time of the English marriage to Mary Tudor. It had several obvious advantages: it provided for the Infanta; it ensured a measure of Austrian support; and it appealed to that loyalty the Netherlanders had traditionally given to women rulers of the Spanish royal house. Some reservations were attached to the settlement. Certain key bases were retained. The provinces were not given freedom to trade with the Indies. If there were no issue of the marriage, the link with Spain would be restored. But even though the northern rebels totally ignored this change of sovereignty which supposedly included them, it was at least a kind of solution.

For well over thirty years the Escorial had been the King's one hobby and his ruling passion. In Portugal, beset by problems of administering a new empire, he had worried about the design of its choir stalls, and on his way back to Spain in the summer of 1583 he had hurried there to inspect the progress of the works.

The frontispiece of Philip's family papers.
University Library, Valladolid. Photograph MAS, Barcelona.

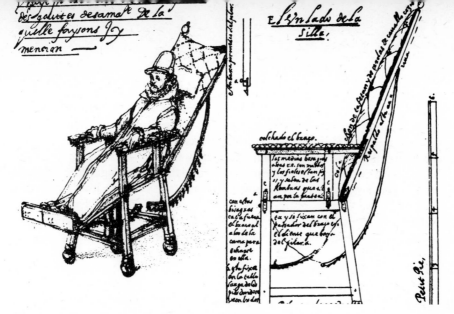

The designs for a gout-sufferer's chair made for Philip.
Biblioteca Nacional, Madrid. Photograph MAS, Barcelona.

During the next few years fifty altars were erected, and once the bodies of his ancestors and family had been moved from temporary storage into the funeral vaults and the internal decor reached completion, the basilica was dedicated amid a blaze of illuminations.

By then the King had only three years to live. In Anne of Austria's time he had made a practice of attending the great ceremonies of the Christian year, the Nativity, Easter, Pentecost and *Corpus Christi*, walking through the cloisters in procession with his monks. On Easter Sundays he would dine with them; and on St. Luke's Day the candles were lit at every altar and the King would kneel in supplication, dressed in a gown as sombre as the habits around him. Perhaps he had never seen his own role at San Lorenzo as being more than that of a worshipper or a penitent at a shrine, and as time went on his presence there shrank to the occupancy of what was little more than a cell with whitewashed walls, a plain ceiling and a tiled floor, furnished with a bookcase and a bureau, two marble-topped tables, a small library of religious texts, some sacred images, an altar, a crucifix, and a bed in an alcove – a humble camp-follower of God.

The King was sometimes in Madrid. But during the last years it was largely from that small and uncomfortable room that the Spanish empire was administered. As he grew older, he attempted more and more to oversee everything, to provide for everything – endlessly reading, dictating, annotating, a slave to his own method. Under the strain of it even that astonishing physique and endurance had begun to fail. His eyesight was bad; he suffered from gout, arthritis, and a serious blood infection. A year and a half before his death running sores appeared on his hands and feet. They healed slowly. His taste for the ceremonies of the Church remained insatiable, and in the spring of 1598 he had himself carried from his sick-bed to a window in the palace at Madrid to watch the arrival of several huge packing-cases of sacred relics collected from all over Europe which were passing through the city on their way to the Escorial.

When summer came he himself followed, impatient of the advice of those who begged him not to make the journey. He wished, he said, to lay his bones in his own house. Borne in a litter by a roundabout route that took six days, he reached San Lorenzo apparently refreshed and strong enough to take part in a procession and hear a *Te Deum* sung. And for the last time he went the round of the treasures he had collected over so many years – the collections of wild life and flowers, the war trophies taken at St. Quentin and Lepanto, the altars and crucifixes, the visions of Hieronymus Bosch, and the Titians dating back to the days of the Emperor and his own triumphant accession. The excitement brought on a fever, and late in July the long agony of his death struggle began.

It was to last for fifty-three days. Symptoms of dropsy had appeared. A tumour on the thigh was lanced, and to the horror of the surgeons sprouted boils on either side of it which rapidly spread to the whole body. He could not bear to be touched; his bandages and linen could not be changed; a man of delicate refinement, he had to endure the onset of physical corruption in its way as terrible as anything he had imposed on his victims in the fire. His whole body was visibly rotting, till the moment came, in Sepulveda's words, when nothing was left of him but his eyes and tongue and spirit.

Throughout his ordeal he remained rational and serene. He showed no sign of fear; regarding death as merely a journey longer than others – indeed he was making the last of the 'Great Journeys of Don Philip' at which his eldest son had scoffed. When his confessor told him he was dying he greeted the news with joy. But there was still work to be done: charitable bequests to be made, his own funeral arrangements to be settled.

The lead coffin in which he was to lie was brought to his room. The outer wooden shell was to be made from the timbers of a ship, 'The Seven Wounds', which had fought against the Turk – a symbolic but strange lodging for a man who had so seldom ventured to sea. In these final days his thoughts were concerned with his own redemption through the offices of the Church, but also with the future of the empire he was leaving to his children, the Prince and the Infanta. The recipient himself in his early days of so much advice, he was free with his own now, as he begged these pale successors to love one another, to govern justly and to defend the Catholic faith. 'Alas, Don Cristobal, I fear that they will rule him,' he murmured to de Moura of his son, for he had not even the consolation of knowing that his kingdom would be in strong hands when he was gone.

He was given Extreme Unction; he confessed and took communion; but still he lingered – his tenacious will and spirit survived the virtual destruction of the living body that housed them. On 11th September the Prince and the Infanta were brought to the bedside for the last time and he commended them to one another, begging the Prince to have 'a great care and regard' for Isabella, 'because she was my looking-glass and the light of my eyes'. Two days later, in the early hours of the morning of 13th September, he died. Almost the last thing he must have seen was the crucifix which had been held up for his father's dying gaze forty years earlier at Yuste and which he had carefully kept at the Escorial for the occasion.

> The King is dead [reported the Venetian ambassador, Francesco Soranza, later that day]. His Majesty expired at the Escorial this morning at day-

A silver reliquary made in Barcelona in the third quarter of the 16th century.
Crown copyright, the Victoria and Albert Museum, London.

break, after having received all the sacraments of the church with every sign of devoutness, piety, and religion.

Although change is usually popular, yet nobles and people, rich and poor, universally show great grief.

His Majesty lived seventy-one years, three months, and twenty-four days; he reigned forty-two years, ten months and sixteen days. He was a Prince who fought with gold rather than with steel, by his brain rather than by his arms. He has acquired more by sitting still, by negotiation, by diplomacy, then his father did by armies and by war. He was one of the richest Princes the world has ever seen, yet he has left the revenues of the kingdom and of the crown burdened with about a million of debts. . . . Profoundly religious, he loved peace and quiet. He displayed great calmness, and professed himself unmoved in good or bad fortune alike. . . .

On great occasions, in the conduct of wars, in feeding the civil war in France, in the magnificence of his buildings, he never counted the cost; he was no close reckoner but lavished his gold without a thought; but in small matters, in the government of his household, in his presents and rewards, he was more parsimonious than became his station. . . . He held his desires in absolute control and showed an immutable and unalterable temper. He has feigned injuries and feigned not to feel injuries, but he never lost the opportunity to avenge them. He hated vanity, and therefore never allowed his life to be written. No one ever saw him in a rage, being always patient, phlegmatic, temperate, melancholy. In short, he has left a glorious memory of his royal name, which may serve as an example, not only unto his posterity and his successors, but to strangers as well.

It was an obituary of which the dead man would have approved. Roman *gravitas* had always been his style. Tribute had been paid to the earnestness of his faith. He would probably not have been too put out by accusations of extravagance or parsimony, for he knew he had always acted in the interests of his country. But in the light of history, how true a portrait was it of the living man?

On the whole Soranza clearly intended it as an admiring tribute. One can still sense in it the awesome weight of Philip's patient and persevering nature which so impressed contemporaries, including those who were his enemies or who had suffered at his hands. Egmont had prayed for him on his way to the scaffold; Alva had accepted disgrace without a murmur; and even Elizabeth of England kept a portrait of her one-time suitor in her boudoir.

The other side of the coin is the slow-burning implacable fire of the King's resentment of those who crossed him. Not naturally cruel, he was capable of monstrous cruelties in defence of what he conceived to be God's kingdom on earth and the salvation of souls. The murders of Montigny and Escovedo and the commission to Alva to root out heresy in the Netherlands in blood were crimes by any standard, but that Philip felt they were justified is shown by his claim on his death-bed that he had never consciously done an injustice to anyone. It was not casuistry. He believed it with every fibre of his being.

Even his apologists have found it hard to square the circle and account for the strange mixture of kindliness and vengefulness in his nature. Perhaps narrowness of vision is the key – his outstanding trait and hallmark. Brought up in a mental straightjacket, he had none of his rival Navarre's natural scepticism of mind. He was a zealot for a cause, always more Papist than the Pope, but Catholic in a specially Castilian sense that was bound up with the glory of his family and his country. Dealing with world problems, he remained provincial. Even Aragon was foreign territory to him. It was very reluctantly that he went on his travels. And as he grew older his life narrowed still further till it became centred in those small bleak apartments in San Lorenzo.

The marvel is that with such handicaps he did as well as he did. For he was a man of limited accomplishments. His vast correspondence on almost every topic under the sun generates hardly a fraction of the fire and originality which Queen Elizabeth throws into ten minutes berating of an ambassador. One can search his letters in vain for a spark of humour. Gifted with servants of genius, he misused them. Endowed with the wealth of the Indies, he spent it unproductively. Under his rule hardly a thing was done to improve the roads or navigable rivers of Spain. Rural depopulation left the countryside poorer at his death than at his birth. The great outburst of creativeness in the Arts which was to mark the next two reigns owes very little to his patronage. A faithful son of the Church, he was hostile to its most potent force, the Jesuits.

A pedestrian mind. But his spirit was not pedestrian. He met terrible adversities without flinching. He never despaired, except perhaps momentarily over the state of the finances. Faced with political, social and military problems as great as if not greater than those that had broken his father, he never abdicated even in thought. If he cost Spain the seven northern provinces of the Netherlands, he won her Portugal and a vast new empire in Brazil and the East. Under his rule the prestige of the Spanish people reached heights never to be repeated. A fallible human, he had to wear the cloak of infallibility – a secular Pope. And at the end, when all the trappings of grandeur were stripped down to the grim realities of a sick-bed in which he was drowning in his own excreta, he showed the spirit of a brave and steadfast man.

References

The following are the main sources given in the list of references. Where an abbreviation is used later, it is given here in square brackets.

BERTRAND, L. *Philippe II à l'Escorial*. Paris, 1929.

BRANDI, K. *The Emperor Charles V.* (trans. C. V. Wedgewood). London, 1939.

Calendar of State Papers (Spanish). HMSO, London. [CSP (Spanish)]

DHANYS, M. *Les quatre femmes de Philippe II*. Paris, 1933.

FLANAGAN, L. N. W. *The Wreck of the Girona*. (Pamphlet, reprinted from 'Ireland of the Welcomes', Jan./Feb. 1973.)

FREER, M. W. *Elizabeth of Valois*. London, 1857.

GACHARD, L. P.
  (ed.) *Correspondance de Philippe II sur les affaires des Pays Bas* (first part). Brussels, 1848-79. [CPB]
  (ed.) *Relations des ambassadeurs vénitiens*. Brussels, 1855. [RAV]
  Don Carlos et Philippe II. Brussels, 1867.
  (ed.) *Lettres de Philippe II à ses filles les Infantes Isabelle et Catherine écrites pendant son voyage en Portugal*. Paris, 1884. [Letters to Infantas]

LEFÈVRE, J. (ed.) *Correspondance de Philippe II sur les affaires des Pays Bas* (second part). Brussels, 1940 [CPB]

MARAÑON, G. *Antonio Perez* (trans. C. D. Ley). London, 1954. (With acknowledgement for quotation to the publishers, Hollis and Carter Limited.)

MARIÉJOL, J. H. *Master of the Armada*. London, 1933. (With acknowledgement for quotation to the publishers, Hamish Hamilton Limited.)

MATTINGLY, G. *The Defeat of the Spanish Armada*. London, 1959. (With acknowledgement for quotation to the Executors of the Garrett Mattingly Estate, and the publishers, Jonathan Cape Limited and the Houghton Mifflin Company.)

MAXWELL, Sir W. Stirling. *Don John of Austria*. London, 1883.

MOTLEY, J. L.
  History of the United Netherlands.
  Rise of the Dutch Republic.

PRESCOTT, W. H. *History of the Reign of Philip II*. London, 1855.

List of References

page	line	
20	35	see Brandi, p. 485.
21	2	see Prescott, vol. 1 p. 15.
23	33	see Brandi, p. 383.
31	36	RAV (Suriano), p. 123.
35	3	CSP (Spanish), 2 April 1553.
35	43	CSP (Spanish), 29 July 1553.
37	12	CSP (Spanish), 22 August 1553.
37	27	CSP (Spanish), 20 September 1553.
37	33	CSP (Spanish), 20 September 1553.
38	3	CSP (Spanish), 20 October 1553.
38	11	CSP (Spanish), 15 October 1553.
42	14	CSP (Spanish), 1 April 1554.
42	21	CSP (Spanish), 6 January 1554.
42	34	CSP (Spanish), 9 April 1554.
42	42	CSP (Spanish), notes by Simon Renard, June 1554.
45	10	CSP (Spanish), 26 July 1554.
45	21	CSP (Spanish), 17 August 1554.
45	23	CSP (Spanish), 12 August 1554.
46	36	CSP (Spanish), 17 August 1554.
46	46	CSP (Spanish), November 1554.
48	12	CSP (Spanish), 12 March 1555.
49	6	CSP (Spanish), 8 June 1555.
49	31	CSP (Spanish), 1 August 1555.
53	20	RAV (Badovaro), p. 36.
54	4	RAV (Suriano), p. 125.
54	47	CSP (Spanish), 6 April 1556.
55	8	CSP (Spanish), May 1556.
55	14	CSP (Spanish), 15 July 1556.
64	19	CSP (Spanish), 21 November 1558.
66	9	CSP (Spanish), 14 December 1558.
68	3	CSP (Spanish), 11 April 1559.
72	45	see Motley, *Rise of the Dutch Republic*, vol. 1 p. 202.
78	26	see Cabrera, vol. 5 p. 326.
80	24	see Brantôme, vol. 5 p 131.
82	38	RAV (Suriano), p. 130.
84	13	RAV (Tiepolo), p. 154.
87	31	CPB, i, 230.

page	line		page	line	
89	44	see Motley, *Rise of the Dutch Republic*, vol. 1 p. 455.	164	13	Letters to Infantas, 16 April 1582.
91	30	CPB, introduction for 1566.	164	42	Letters to Infantas, 10 July 1581.
95	9	CPB, 27 November 1566.	165	16	Letters to Infantas, 5 March 1582.
95	20	CPB, 11 April 1567.			
97	12	see Gachard, *Don Carlos et Philippe II*, p. 327.	165	22	Letters to Infantas, 7 May 1582.
99	12	RAV (Badovaro), p. 63-5.	166	13	Letters to Infantas, 23 October 1581
99	21	see Gachard, *Don Carlos et Philippe II*, p. 137.	166	19	Letters to Infantas, 15 January 1582.
99	24	RAV (Tiepolo), p. 151.	166	25	Letters to Infantas, 1 October 1582.
101	15	see Freer, vol. 2 p. 217.			
102	40	see Gachard, *Don Carlos et Philippe II*, p. 364.	166	39	see Dhanys, p. 231.
107	36	see Freer, vol. 1 p. 253.	175	12	CPB, 15 August 1583.
114	11	CSP (Spanish), January 1560.	184	21	CPB, 12 September 1583.
114	13	CSP (Spanish), 25 March 1561.	187	2	CPB, 4 September 1587.
115	15	CSP (Spanish), 17 March 1561.	189	10	CSP (Spanish), 1 April 1588.
115	19	CSP (Spanish), 3 April 1562.	189	23	CSP (Spanish), 1 April 1588.
116	22	CSP (Spanish), February 1569	189	31	CSP (Spanish), 5 April 1588.
117	12	CSP (Spanish), 23 May 1569.	190	13	CSP (Spanish), May 1588.
125	15	see Maxwell, vol. 1 p. 183.	190	30	CSP (Spanish), 22 June 1588.
125	41	see Maxwell, vol. 1 p. 238.	191	13	CSP (Spanish), 24 June 1588.
127	39	see Maxwell, vol. 1 p. 82	191	31	CPB, 25 October 1587.
132	8	see Maxwell, vol. 1 p. 450.	192	8	CSP (Spanish), 30 July 1588.
132	10	see Maxwell, vol. 1 p. 461.	193	27	CSP (Spanish), 6 August 1588.
136	33	CPB, 8 January 1573.	193	30	CSP (Spanish), 7 August 1588.
136	38	CPB, 18 March 1573.	195	26	CSP (Spanish), 21 August 1588.
143	1	RAV (anonymous), p. 182.			
144	6	see Marañón, p. 12.	195	40	CSP (Spanish), 21 August 1588.
144	34	see Marañón, p. 17.			
144	36	see Marañón, p. 17.	197	44	see Flanagan, *The Wreck of the Girona*.
144	38	see Marañón, p. 17.	199	27	CPB, 3 September 1588.
144	41	see Marañón, p. 19.	199	38	see Mattingly, p. 327.
145	29	see Maxwell, vol. 1 p. 190.	202	6	CPB, 26 November 1589.
147	2	CPB, 22 December 1576.	202	31	CPB, 24 June 1590.
147	6	CPB, 6 January 1577.	203	21	CPB, 4 August 1591.
147	11	CPB, 10 January 1577.	207	43	CPB, 6 December 1592.
147	14	CPB, 26 November 1576.	210	29	see Marañón, p. 196.
147	22	CPB, 31 January 1577.	210	43	see Mariéjol, p. 303.
147	34	CPB, 3 February 1577.	212	2	see Marañón, p. 202.
151	11	CPB, 16 March 1577.	212	14	RAV (Contarini), p. 219.
152	6	CPB, 22 June 1577.	213	32	see Marañón, p. 238.
153	26	see Mariéjol, p. 225.	214	16	see Marañón, p. 254.
156	38	see Maxwell, vol. 2 p. 331.	215	43	see Marañón, p. 277.
157	6	RAV (anonymous), p. 183.	217	9	RAV (Contarini), p. 220.
157	27	see Bertrand, p. 73.	217	21	RAV (Vendramino), p. 230.
161	44	Letters to Infantas, 3 April 1581.	218	19	RAV (Vendramino), p. 233.
162	32	Letters to Infantas, 3 January 1583.	219	17	RAV (Contarini), p. 216.
			220	43	Letters to Infantas, introduction p. 45.
162	43	Letters to Infantas, 8 November 1582.	221	12	see Mariéjol, p. 330.
163	4	Letters to Infantas, 1 October 1582.	221	24	Letters to Infantas, appendix p. 75.
163	20	Letters to Infantas, 1 March 1581.	222	17	see Mariéjol, p. 331.
163	27	Letters to Infantas, 15 January 1582.	227		see Motley, *History of the United Netherlands*, vol. 3 p. 414.
164	4	Letters to Infantas, 19 March 1582.	230	45	CSP (Venetian), 13 September 1598.

Index

Page numbers in *italics* indicate
Colour Plates